THE CANADIAN FUR TRADE
IN THE INDUSTRIAL AGE

Throughout much of the nineteenth century the Hudson's Bay Company had a virtual monopoly on the core area of the fur trade in Canada. Its products were the object of intense competition among merchants on two continents — in Leipzig, New York, London, Winnipeg, St Louis, and Montreal. But in 1870 things began to change, and by the end of the Second World War the company's share had dropped to about a quarter of the trade. Arthur Ray explores the decades of transition, the economic and technological changes that shaped them, and their impact on the Canadian north and its people.

Among the developments that affected the fur trade during this period were innovations in transportation and communication; increased government involvement in business, conservation, and native economic welfare; and the effects of two severe depressions (1873–95 and 1929–38) and two world wars.

The Hudson's Bay Company, confronting the first of these changes as early as 1871, embarked on a diversification program that was intended to capitalize on new economic opportunities in land development, retailing, and resource ventures. Meanwhile it continued to participate in its traditional sphere of operations. But the company's directors had difficulty keeping pace with the rapid changes that were taking place in the fur trade, and the company began to lose ground.

Ray's study is the first to make extensive use of the Hudson's Bay Company archives dealing with the period between 1870 and 1945. These and other documents reveal a great deal about the decline of the company, and thus about a key element in the history of the modern Canadian fur trade.

ARTHUR J. RAY is Professor of History at the University of British Columbia. Among his other books are *Indians in the Fur Trade; 'Give Us Good Measure': An Economic Analysis of Relations between the Indians and the Hudson's Bay Company before 1763*, with Donald Freeman; *Early Fur Trades*, with C.E. Heidenreich; and *Illustrated History of Canada*, with five other historians.

ARTHUR J. RAY

The Canadian Fur Trade in the Industrial Age

UNIVERSITY OF TORONTO PRESS
Toronto Buffalo London

© University of Toronto Press 1990
Toronto   Buffalo   London
Printed in Canada
ISBN 0-8020-2699-0 (cloth)
ISBN 0-8020-6743-3 (paper)

Printed on acid-free paper

Canadian Cataloguing in Publication Data

Ray, Arthur J., 1941–
   The Canadian fur trade in the industrial age

   Includes bibliographical references.
   ISBN 0-8020-2699-0 (bound) ISBN 0-8020-6743-3 (pbk.)

   1. Fur trade – Canada, Northern – History.
   2. Hudson's Bay Company – History. 3. Indians of
   North America – Canada – Economic conditions.
   I. Title.

   HD9944.C22R39 1990   380.1'439   C89-095478-X

This book has been published with the help of a grant from the Social
Science Federation of Canada, using funds provided by the Social
Sciences and Humanities Research Council of Canada. Publication has
also been assisted by the Canada Council and the Ontario Arts Council
under their block grant programs.

For S.A.S.

Contents

Figures and tables

TABLES

Acknowledgments

I am very grateful to the staffs of the British Library official publications and periodical sections, the Public Record Office, the National Archives of Canada, the Provincial Archives of Alberta, British Columbia, and Ontario. I owe a particular debt of gratitude to Shirlee Anne Smith, keeper of the records, Judith Beattie, Debra Moore, Anne Morton, and Michael Moosburger of the Hudson's Bay Company Archives in the Provincial Archives of Manitoba. Without their cheerful help and numerous suggestions this study would not have been possible. My research assistants, Paulette Falcon, Arif Lalani, Ramona Rose, David Dmitrisanovic, and Brian Foreman, have done yeoman service. I would like to thank Brian Gallagher and Frank Tough for reading and commenting on earlier drafts of this manuscript. On a more personal note I would like to extend a special thanks to Dianne Newell and Shirlee Anne Smith for much needed encouragement, countless suggestions, and a great deal of patience.

A leave fellowship and research grants provided by the Social Science and Humanities Research Council of Canada made this work possible. This assistance is greatly appreciated.

Preface

In his classic study, *The Fur Trade in Canada*, Harold Innis observed that the era after 1869 was 'one of the most interesting periods in the history of the trade.'[1] Contrary to popular impressions, the fur trade did not remain a static business which slowly faded away during this time. Rather, with fur prices soaring, it remained strong and vibrant and expanded in the north until after the Second World War. But the character of the enterprise changed markedly during this period because of the impact of the expanding industrial economies of Europe and North America.

The diversification of the Hudson's Bay Company and the decline of its hegemony were among the most striking changes. At the time the company surrendered its chartered territorial rights to Rupert's Land during its bicentennial in 1870, it dominated the trade to the near exclusion of other operators in the subarctic woodlands. By the end of the Second World War the Hudson's Bay Company's posts barely secured one-quarter of the total returns, and the organization was under attack by opponents on all fronts.[2] Ultimately the fierce competition that took place led to the depletion of fur and game resources and the 'pauperization' of the native peoples.[3]

Comparatively little has been written about the modern fur trade. Certainly there are no histories of the Hudson's Bay Company that are comparable to those covering the years before 1870.[4] Consequently we have a poor understanding of how and why the venerable company fell from power. And, whereas a great deal has been written about the company's pre-Confederation rivals, only scant information is readily available about its twentieth-century challengers such as Lamson and Hubbard, the Northern Trading Company, or Revillon Frères.[5]

Similarly, biographies have been written about most of the fur traders who played significant roles in the fur trade before 1870, but few exist for those who shaped events in the later era. Details about the lives of most of the leaders now are sketchy at best. However, a handful of excellent reminiscences have been published. Two of the most useful and widely cited accounts of Hudson's Bay Company traders are J.W. Anderson's *Fur Trader's Story* and Philip H. Godsell's *Arctic Trader*. Anderson provides rich descriptions of all aspects of life at headquarters posts and outposts in the James Bay District between 1910 and the early 1940s. On the other hand, Godsell, who loved to tell a good story, provided lively insights into the relationships that developed between traders, Indians, and government officials. His narrative ranges over much of the north. More recently available are the account of Hugh Mackay Ross, *The Apprentice's Tale*, which provides good descriptions of life at small posts in northern Ontario in the 1930s, and that of Sydney Augustus Keighley, *Trader-Tripper-Trapper: The Life of a Bay Man*, covering northern Manitoba and Saskatchewan between 1917 and 1963.

There are few narratives that depict the fur trade from the perspective of the company's opponents. One of the most interesting of these is Peter Baker's *Memoirs of an Arctic Arab: The Story of a Free-Trader in Northern Canada*. Baker was a Christian from Lebanon who battled the Hudson's Bay Company in the Mackenzie River area between 1907 and 1927. He was one of a new breed of traders from central and eastern Europe and the Mediterranean who arrived in Canada in the great waves of immigration that took place at the turn of this century. These newcomers proved to be innovative and tenacious competitors against the Hudson's Bay Company. John Tetso, a Slavey Indian, offered a rare native glimpse of life on the trapline in the Mackenzie River region during the 1940s and 1950s in his *Trapping Is My Life*. In *An Indian Remembers*, Tom Boulanger talks about the changing nature of the fur trade in northern Manitoba in the 1920s and 1930s. Although they are insightful, these few published first-hand accounts do not provide a good overview of the development of the industry after Confederation.

Until very recently it was not possible to study the changing role of the Hudson's Bay Company in the industrial fur trade because its records were not available to scholars.[6] The company's 250th anniversary in 1920 provided the catalyst for establishment of an archive, and throughout that decade records were brought in to Winnipeg from various Canadian locations and sent to London. An archivist and staff began the slow process of sorting and organizing the records up to 1870. The directors of the company approved their being made available to scholars in 1931.[7] In the Hudson's Bay Company tercentennial year the records from 1870 to 1900 were opened (there are over 4,900 linear feet of post-1870 documents). After the transfer from London to the Provincial Archives of Manitoba an accelerated effort was made to classify the post-1900 records to enable the archives to follow the thirty-year ruling of making records available to the public. The goal is slowly being achieved.

Now that these voluminous accounts are accessible, we can address a number of important questions. To what extent did the Hudson's Bay Company's Fur Trade Department undergo a metamorphosis as the industrial age advanced in Canada and the organization diversified? What kinds of business innovations did the newcomers introduce? How did changes in the industry and the company affect native peoples? I shall address these central issues by focusing on the Hudson's Bay Company's activities in the central Subarctic – the core area of its traditional operations covering nearly one-half of Canada. Although the Hudson's Bay Company expanded into the Arctic during the second half of this period, space precludes an extended discussion of this move and its impact on the Inuit.[8] Highlighted are the ways in which international, national, and regional economic developments influenced the subarctic fur trade and the company's fortunes within it. The major developments I consider include the diversification of the Hudson's Bay Company, the increasing involvement of the state in the region through conservation programs and the activities of the Department of Indian Affairs, the maturation of the North American industrial economy and the concomitant shift of the centre of global economic power from England to the United States, the integration of regional markets through improvements in transportation and communication technologies, and the impacts of the two world wars. I shall address these topics in ways that clarify the geography of change. Although the focus is on the company rather than native peoples, none the less this study does have great relevance for their history.

Ultimately it challenges the commonly held notion that continuities of native traditions between 1870 and 1945 are largely to be explained in terms of a stable fur industry.[9]

University of British Columbia
1989

THE CANADIAN FUR TRADE
IN THE INDUSTRIAL AGE

1
Does the fur trade have a future?

Now gentlemen, this company has not been very celebrated for doing things in a hurry. It is really very much like Rip Van Winkle waking up in the year 1871 and finding out that steam engines and steam boats will be of advantage to the trade. The policy of the Hudson's Bay Company from the beginning was to keep out every vestige of civilization and every attempt at colonization. (Anonymous shareholder, General Court, the London Tavern, 12 July 1871)

In a series of crucial meetings held on 28 and 29 June and 12 July 1871 Hudson's Bay Company stockholders hotly debated the company's future. Opinions were sharply divided over the central question of whether the company should abandon its traditional fur trade roots and concentrate all its resources on new business ventures. The London directors (called the governor and committee) provoked the dispute by presenting their blueprint for the company's future at the 28 June meeting. They wanted to build a diversified organization from its fur trade base. The assembled stockholders were unreceptive to this idea. Most of them were in a rebellious mood; they had come with the intention of vetoing the committee's scheme. A handful of the dissidents drafted and circulated a counter-proposal before the first meeting began.[1] Although they were not a unified group, most of the dissenters wanted to sever the connections with the past. They regarded the fur trade as a dying industry which would be swept away by the advance of civilization. For them the company's future was in land development and promotion schemes. This tension within the company persisted throughout the period before 1945.

The governor and committee closely modelled the scheme they put forward along the lines recommended in a planning report they had asked Cyril Graham (later Sir Cyril), vice-president of the Transatlantic Telegraph Company, to prepare.[2] For this purpose the directors had sent Graham to Canada in 1870 with instructions to survey the country and suggest business activities the Hudson's Bay Company should pursue in the light of the rapidly changing economic and political scene. In keeping with the committee's wishes, Graham paid particular attention to (a) the fur trade, (b) the relations between the company and its officers, and (c) general business prospects. Accordingly, he criss-crossed the country talking to leading businessmen, politicians (including Prime Minister Sir John A. Macdonald), and Hudson's Bay Company officers. Graham filed his report from Fort Garry in two instalments.[3]

His survey convinced him that the company should remain active in the fur trade. He cited three major reasons. First, Graham thought that the future prospects of the industry were excellent. Second, he estimated that it would take at least fifteen years to complete the proposed transcontinental railway. Until then large-scale immigration and agricultural development were not possible. Meanwhile the fur trade would have to provide the company with most of its revenue. Third, Graham believed that the continued involvement of the Hudson's Bay Company in the fur trade would enable its officers to retain their powerful influence over the Indians. In this way these men could promote peaceful relations between the native peoples and incoming settlers. If bloodshed on the frontier was avoided, agricultural development could proceed rapidly, bringing an earlier return to the company on the sales of its land holdings in the fertile belt.

Certainly the Canadian government wanted the company to act as a peacekeeper and as an agent of the government in the northwest. At the 28 June 1871 meeting company governor, Sir Stafford Northcote, stated he had received a communiqué in which Prime Minister John A. Macdonald wrote: 'I am very anxious, indeed, that we should be able to deal with the Indians upon satisfactory terms. They are the great difficulty in these newly civilized countries. They are the great difficulty with which the Americans have to contend in their new countries. The Hudson's Bay Company have dealt with the Indians in a thoroughly satisfactory way. The policy of Canada is also to deal with the Indians in a satisfactory manner.'[4] Macdonald continued: 'It would be of advantage to us, & no doubt it would be of advantage to you, that we should be allowed to make use of your officers & your posts for the purpose of making those payments to the Indians which will have to be made annually by the Government of Canada in order to satisfy their claims & keep them in good humour. The Indians had a title to some of these lands which is now extinguished – upon which certain terms which involve annual payments; & it would be of great advantage that we should be able to employ officers who are known to these Indians in order to make these payments & keep the Indians in good humour.'

Graham favoured the idea of having the company officers distribute government annuities to the Indians. He firmly believed that these men would be more trustworthy than government agents. This distinction was very important to him, since he believed that in the United States unscrupulous government agents were defrauding American Indians of their annuities. In Graham's opinion these abuses were provoking the unrest that was taking place south of the border. Besides this political consideration, he knew that the company stood to reap economic benefits from having annuity payments made at its trading posts.[5]

measures to reduce costs + increase profits

After examining fur-trading operations first hand and holding discussions with senior company officers, Graham concluded that ways had to be found to halt spiralling costs and declining profits. Otherwise the company would not be able to meet the competition that was sure to develop as soon as the northwest was opened by railways and the telegraph. The traditional fur trade was expensive to operate compared with other types of merchandising. Nearly all transactions were of a credit-barter nature. This meant that every year considerable capital was invested in both Indian debts and post inventories. This capital turned over very slowly, given the long delays that took place (up to five years) between the time the company first bought the goods and when it sold the furs it received in exchange for them. This sluggish turnover added to the cost of doing business. There were other *gift-giving* expenses. Gift-giving, a central aspect of the trade of the mercantile era, continued to be important in the late nineteenth century, even though the presents were not as lavish as in former times.[6] In addition, the company still provided economic aid to elderly, sick, and infirm natives in the form of gratuities of merchandise.[7] It was tempting for industrial capitalists to eliminate these traditional fur trade practices for the sake of cost cutting. But, Graham cautioned, it would be a serious mistake to do so. No doubt swayed by the advice of the officers, he argued that these men had to have the authority to give credit to deserving Indians and to extend it generally whenever local conditions warranted. He also expressed the opinion that gift-giving costs were insignificant, considering the good will that the Hudson's Bay Company earned in return.

Graham thought that investing capital in the development of steamboat service on Lake Winnipeg and the Saskatchewan, Peace, Athabasca, and Mackenzie rivers offered the best way to trim expenses and place the fur trade on a more secure footing. The old Red River cart / York boat / canoe system developed in the pre-industrial era was simply too labour intensive. Furthermore, the Métis labourers, who were the backbone of the service, were becoming 'unruly.' The company's commissioner in Canada, Donald A. Smith, had already written to the directors about this problem on 1 August 1870. In his letter Smith noted that the Portage la Loche Brigades (the Yorkboat brigades that hauled cargoes between Red River, Norway House, and Portage la Loche) routinely refused to carry loads as large as those they formerly had done, and they travelled more slowly. This meant the Métis brigademen were costing the company money, and they were causing great inconvenience in Red River, where supply shortages were the result.[8] The issue came to a head in 1869–70. The boat crews from Red River mutinied on the Saskatchewan River during the summer of 1869; one year later eight of nine Red River crews did likewise. In these particular instances the job actions were politically motivated. None the less, they served to underscore the company's vulnerability to its native labour force and, as such, served as a catalyst for dealing with a long-simmering business problem. Smith had already decided how he wanted to proceed. He wrote: 'for all these evils the only remedy is the employment of steam.'[9] Being more specific, Smith added: 'Were a steamer placed on Lake Manitobah [sic], a second on the lower reaches of the Saskatchewan and a third on its upper waters, we would be comparatively independent of the disturbing causes which presently annoy us.'

Obviously Graham accepted Smith's ideas completely, and he included them in his own set of recommendations. Additionally, he argued that by taking the initiative in building a network of steamboat routes in the northwest, the company would be able to profit from the traffic that settlement and commercial development were sure to generate.

Some of Graham's cost-cutting proposals did not require the initial outlay of additional capital. For example, he recommended eliminating the food ration allowances that traditionally were given to men and their families in the Northern Department. Graham noted that these rations were not too costly when pemmican could be bought for merely two pennies per pound. However, by 1870 prices had risen to more than seven times that amount. Even worse, in many areas beef, which was more expensive, had to be substituted. These changed circumstances meant that the labour force was eating the company out of house and home. Graham thought it made better sense to offer a modest increase in salary to employees stationed in the prairies and parklands to compensate them for the elimination of these allowances. He favoured continuing the old practice only in remote districts where employees were not able to purchase food locally.

After studying the company's merchandise-pricing policies, Graham advocated replacing the old 'gross system of valuation' with a more finely tuned pricing scheme. He concluded that in 1870 the company sold some articles for reasonable profits, but many of the more valuable stock items were priced too low. Graham claimed that competitors bought some of these goods and resold them for a profit.

Despite the company's long experience as a trading firm Graham was quite surprised to discover that its managers had not developed a good system for requisitioning trading merchandise at the lowest possible rates. He claimed that virtually any merchant could get better wholesale prices than the company did for most of the articles it routinely carried on inventory. No doubt merchants could do so partly thanks to the revolution that was taking place in mass wholesaling in North America, made possible by the telegraph and railway.[10] In view of this development, the Hudson's Bay Company needed to obtain any advantages it could from volume buying. Graham correctly noted that it was imperative to address this problem immediately, given that it was likely competitors would soon be taking to the field in force.

He was also highly critical of the manner in which fur-buying operations were conducted in the field. He noted that in many of the districts where opposition was weak or non-existent company traders were sending men out to Indian camps to collect furs. Originally traders used this tactic, known as 'tripping,' to secure furs from those Indians already in debt to the company before opponents bought them. When men 'tripped' without competition they were not protecting their credit; instead, they were 'poaching' on each other's territory and needlessly fuelling Indian demands for better fur prices. In addition to these problems, salary and provision costs for 'tripping' often exceeded the value of the returns.

During his visit to Canada Graham became aware that the company's senior officers were very demoralized. They were outraged about the manner in which the directors and stockholders had treated them over the sale of the Hudson's Bay Company's title to Rupert's Land in 1870. The officers had not been kept informed during the lengthy negotiations that had begun in 1863.[11] They were particularly angry that they were not given a share of the compensation the company had received. This deal included a $1.5 million cash payment, a one-twentieth share of the lands in the fertile belt, and title to the developed properties surrounding the company's many trading posts. The stockholders justified excluding the commissioned officers from this windfall by narrowly interpreting the 'deed polls' (employment contract agreements) of 1821 and 1834, which specified that collectively these men were entitled to only a 40 per cent share of the trading profits. Some of the stockholders expressed the view that in the future this old scheme should be withdrawn and all the officers placed on straight salaries.

By 1871 it was clear that disaffected officers could form an opposition company with Canadian and American financial backing.[12] Graham knew that any such action could strike a critical blow to the Hudson's Bay Company, so he sought to appease the officers. Accordingly, he opposed the idea of abandoning the profit-sharing system. Instead, he recommended extending it to any men whom the company might hire in the future to manage new business ventures. In addition, Graham recommended taking a number of steps to provide better incentives. One of his suggestions involved replacing the existing two-tiered system of commissioned officers with a four-tiered one having the ranks of chief factors, factors, chief traders, and traders. According to the proposed scheme, men holding the senior-most ranks would superintend departments and report directly to the commissioner. Factors would oversee districts and chief traders would manage subdistricts. The best qualified clerks and non-commissioned men whose service deserved recognition would be selected to fill the trader ranks. Graham reported that a serious problem with the current hiring and promotion system was that many good servants received promotions to positions for which they were unqualified. Conversely, many men who should have been rewarded for good and loyal service did not obtain their due because their superiors feared making inappropriate promotions.

9 Does the fur trade have a future?

Graham thought that the adoption of the reforms he proposed offered the company the possibility of recruiting servants of higher quality than those it had obtained in the 1860s.

potential for retail trade

Concerning potential alternative business prospects, Graham noted that the Hudson's Bay Company was particularly well situated to develop a general retail trade. Already it had a reputation for carrying high-quality merchandise. A substantial portion of the basic inventories carried at the trading posts included items that would be in demand by pioneers. Many of the more southerly posts were ideally located to serve settlers in the future. By developing saleshops at these locations the company could draw settlers around them, thereby enhancing the value of the contiguous property. Regarding the one-twentieth share of prairie lands that the company was to receive from the government, Graham favoured taking a 'moderate course.' He thought the best strategy would be to hold on to those lands that likely would draw settlement rapidly and to sell other blocks quickly at a minimum price. To facilitate and profit from the financing that would be needed for land sales and development projects Graham favoured forming a northwestern bank in which the Hudson's Bay Company would hold most of the shares.

Central to Graham's series of recommendations was the notion that the company should diversify in a way in which the traditional and newer lines of business activity reinforced one another. The governor and committee accepted the wisdom of this basic premise and included most of his suggestions in the plan they presented to the stockholders on 28 June 1871. The principal exceptions were that the governing committee did not adopt Graham's proposal to enter into the banking business (banking laws prohibited land development companies from doing so), and they went further than he envisioned in their effort to regain the goodwill of the officers. To appease these men the committee advocated paying to them the compensation the company was about to receive from the United States for the losses it had suffered as a result of the 1846 Oregon boundary settlement. This amounted to $450,000 for the possessory rights and $200,000 for the Puget Sound Agricultural Company.[13]

Stockholder opposition

The stockholders vociferously opposed the modified Graham plan when it was presented to them, because they strongly objected to investing more money in the fur trade, and they adamantly opposed distributing the Oregon compensation package to the officers. Their opposition was understandable. Most of those present on 28 June 1871 had invested in the company during or after the 1863 public share offering promoted by the International Financial Society. This society bought a controlling interest in the Hudson's Bay Company in June of that year, and it promptly raised the capital of the company from £1,393,569 to £2 million by offering shares to the public in £20 units.[14] The prospectus issued at the time stressed that a substantial portion of the company's chartered territory included rich mineral deposits, lands that were ideal for agricultural and urban development, and waterways that would become part of an east-west transportation system in British North America.[15] The promoters stressed that the capital raised by the common share offering would be earmarked for the development of these resources. In other words, the recapitalized Hudson's Bay Company was going to turn its attention to the construction of communication and transportation systems and the promotion of land sales.[16]

Most of the newer shareholders held these expectations when they purchased their shares, and therefore they regarded the directors' proposal to invest more money in the fur trade as a breach of faith. Furthermore, this group of investors believed that the industry had no future, given that the anticipated advance of 'civilization' (the agricultural frontier) would destroy the resource base upon which the trade depended.[17] Of course these ideas were borne out of ignorance about the geography of Rupert's Land and the fur industry of the late nineteenth century. The governor and committee attempted to correct this mistaken picture by pointing out that many areas of northern Canada would never be developed for agriculture because of environmental constraints. They presented data from the company's archives (fig. 1) to show that fur volumes were not declining and therefore there was no reason to worry about resource depletion. Despite these reassurances, many stockholders remained unconvinced.

While some worried about the future of the industry, others doubted that investing money to improve the company's transportation system would reverse the downward trend in profitability. At least one anonymous shareholder heaped scorn on the idea by drawing an analogy between the company and Rip Van Winkle.

The £39,790 Oregon settlement money was an even more contentious issue than the investment proposal. While the negotiations for the sale of Rupert's Land dragged on from 1863 to 1869, the governor and committee had led the stockholders to anticipate that the company would receive as much as £5 million for the surrender of its chartered

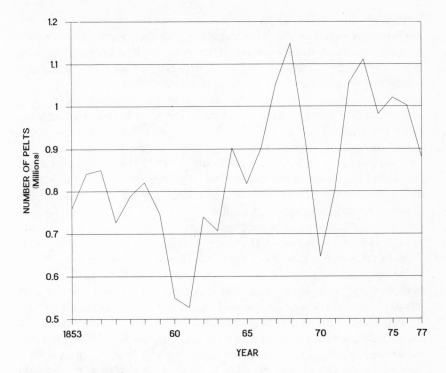

Figure 1
Hudson's Bay Company fur sales, 1853–77

territory.[18] The agreement struck between the company and the governments of Canada and Great Britain dashed these lofty dreams. The
1863 share offering raised more money for the company than was
realized in the £300,000 settlement. For these reasons many of the
stockholders wanted the company to distribute the £39,790 as an
extraordinary dividend. Certainly they had a strong case. After all, the
company had listed this outstanding claim among the company's assets
in the 1863 prospectus.[19]

As would be expected under the circumstances, the assembled stockholders also attacked the proposal to expand operations into general
merchandising. It was no more compatible with the investment goals
of most of those who were present than any of the other recommendations were. One of them challenged Governor Northcote on the subject,
saying: 'there is a legal question involved ... We are not general traders.

I have never seen any charter which authorizes us to become general factors.'[20] He continued: 'Our business was the fur trade ... you are going on a totally different basis ... we are to be storekeepers, carriers, shopkeepers or anything. Well, now Sir, I beg, without intending any offence, to express my belief that it is a wild project.'[21]

After a protracted and heated debate the governor put the plan to a vote. Those present defeated it by a show of hands. Undaunted, Northcote called for a paper ballot, and he sent runners down the street to rustle up more votes. Using this tactic, the governor obtained the support he needed. The dissidents raised a howl of protest, and they challenged the legitimacy of the second ballot. Given the importance of the issue, the governor and committee decided to settle the matter by conducting a mail ballot. The committee carried the day once more.[22] Although they were victorious, throughout the 1870s the directors had to face a vocal group of disaffected stockholders who closely monitored, and often criticized, the committee's management.

The first task facing the London directors after clearing the hurdle of the stockholders was that of developing a suitable structure and strategy for managing a diversified business. On 1 June 1870 they had appointed Donald A. Smith (later Lord Strathcona) commissioner and the following year elevated him to chief commissioner. As chief commissioner he was given the responsibility for all the company's operations in Canada and the Northwest Territories. Smith was fifty-two years old and had begun his career with the company thirty-two years earlier in Labrador. In June 1869 the company placed him in charge of the combined Montreal and Labrador departments. One year later he became president of the Northern Department which included most of the western interior of Canada.[23]

Shortly after Smith assumed his new position it became clear to the governing committee that one man could not effectively supervise the company's fur trade, saleshops, and land interests. Accordingly, in 1874 the position of land commissioner was created. Smith resigned as chief commissioner and took up the new position which was more compatible with his current business interests.[24] Since 1869 he had been investing his own retirement money and that of many of his fellow officers in a variety of industrial, commercial, and land development ventures. He was one of the principal investors in the Canadian Pacific Railway, and he played a key role in pushing the project through to completion in 1885. Eventually he amassed one of the largest personal fortunes in Canada. The governor and committee authorized Smith to deal directly with them on any aspect of his responsibilities. James A. Grahame replaced Smith as chief commissioner; he was another long-time fur trader.[25] Grahame's primary responsibilities were the fur trade and saleshops.

conflicts bet. Smith + Grahame

The deteriorating economic climate of the early 1870s compounded the problems inherent in the arrangement. Smith was a domineering and revengeful individual – a 'good hater,' as one of his biographers has observed.[26] To make matters worse for Grahame, Smith held the confidence of the profit-sharing officers. The governor and committee anticipated that a clash of authority and personality might take place.[27] They encouraged Grahame to co-operate with Smith but cautioned him not to let Smith interfere. Smith refused to be contained, however, and on several occasions he wrote to London making suggestions for the improvement of various aspects of company operations under Grahame's jurisdiction. Smith's criticisms of Grahame increased as the economy slid into depression, and land sales slumped as a result (fig. 2). Smith was particularly upset about what he considered to be the chief commissioner's lack of initiative in seeking out new business opportunities outside the fur trade.[28] Whenever disputes arose between Grahame and Smith, the governor and committee always supported Grahame even if Smith's critical remarks were well founded. In 1879 Smith resigned and the governor and committee appointed Charles Brydges.[29] Smith's departure from the scene was only tempo-rary. In the 1870s he began buying stock in the company, becoming an important shareholder by the early 1880s. In 1883 he gained a position on the governing committee. In 1888 the stockholders elected Smith deputy governor and one year later he secured the governorship. He served in that capacity until his death at the age of ninety-four in 1914 (fig. 3).

The clashes that took place between Smith and Grahame served to highlight the fundamental defects of the company's administrative structure in the late nineteenth century. The various branches of the business were diverging from a common base, and they were differen-tially affected by the volatile economic climate of the late nineteenth century. It became increasingly difficult for one or two men to manage all the company's affairs. For instance, a man trained in the fur trade and committed to this industry was poorly equipped or little inclined to take the initiative in retailing and government contracting. Grahame was a good example of this phenomenon. There is no doubt that he was slow to respond to these new opportunities;[30] he gave priority to

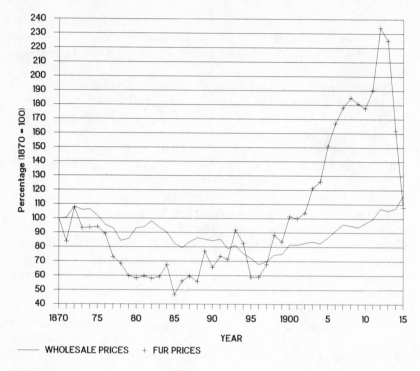

Figure 2
Wholesale price indices, 1870–1915

the business he knew best – the fur trade. Smith's outlook was just the opposite. As his business horizons widened, he came to the conclusion that there was little future in the fur trade, and he thought that the Hudson's Bay Company should channel its energies elsewhere. For this reason it is not surprising that under his governorship between 1889 and 1914 the company failed to keep pace with the developments that were taking place in the industry.

Another problem was that the governor and committee were not consistent in the way they delegated authority to their senior managers in the 1870s and 1880s. After steadfastly backing Grahame even when Smith offered sound criticisms of him, they reversed course when they appointed Charles J. Brydges to succeed Smith as land commissioner in 1879.[31] By this date the committee members were eager to pursue new business ventures and had concluded that Grahame was too

TABLE 1
Ranks of commissioned officers in the Hudson's Bay Company

Rank	Pre-1870	1871	1876
Inspecting chief factors		4	3
Chief factors	28	8	8
Factors		10	15
Chief traders	28	10	10
Junior chief traders		8	21

SOURCE: GD HBCA PAM A 104/282–7

conservative. But they were not willing to sack him. They feared that such a move would alienate the fur trade officers. To avoid this possibility the governor and committee encouraged Brydges to master all aspects of the company's affairs without informing Grahame they had given Brydges this mandate.[32] The committee hoped their action would give Brydges a chance to gain the support of the fur trade officers. Conflicts were inevitable as Brydges exercised his confidential mandate and 'meddled' in Grahame's affairs. Meanwhile, Smith was working behind the scenes to undermine Brydges, whom he hated. On the day Smith assumed the governorship the committee informed Brydges that they were going to terminate his appointment as land commissioner.[33]

In keeping with the spirit of Cyril Graham's 1870 plan, the governing committee introduced new commissioned officer ranks in 1871 in order to expand career opportunities. They created the positions of factor and junior chief trader, and they introduced the position of inspecting chief factors, giving the company a five-tiered system of ranks.[34] The number of positions in each rank is shown in table 1. From the perspective of business management the new position of the greatest importance was that of inspecting chief factor. The inspecting factors visited the fur trading districts, auditing books, reporting on the condition of the company's physical plant, evaluating personnel, and making recommendations for improvements. Previously the district managers had made these assessments. For the first time the directors provided for the systematic external auditing of the company's local fur trading operations. The change was not well received by district and post managers, who regarded the inspecting factors as threats to their authority.

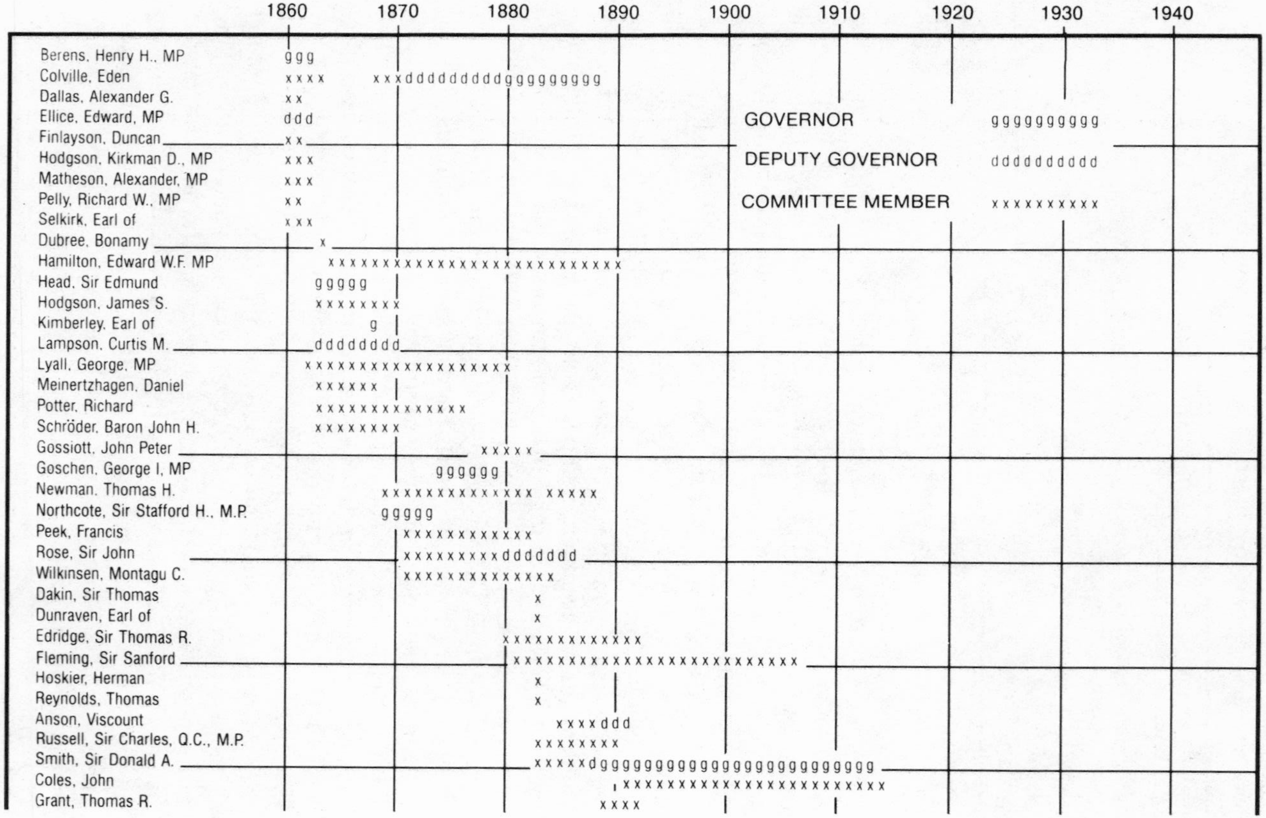

GOVERNOR g g g
DEPUTY GOVERNOR d d d
COMMITTEE MEMBER x x x

	1860	1870	1880	1890	1900	1910	1920	1930	1940

Berens, Henry H., MP
Colville, Eden
Dallas, Alexander G.
Ellice, Edward, MP
Finlayson, Duncan
Hodgson, Kirkman D., MP
Matheson, Alexander, MP
Pelly, Richard W., MP
Selkirk, Earl of
Dubree, Bonamy
Hamilton, Edward W.F. MP
Head, Sir Edmund
Hodgson, James S.
Kimberley, Earl of
Lampson, Curtis M.
Lyall, George, MP
Meinertzhagen, Daniel
Potter, Richard
Schröder, Baron John H.
Gossiott, John Peter
Goschen, George I., MP
Newman, Thomas H.
Northcote, Sir Stafford H., M.P.
Peek, Francis
Rose, Sir John
Wilkinsen, Montagu C.
Dakin, Sir Thomas
Dunraven, Earl of
Edridge, Sir Thomas R.
Fleming, Sir Sanford
Hoskier, Herman
Reynolds, Thomas
Anson, Viscount
Russell, Sir Charles, Q.C., M.P.
Smith, Sir Donald A.
Coles, John
Grant, Thomas R.

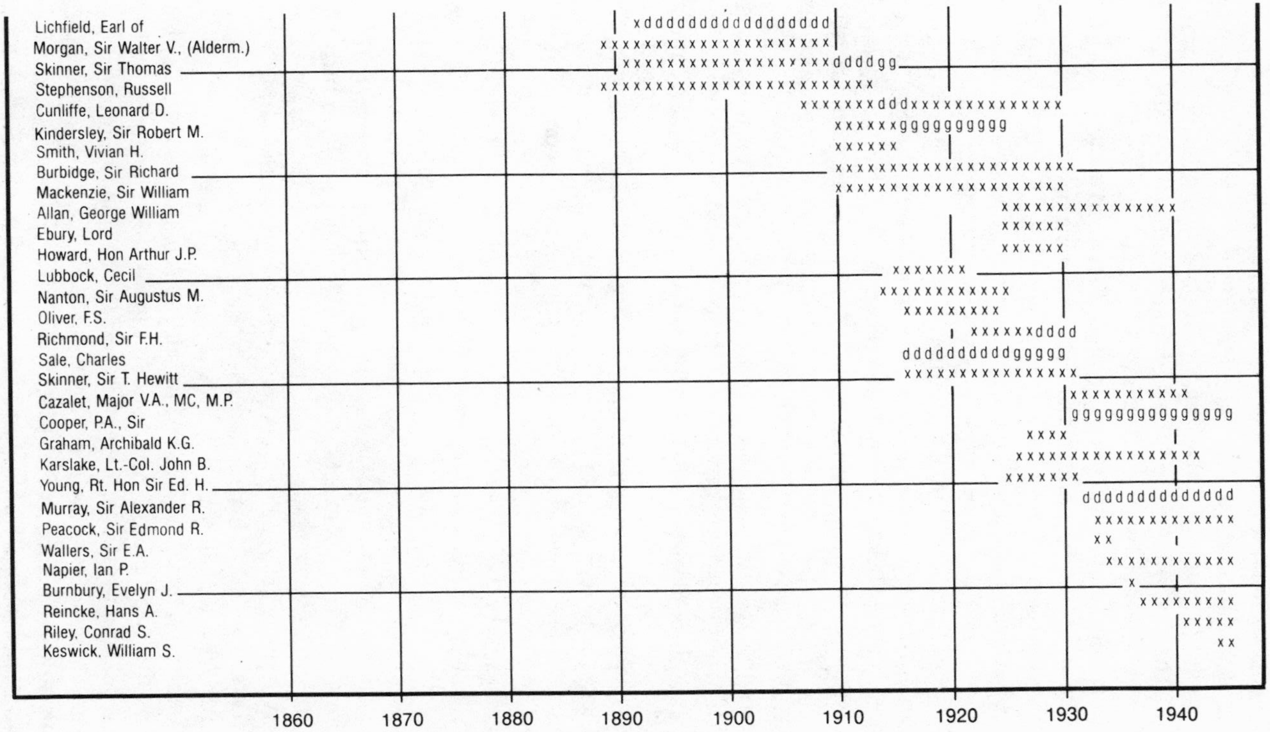

Figure 3

Governors and committees of the Hudson's Bay Company, 1870–1945. Source: Hudson's Bay Company Annual
Reports to Shareholders, HBCA PAM. © Arthur Ray 1988

Lichfield, Earl of
Morgan, Sir Walter V. (Alderm.)
Skinner, Sir Thomas
Stephenson, Russell
Cuniffe, Leonard D.
Kindersley, Sir Robert M.
Smith, Vivian H.
Burbidge, Sir Richard
Mackenzie, Sir William
Allan, George William
Ebury, Lord
Howard, Hon Arthur J.P.
Lubbock, Cecil
Nanton, Sir Augustus M.
Oliver, F.S.
Richmond, Sir F.H.
Sale, Charles
Skinner, Sir T. Hewitt
Cazalet, Major V.A., MC, M.P.
Cooper, P.A., Sir
Graham, Archibald K.G.
Karslake, Lt.-Col. John B.
Young, Rt. Hon Sir Ed. H.
Murray, Sir Alexander R.
Peacock, Sir Edmond R.
Wallers, Sir E.A.
Napier, Ian P.
Burnbury, Evelyn J.
Reincke, Hans A.
Riley, Conrad S.
Keswick, William S.

1860   1870   1880   1890   1900   1910   1920   1930   1940

In 1884 the governor and committee made another change in the company's administrative structure when they created a two-man Canadian subcommittee consisting of Donald Smith and Sandford Fleming. This act represented the London directors' first attempt to give Canadians some control over company affairs. However, the governor and committee did so largely in order to deal with Smith's allegations that the company's land and commercial interests were being mismanaged by Brydges. Accordingly, a copy of all correspondence between Canada and London was supposed to be submitted to Smith and Fleming, and they were given the responsibility for approving all purchases of goods in North America.[35] This new administrative arrangement proved to be impracticable, however, since Smith and Fleming rarely met because they were preoccupied with other business ventures. Once Smith was elected governor of the company in 1889 and the governor and committee terminated Brydges' contract as land commissioner, there was no further need for the subcommittee. It ceased to operate after 1892. Although this experiment born of power struggles within the company was short lived, it did foreshadow the creation of a Canadian management committee in the twentieth century.

Joseph Wrigley's appointment as trade commissioner in 1884 to replace Grahame represented a more important and long-term departure from company tradition. Wrigley was the first trade commissioner who did not apprentice in the company's fur trade service. Rather, he had worked in his family's woollen textile manufacturing business in Huddersfield, England. The decision to hire a man outside the service reflected the governor and committee's determination to expand its retailing activities beyond the fur trade.[36] In spite of this interest, the directors did expect Commissioner Wrigley to place the fur-trading operations on a more competitive footing. He was unable to turn his attention to this task immediately. Instead, during his first year in office, Wrigley was largely absorbed with handling the company's contracts to supply the troops that the government sent to put down the North-West Rebellion.[37]

While the directors struggled to find solutions to their administrative problems, they wasted no time in embarking on their plan for updating the transportation system. On 7 May 1872 the company launched the first inland steamboat – the *Chief Commissioner*. There were problems with this new venture from the outset. The Saskatchewan River, which was crucial to the development of any successful steamboat network, *transportation*

proved unsuitable for safe, reliable navigation unless considerable investments could be made in navigation improvements. Neither the Canadian government nor the Hudson's Bay Company would spend the money that was needed. Also, the company discovered that the *Chief Commissioner* was not properly designed for the routes it plied.[38] In the light of these early problems and in the anticipation that the expanding railway system would render steamboat transportation in the prairies obsolete, the company abandoned its effort to develop the business on the Saskatchewan River. Instead, the directors took advantage of the close links that existed between Donald Smith and the Canadian Pacific Railway, and they negotiated a preferential freight rate agreement in 1884 which gave the Hudson's Bay Company a 12.5 per cent discount on its rail shipments, excluding flour.[39]

Grahame

The Hudson's Bay Company had better luck with steamboats in the Athabasca River/Mackenzie River area. Preparations were begun at Lake Athabasca in 1881, and two years later the company launched the *Grahame* at Fort Chipewyan.[40] This vessel proved a success from the outset. It carried 200 tons of freight and steamed with little difficulty between Fort Chipewyan and Fort McMurray on the Athabasca River and Fort Vermilion on the Peace River. The *Grahame* was also able to travel sixty miles up the Clearwater River to the rapids at the north end of the old Methy Portage. As a result, canoes, scows, and York boats were no longer needed at this historic portage. Many of the displaced men found alternative employment cutting and stacking cordwood along the route. Three years after launching the *Grahame* the Hudson's Bay Company put the *Wrigley* into service. This was a much smaller, propeller-driven craft which was well suited for service between Great Slave Lake and the lower Mackenzie River.

Wrigley

The only remaining transportation bottleneck in the region was a reach of the Athabasca River between Fort McMurray and Athabasca Landing. The Hudson's Bay Company built another sternwheeler, the *Athabasca*, to tackle this section. The *Athabasca* made its first trial run in 1888. The vessel was not able to haul cargo upriver to Lesser Slave Lake because difficult rapids blocked the way on the Lesser Slave Lake River. Travel between Athabasca Landing and Grand Rapids, nearly two-thirds of the distance to Fort McMurray, was much easier, and it was here that the *Athabasca* proved useful. Scows were even more important for the downstream shipment of cargo.

Elsewhere in the north the Hudson's Bay Company made few changes in its transportation arrangements. The most important one affected York Factory, the traditional port of entry for the western interior. In 1874 the company moved the depot of the Northern Department from York Factory to Winnipeg in anticipation of the development of railway and steamboat systems.[41] Cargoes continued to be sent inland from the post after that date, but the quantities diminished steadily, since the factory's hinterland now included only the immediate district. Moose Factory remained the headquarters and port of entry for the Southern Department.

In 1870 muskrat, beaver, and marten still dominated Canadian fur production. At the time muskrat pelts were of low value, being used primarily to make coat linings in expensive garments or as the exterior fur in low-grade winter wear. Beaver pelts, the staple of the fur trade before the middle of the nineteenth century, were still prized by felt makers who used the high-quality wool and by fur manufacturers who fashioned the skins into coats and muffs. Marten, often called Hudson Bay sable (it is closely allied to the Siberian sable), was a luxury fur. Fur garment manufacturers primarily used it to trim fancy garments and to make scarves and neckpieces.[42] In the Northern and Southern departments of the Hudson's Bay Company, which included most of the territory of Old Rupert's Land and the northwest (figs 4 and 5), the volume of muskrat production dwarfed that of all other species (table 2). Nearly two times more muskrat were taken than beaver, the second-ranked fur in terms of volume, and four times more than marten. These three furs, along with lynx, mink, red fox, river otter, buffalo robes, hair seal, skunk, and brown bear accounted for nearly 95 per cent of the total output. Apart from the overwhelming dominance of these eleven varieties of peltry, there are some other striking aspects about the 1870 fur trade that warrant comment. Buffalo robes were still important in the Northern Department, ranking fifth in terms of numbers; and, except for muskrat skunk, the production of low-value furs, ermine, rabbit, squirrel, hare, and raccoon, was very limited. Collectively these five fur-bearing species accounted for slightly more than 1 per cent of the total returns.

Reflecting the size and ecological diversity of the Northern and Southern departments, there were distinctive spatial patterns of production. Figures 4 and 5 show the volume and composition of Hudson's Bay Company district fur returns in 1870. They reveal that most of the muskrat came from the southern boreal forests and parklands between the Rainy River and the upper Saskatchewan River, including the districts of Lac la Pluie, Red River, Norway House, Swan River, Cum-

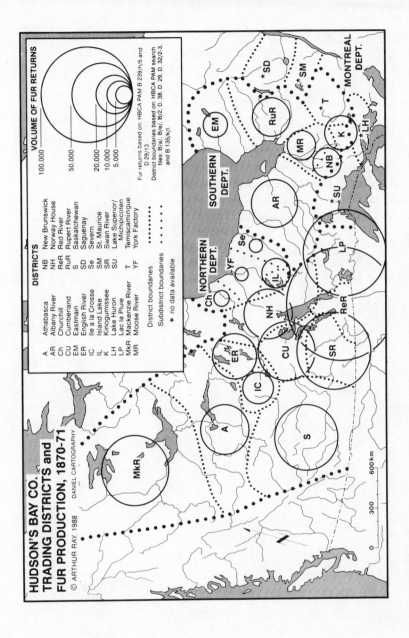

Figure 4
Hudson's Bay Company trading districts and fur production, 1870–1

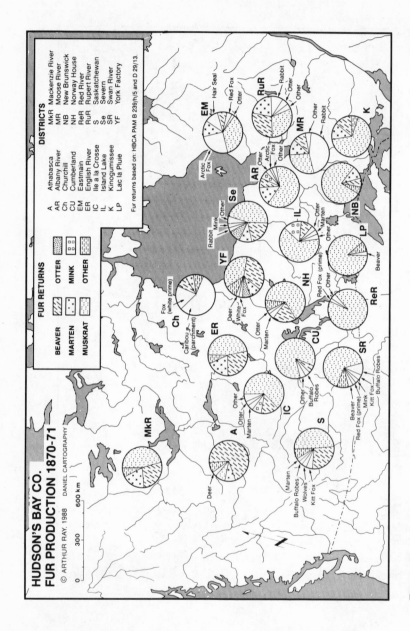

Figure 5
Hudson's Bay Company fur production, 1870–1

TABLE 2
Composition of Hudson's Bay Company returns, 1870

Fur species	Number	Per cent of total	Cumulative percentage
Muskrat	232,251	41.074	41.07
Beaver	124,000	21.930	63.00
Marten	52,308	9.251	72.25
Lynx	37,447	6.623	78.88
Mink	27,708	4.900	83.78
Fox, red	13,058	2.309	86.09
Otter, river	10,973	1.941	88.03
Buffalo robes	10,729	1.897	89.92
Seal, hair	9,917	1.754	91.68
Skunk	9,606	1.699	93.38
Bear, brown	8,420	1.489	94.87
Fisher	7,959	1.408	96.27
Wolf	5,856	1.036	97.31
Fox, white	4,629	0.819	98.13
Fox, cross	3,436	0.608	98.74
Ermine	2,223	0.393	99.13
Raccoon	1,696	0.300	99.43
Wolverine	1,421	0.251	99.68
Fox, silver	914	0.162	99.84
Seal, fur	688	0.122	99.96
Otter, sea	89	0.016	99.98
Wild cat	68	0.012	99.99
Fox, blue	48	0.008	100.00
Musk ox	0	0.000	100.00
Total	565,444	100.000	

SOURCE: Jones, *Fur farming* and GD HBCA PAM A 104/282–7

berland House, and Saskatchewan. This is why the fur traders referred to this area, particularly the Manitoba portion, as 'muskrat country.'[43] Without doubt it was one of the world's greatest prime muskrat-producing areas. Beyond muskrat country, large numbers were taken in the Mackenzie River and Albany River districts. In the latter district, most of the muskrat returns came from the upper Albany River area towards Rainy River.

The striking feature of beaver trapping was the overwhelming importance of the Athabasca, Mackenzie River, and Saskatchewan districts (fig. 5 and table 2). In the case of Saskatchewan, most of the beaver obtained came from the woodlands to the north of the Saskatchewan River. Obviously the primary beaver-trapping area had receded towards the western and northwestern fringes of the Northern Department. Trapping pressure was responsible for this retreat. Except for Norway House and Rupert River, all the remaining districts produced fewer than 4,000 beaver pelts; ten of these yielded less than 2,000.

Marten trapping was highly concentrated in the Mackenzie River District. This district overshadowed all others by a considerable margin, yielding just under 11,000 pelts or almost 40 per cent of the total. Seven other districts supplied 1,000 or more pelts in 1870; these were Athabasca, English River, Saskatchewan, Norway House, Albany River, and Kinogumissee. The remaining districts accounted for only limited amounts. In contrast to marten, mink output was more evenly distributed. The leading districts included many of the same ones that were heavy muskrat producers, except for Trout Lake, where few muskrat were included in the returns. At the time, mink was a low-grade utility fur used in coat linings.

Not surprisingly, buffalo robes, the eighth-ranked commodity, came exclusively from the parkland / grassland area, with the returns of the Swan River District dwarfing those of the Saskatchewan and Cumberland districts. The Hudson's Bay Company received only a small share of this declining business. Instead, American traders situated on the upper Mississippi and upper Missouri rivers handled the bulk of the traffic. They were able to offer the highest prices thanks to their lower shipping costs.[44]

Kitt fox returns came mostly from the parkland / grassland area, with the Swan River District predominating, followed by the Saskatchewan, Red River, and English River districts. Because this fox is primarily a creature of sandy shrubby environments, few were taken in the rocky English River District.

River otter (an aquatic member of the weasel family that feeds mostly on fish and frogs) was at this time a luxury fur. Natives trapped substantial numbers in all districts. None the less, the boreal forests between the Rupert River and Isle à la Crosse on the upper Churchill River were the prime areas, overshadowing all others. Similarly, red fox (an animal that is common to most environments lying between the Arctic Circle and the equator) were taken in all districts, although the southern James Bay region did not provide many pelts. As in the kitt fox situation, the prairie districts accounted for most of the returns.

In 1870 the Hudson's Bay Company consolidated the returns of coyote, ordinary wolf, and timber wolf pelts under the single category 'wolf.' This explains why the bulk of wolf returns came from the parklands and grasslands, particularly in Saskatchewan, followed by the Swan River and Red River districts. The returns of these three districts included large numbers of coyote, or prairie wolf. Traditionally coyote were taken by plains Indians and Métis partly because they were readily available. These wolves followed the buffalo herds closely and preyed on the old, sick, and immature animals. After natives had exhausted the beaver of the river valley forests, in the prairies coyote were among the few remaining fur-bearers.[45] In contrast, a variety of more valuable fur-bearers were still present in the woodlands in reasonable numbers, so there was little incentive for woodland Indians to go after timber and common wolf before 1870.

Lynx, a clever and elusive creature of the deep forests, where it preyed mostly on hare, has long, silky-haired, highly prized pelts. Taken in comparatively small numbers, it was the fourth-ranked fur in 1870. Most returns came from the parklands and southern boreal forests. Hunters obtained very few of them in the Hudson Bay and James Bay lowlands.

One of the striking features of the aggregate fur returns in 1870 is the extent to which the trade of the late nineteenth century contrasted sharply with that of the late eighteenth century. In 1770 beaver, marten, and muskrat were the leading furs, in that order of importance, which meant that there was a high ratio of luxury to utility furs. But by 1870 muskrat was the leading fur throughout the Southern Department beyond the Hudson Bay and James Bay lowlands and in the Northern Department except for the Churchill and Athabasca districts. In the heart of muskrat country, between one-half and two-thirds of all animals trapped were muskrat. In the southern James Bay area rabbit, rather than muskrat, dominated the returns, because natives had over-trapped the more valuable species. At Moose Factory rabbit pelts accounted for over one-half of the furs produced. Unfortunately for the native trappers, muskrat and rabbit skins fetched low prices, and these two animal species underwent cyclical population fluctuations that were much greater than those of beaver and most other fur-bearers. This problem was most acute in the Hudson Bay and James Bay lowlands, muskrat country, and in the tracts of land along major transportation corridors.[46] In these areas there was a greater need than ever before for the Hudson's Bay Company to offer to its regular trading partners gratuities, uncollectable debts, and relief for the sick and destitute.

competition in trade

In the early 1870s the Hudson's Bay Company faced competitors primarily along a front extending from the Athabasca River / Peace River region through the prairie / parkland district and eastward along the Rainy River. Opponents were also active east of Lake Superior. In the early 1860s the Cariboo Goldrush drew a large population of miners and prospectors to the Quesnel Lake area of British Columbia. As the goldrush faded, 'free traders' began to fan out from the region, and by 1865–6 they had worked their way into the Athabasca River / Peace River country in search of beaver.[47] The Hudson's Bay Company took immediate steps to counter the threat by building a post at Quesnel Lake which became the major outfitting base for these traders. Here the company could monitor their movements. In addition, Chief Trader Peter Ogden was given 'strict orders' to place his best men at McLeod's Lake and the Peace River Portage to oppose vigorously all those who were heading east.[48] Despite these aggressive steps, the 'free traders' (a term the company applied to its small opponents) continued to expand their operations. To draw Indian trappers away from the Hudson's Bay Company they sold illicit alcohol and undercut the company's prices for other goods.[49]

The success that these competitors were achieving caused problems for the Hudson's Bay Company beyond the Athabasca River / Peace River district. 'Frontier Natives' living in the Mackenzie River District wanted the company to lower its tariffs in their country to levels comparable with those of Peace River. Richard Hardisty, who was managing the Mackenzie River District at the time, warned against complying with the Indians' request. According to Commissioner Grahame: 'Mr Hardisty acknowledges the impossibility of altering the Tariff from the inability to supply the extra consumption of imports that would at once arise.'[50] The issue Hardisty raised was an old one. Throughout the period after 1821 the limited capacity of the Hudson's Bay Company's transportation system meant that the quantities of supplies sent to the Mackenzie River area often were inadequate to meet Indian demand. So long as competition was weak, the company did not have to address the problem. However, in the face of growing opposition, it needed to find a solution. Grahame wrote that the company's officers, Hardisty included, 'see steam as [the] cure all.'[51] For this reason, the need to meet the opposition served as a major incentive for the modernization of the company's transportation system in the northwest.

In the woodlands to the east of Athabasca country traders were active in the Green Lake area, where they were 'upsetting the tariff of the trade and unsettling the minds of the Indians.'[52] Also, opponents in the Cumberland District were 'demoralizing' the Indians. To deal with this problem commissioner Grahame authorized the introduction of tariffs that were more favourable to the Indians. He instructed the Cumberland District head, Horace Belanger, to let him know if the change had the desired effect, and he warned him to make sure that the new standard did not adversely affect the business of the adjacent English River District.[53]

Even the isolated York Factory District was feeling the pull of the 'free traders.' In 1874 Chief Factor James Fortescue complained that 'his Indians' were being drawn southward towards Oxford House and Norway House, where they could obtain better prices for their marten and silver fox from company posts and from the opposition.[54] In order to deal with this problem, Grahame authorized the raising of the York Factory District prices for marten and silver fox by 50 per cent.[55] He also ordered Fortescue to work with neighbouring district managers to prevent Indians from obtaining credit in one district and trading in another.[56]

In the prairie / parkland region opposition was particularly strong. Buffalo were still plentiful in the Edmonton area in the early 1870s, but Grahame complained that the selling prices for robes and furs were 'exorbitant.'[57] To combat the opposition in this quarter the commissioner proposed reducing the number of outposts that the company operated and reverting to the older practice of tripping by sending off energetic officers with carts to deal with natives in their buffalo hunting camps.

The prices the natives demanded for robes were also high in the Saskatchewan District near Fort Carlton and at Red River. In contrast to the situation around Edmonton, buffalo were scarce in Saskatchewan and absent in Manitoba. The hunters from the latter district travelled as far as the Cypress Hills area in search of the herds.[58] In order to secure the robe trade of Saskatchewan country the company adopted the policy of 'establishing a cordon of people on the Plains toward the Buffalo country.'[59] Grahame thought this policy would work well. In the Red River settlement the company was receiving its fair share of the robe business. Current prices were $10 per robe and Americans were paying cash for them. Apparently this was the only place in the prairie region in the early 1870s where cash buying took place.

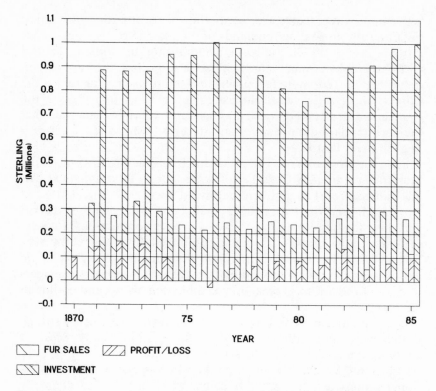

Figure 6
Investments, fur sales, and net returns: Hudson's Bay Company, 1870–85

Besides robes, there was a strong market throughout the prairie/
parkland region for hides and provisions. The vast majority of the
hides were taken south of the border by Indian and Métis hunters. The
Hudson's Bay Company and Red River settlers purchased most of the
available dried meat, grease, and pemmican.

Clearly the stockholders' decision to commit the Hudson's Bay Company to remain in the fur trade was risky and of fundamental importance to the subsequent course of northern and native history. On
balance, the company's experience in the fur trade during the first few
years after the adoption of the 1871 plan was not encouraging. It
was a poor time to be investing substantial additional capital in new
transportation equipment. The severe world-wide depression which
began in 1873 and lasted until the mid-1890s hit fur markets very hard

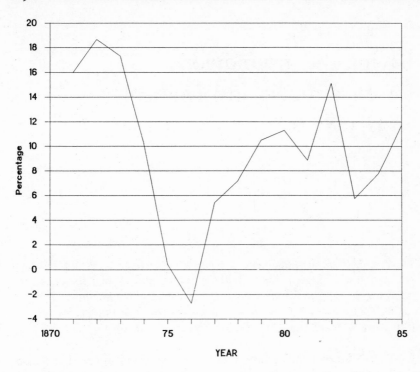

Figure 7
Net return on fur trade investment: Hudson's Bay Company fur trade,
1870–85

(fig. 2). The value of fur sales and the returns on investments slumped
until the late 1870s (figs 6 and 7). Profit margins paralleled the trend,
and the Fur Trade Department registered a net loss in 1876 when fur
prices hit a twenty-year low. In 1877 Governor George Goshen believed
it was necessary to point out to stockholders that the current price
levels were not likely to be the new norm. He cautioned them 'not to
see the present situation as the end of the company.' His forecast was
correct. By 1885 sales and the returns on investments had not recovered
to the levels of 1871 – the year of decision. None the less, the company
survived this trial and in subsequent years it acted as the most conservative force in the industry. But, as we shall see, this conservatism in
the face of rapidly changing circumstances meant that it steadily lost
ground to a growing array of opponents.

2
Laying the groundwork for government involvement, 1870–1885

The Whites think the Indians get too much and Indians think they do not get enough. Government has to hold the balance and see that the Indian is protected. In fact the Government is the guardian of the Indians ... We cannot allow them to starve, and we cannot make them Whitemen.
(Sir John A. Macdonald, House of Commons, 1880)[1]

Once the Canadian government had obtained Old Rupert's Land from the Hudson's Bay Company, it faced the task of extinguishing aboriginal title to those territories needed for agriculture development and for telegraph and transportation rights of way. Government officials wanted to achieve this objective as quickly and as cheaply as possible through the established custom of negotiating treaties. The native peoples, on the other hand, were anxious about their future, and they hoped to use the negotiations to obtain concessions that would enable them to improve their economic position under rapidly changing circumstances. The specific objectives of the bands varied a great deal depending on their local situation. The treaties that Indians signed between 1871 and 1877 (Treaties 1–7) served as models for those concluded between 1899 and 1920 (Treaties 8–11) (fig. 8).

The treaties had their most immediate impact on the Indians and the Hudson's Bay Company through the compensation packages the parties agreed upon. Reflecting their varied economic circumstances and objectives, native groups wanted different amounts of compensation for the extinguishment of their title. During the negotiations for Treaties 1 and 2 in 1871, the Indians of southern Manitoba agreed to a

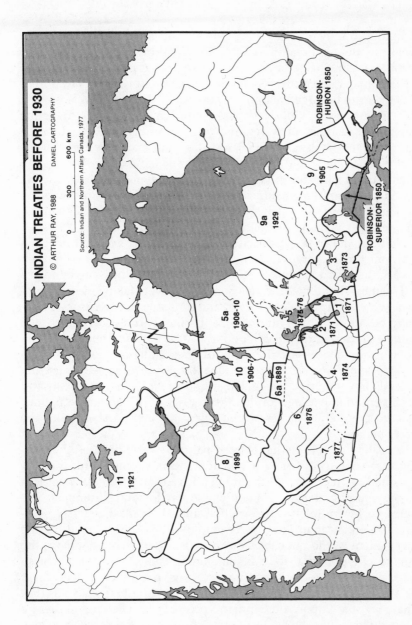

Figure 8
Indian treaties before 1930

$3 annual annuity for every man, woman, and child. Wemyss Simpson, superintendent-general of Indian Affairs and one of the government negotiators for Treaties 1 and 2 expressed the view that this amount was adequate. According to Simpson: 'the sum of three dollars does not appear to be large enough to enable an Indian to provide himself with many of his winter necessaries, but as he receives the same amount for his wife, or wives, and for each of his children, then the aggregate sum is usually sufficient to procure many comforts for his family which he would otherwise be compelled to deny himself.'[2] In other words, Simpson thought an annuity payment of between $12 and $16 per family was sufficient for a hunter to obtain his outfit. In 1870 outfits were still relatively modest, consisting mostly of ammunition, tea, biscuits, traps, traplines, and fishing equipment.

Although the annuity provisions of Treaties 1 and 2 might have been sufficient for these purposes at the time, the Ojibwa living between Lake of the Woods and Lake Superior demanded more. These Indians had seen first hand the kinds of changes that were taking place. Steamboats were plying the Rainy River, and settlements were springing up along both sides of the international border. Farther eastward in the country bordering on Lake Superior, prospectors and miners were at work.[3] The Ojibwa saw the opportunities and problems that these developments created. These Indians did not want to sell their land. Instead, they preferred to negotiate rights of access for the railway and a compensation package for their timber rights.[4] Given their economic agenda, these Ojibwa were in no hurry to come to terms with the government.

In dealing with these hard-nosed bargainers, Morris took the position that he and his fellow negotiators did not come as 'fur traders.' They had no intention of bargaining on issues other than the amount of compensation the government would pay for land surrenders. Furthermore, Morris told the Ojibwa that since their area had less agricultural potential than that surrendered in Treaties 1 and 2, the government would not pay as much for it. His pitch did not move the Ojibwa. Responding to this bargaining ploy, one chief wisely remarked: 'the sound of the rustling of the gold is under my feet where I stand. We have a rich country; it is the Great Spirit who gave us this; where we stand upon is the Indian's property, and belongs to them ... The whiteman has robbed us of our riches, and we don't wish to give them up again without getting something in their place.'[5]

The government negotiators faced a serious problem. So long as the

Ojibwa bands living beside the Dawson Road (an all-Canadian river and wagon road route leading from Thunder Bay to Red River) were making a good income by selling timber and fuel, they were under no pressure to come to terms quickly.[6] Fortunately for the government those Ojibwa who lived to the northward near Lake Osnaburgh had different objectives. They were much more dependent on the fur trade. Through treaty negotiations these Ojibwa hoped to improve their economic position in the fur trade economy. Annuities offered them the prospect of obtaining the income they needed to purchase their hunting outfits without having to resort to the high-priced credit Hudson's Bay Company traders offered. In addition, they wanted the government to help them in the development of gardens,[7] which they believed would help them reduce the risk of suffering from periodic food shortages. This was becoming a major concern because of the growing problem of game depletion.

Sensing that a division existed between the two groups, Morris decided to 'sweeten the pot' in the hope of getting an agreement from these northerly bands. During a conversation he held with the chief of Lac Seul, Morris queried: 'I mean to ask you what amount you would have in goods, so that you would not have to pay the traders prices for them.'[8] Somewhat later Morris answered his own question, saying: 'I think it is a wise thing to do, that is to give you ammunition and twine for making nets to the extent of $1,500/yr for the whole nation, so that you can have the means of procuring food.'[9]

Even after being offered this small additional benefit, the Indians forced Morris to pay them higher annuities than the government had agreed to in Treaties 1 and 2. Men, women, and children received annuities of $5 per year, headmen $15, and chiefs $25.[10] Furthermore, chiefs and headmen were given triennial clothing allowances which were similar to the 'captain's' and 'lieutenant's' outfits that they formerly received from the fur traders.[11] Still not satisfied, the Ojibwa informed Morris that they wanted the government to guarantee to supply food whenever it assembled them to pay annuities.[12] Morris responded by assuring them that, 'unless the Great Spirit sent the grasshoppers and no wheat was grown in Red River, provisions would always be supplied whenever the government brought them together.'[13] Once they had obtained these various concessions, the northern Ojibwa signed Treaty 3 in 1873. The bands who lived along the Rainy River had little choice but to follow.

Subsequently, the Indians who had previously signed Treaties 1 and

2 benefited from the more generous terms the Rainy River and English River Ojibwa had wrung from the government in 1873. In 1875 the Privy Council of Canada amended the earlier agreements to bring the annuity provisions in line with those of Treaty 3.[14] Indians living in the Saskatchewan and Alberta areas sought even larger settlements, but they were not successful. The annuity provisions of Treaties 4 through 7 signed between 1874 and 1877 were the same as those of Treaty 3. The annual ammunition and twine allowances varied considerably according to treaty (table 3).

By the time negotiations for Treaty 6 began in 1876, the bison economy was collapsing. Fearing famine and pestilence, the Indians of southern Saskatchewan, led by Chief Sweet Grass, sent a petition to the governor of the North-West Territories asking for a treaty that would protect them against years of starvation.[15] During the Treaty 6 negotiations, Chief Poundmaker and other leaders asked the government to help his people settle on their reserves and begin to farm.[16] Morris said he responded to these pleas as follows: 'I explained that we could not assume the charge of their every-day life, but in time of great national calamity they could trust the generosity of the Queen.'[17] The assurances Morris gave to the Indians of the Saskatchewan prairies and parklands were incorporated into a clause in Treaty 6 which guaranteed: 'That in the event hereafter of the Indians comprised within this treaty being overtaken by any pestilence, or by a general famine, the Queen, on being satisfied and certified thereof by her Indian Agent or Agents, will grant assistance of such character and to such extent as her Chief Superintendent or Indian Agent shall deem necessary.'[18] In addition, in Treaty 6 the government pledged to provide medical help to the Indians.

The problem for the government was that the development of the North-West Territories was an expensive undertaking (fig. 9), and the conclusion of Treaties 1–7 added considerably to these expenditures (fig. 10). Between 1868 and 1881 they accounted for over 11 per cent of the total for the new territory, and by 1885 Indian Department expenses accounted for nearly 15 per cent of the total federal expenditures under supply bills.[19] These spiralling costs provoked prolonged and heated debates between MPs in the House whenever the government introduced Indian Department supply bills. In these debates federal politicians expressed their shock and alarm over the magnitude of the financial burden that the government had assumed in Treaties 1 through 7. The MPs were concerned for two reasons. First and fore-

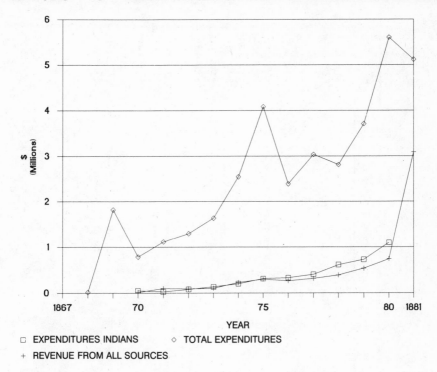

Figure 9
Government expenditures and receipts: Manitoba and the North-West,
1867–81

most, no one in the government had any idea of how many Indians
lived in the surrendered territories. This ignorance came to light in the
controversy that arose over the mounting size of the appropriations
that the Indian Department annually requested for annuity payments
between 1875 and the early 1880s. The large initial expenditures shown
in figure 9 were the result of the government's granting the Indians
the right to wait one or more years after treaties were signed to settle
on reserves and collect their annuities. When they did so they received
their current annuities plus those that were in arrears. The substantial
arrears payments made between 1875 and 1885 largely account for the
upward curve in spending that took place before payments levelled
off at about $140,000 per year. The upsurge in 1899 reflects the impact
of the signing of Treaty 8 in that year.

TABLE 3
Treaty compensation packages

Treaty	Date	Expenses at time of signing	Recurring incidental expenses	Annuities
Robinson-Superior	1850	2,000 [sterling]	Not mentioned	$4/Indian
Robinson-Huron	1850	2,160 [Sterling]	Not mentioned	$4/Indian
Manitoulin Island	1862	$700	Not mentioned	*
Treaties 1 and 2	1871	$3/Indian, farm stock & equipment and buggy to each chief		
Treaty 3	1873	$12/Indian, farm stock & equipment and buggy to each chief	$1,500/year for ammunition & twine	$25/chief $15/headman $5/Indian
Treaty 4	1874	$25/Chief; $15/headman; $12/Indian; ammunition, farm animals & equipment; coats for chiefs & headmen	$750/year for ammunition & twine; triennial clothing allowances	$25/chief $15/headman $5/Indian
Treaty 5 Adhesions 1908–10	1875	$5/Indian; farm stock & equipment; flags & medals chiefs; $500 moving costs for Saulteaux of Sask R	$500/year for ammunition & twine; triennial clothing allowances; additional amounts for the adhesions	$25/chief $15/headman $5/Indian
Treaty 6 Adhesion 1889	1876	$12/Indian; farm animals & equipment; flags, medals & waggons or cars for chiefs	$1,500/yr for ammunition & twine; triennial clothing; $1,000/year for provisions for first 3 years	$25/chief $15/headman $5/Indian

Treaty	Year			
Treaty 7	1877	$12/Indian; farm animals & equipment; flags, medals & for chiefs; rifle for each headman & chief	$2,000 for ammunition; triennial clothing	$25/chief $15/headman $5/Indian
Treaty 8	1899	$32/Chief, $22/headman & $12/Indian; farm animals & equipment; flags & medals for chiefs	$1/family/year for ammunition; triennial clothing	$25/chief $15/headman $5/Indian
Treaty 9	1905	$8/Indian; flag & copy of treaty for each chief	Not mentioned	$4/Indian
Treaty 10	1906	$32/Chief, $22/headman & $12/Indian; medals for chiefs & headmen; flag/chief	Ammunition & twine; triennial clothing & help with farming	$25/chief $15/headman $5/Indian
Treaty 11	1921	$32/Chief, $22/headman & $12/Indian; medals & flags for chiefs; $50/family for hunting equipment	$3/hunter in twine, ammunition and trapping equipment	$25/chief $15/headman $5/Indian

SOURCE: Department of Indian Affairs, *Indian Treaties in Historical Perspective* (Ottawa 1979)

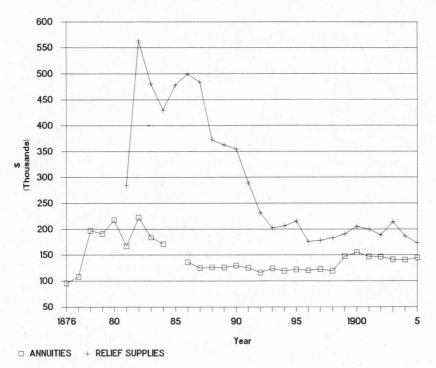

□ ANNUITIES   + RELIEF SUPPLIES

Figure 10
Annuity and relief supply expenses: Manitoba and the North-West,
1876–1905

Annuities

By the late 1870s, members of parliament were clamouring to know
how many more 'stragglers' could be expected; they wanted to know
when the annuity bills would stop increasing. Under intensive ques-
tioning by opposition members in the 1880s successive ministers had
to admit that they had no idea of how many Indians there were, since
no censuses had been taken.[20] Clearly the government had made a
blind commitment, and the dimension of the obligation was still
unknown. This disturbing fact was haunting members of parliament.
    Rather than accept such a painful reality, it seems that some MPS
preferred to believe that widespread fraud by Indians accounted for
the escalating annuity bill. In Ottawa it was widely rumoured that
Indians often presented themselves at two or more payment locations
in order to collect more money than was rightfully theirs. Indian

Department officials acknowledged that a problem existed, but they denied deceptions were commonplace and stated that they definitely did not account for the growing size of the annuity bill.[21] John A. Macdonald's attitudes about the matter and his perceptions of native people did not help to clear the air. In replying to a member of the House who raised the fraud charges, the prime minister quipped: 'they are very clever fellows, and some of the agents cannot know one Indian from another, they look so much alike; but of course frauds will become more difficult by degree.'[22]

Also, the costs of delivering annuity payments were much greater than the government had anticipated. At the outset the government lacked the administrative machinery needed to make the payments, so it turned to the Hudson's Bay Company for help in the manner Macdonald had envisioned in 1871. In the first few years agents distributed the annuities at a few strategically located company posts where the Indian bands assembled. No payments were made at a given post until all appropriate band members were present. Those who arrived early had to be fed. The Hudson's Bay Company charged the provisioning expenses to the government. Very quickly the Indians came to regard the annual treaty feast as a normal part of the payment ceremony. This is not surprising considering that gift exchange ceremonies were still an important aspect of their trading relations with the Hudson's Bay Company. One MP claimed that during a visit he made to Fort Qu'Appelle at annuity time 3,000 to 4,000 Indians already had gathered but they forced the paymaster to wait five days before letting him begin his duties so that they could conduct a feast.[23] In response to mounting pressure from the House to trim the size of the annuity bills, in 1880 Macdonald announced that henceforth the government would pay Indians annuities only on their respective reserves. This would eliminate the need to feed them at treaty time and it would stop the alleged fraud.[24]

Although Indian Department expenditures were causing great concern to Ottawa politicians, Indians and whites alike living in the northwest welcomed them as an economic windfall. The aggregate value of the annuities paid out in each treaty area were substantial, even though the per capita amounts were small. Also, the economy of the northwest was cash poor, which meant that the Indians were among the very few people who had any money to spend during the first couple of decades after Confederation. For this reason travelling pedlars quickly appeared on the scene in search of a share of the lively 'treaty trade' that sprang up. Pedlars closely followed the government treaty parties. Hudson's Bay Company officers resented these intruders and likened them to 'sharks following a sinking ship.' Naturally, company men were among the sharks.[25] By drawing cash merchandisers into the north for the first time, annuity payments served as a catalyst for the movement of native people away from the credit / barter system of the pre-Confederation fur trade and towards a new economic order in which buying furs and merchandising were increasingly separated and cash transactions became more commonplace.

Initially, relief expenditures were even more important than annuity payments in Old Rupert's Land. In the early 1880s these costs greatly alarmed Ottawa politicians. Indians, the Métis, and government officials alike had foreseen the end of the buffalo-hunting economy. But no one had anticipated the speed at which the collapse would take place. The recently independent and proud Plains Indians were suddenly reduced to being wards of the state who were utterly dependent on massive economic assistance to fend off starvation. By the early 1880s government expenditures for this aid had risen to about half a million dollars annually (fig. 9). The young Canadian government had to shoulder this financial burden at the height of a world-wide depression when it was increasingly difficult to borrow money, making fiscal restraint an absolute necessity. In the 1870s the expenditures for development of the northwest exceeded the revenues received by a wide margin (fig. 9).

The government faced legal problems and a moral dilemma in its efforts to hold the line on Indian Department expenditures. It was legally bound to provide famine assistance in the Treaty 6 area. Some members of parliament firmly believed that the government should not have made such a treaty commitment. For instance, in 1880 the controversial Dr John Schultz of Manitoba (1871–82) told the house: 'the necessity for this expenditure commenced with the sanction, by the late Administration, of one of the vicious conditions of Treaty # 6 ... the result of the clause agreeing that the government should furnish food in times of scarcity – was followed by a vote for that purpose at the very next session of Parliament, and we have found the constant occurrence of a similar necessity at every session since.'[26] Donald A. Smith, who at the time was representing the riding of Selkirk, Manitoba, in parliament (the riding was then in the southwestern part of the province), agreed that the clause was 'a most unfortunate one and never ought to have been agreed to by the Indian Commissioners.'[27]

Smith added, however, that the government had little choice but to honour the agreement or run the risk of provoking general unrest in the native population.[28]

Members of parliament were only too willing to 'blame' other parties for the relief clause. In reality the government had no choice but to render aid in the Treaty 6 area or elsewhere. Sir John A. Macdonald bluntly made this point in his address to the House on 11 March 1881: 'Of course the system is tentative and it is expensive, especially in feeding destitute Indians, but it is cheaper to feed them than to fight them, and humanity will not allow us to let them starve ... The vote [for supply bills] is large, but the Indians must be fed, and the country will not allow us to let them starve for the sake of economy.'[29]

Besides worrying about costs, members of parliament feared that their approval of ever larger supply bills encouraged the Indians to become permanent wards of the state. Mr David Mills, former superintendent-general of Indian affairs for the Reform party government, expressed this concern in the commons on 26 April 1882, stating that it was pretty evident that 'the Indians have become pensioners upon the Public Treasury, that we are called upon to feed them, to clothe them, and that they are doing little or nothing for themselves.'[30] This alarmism is not surprising, considering the social ideology of the era. It was not commonplace for governments to provide extensive social assistance on a continuing basis. In this regard the Indian Department was a pioneering government agency which was bound to be sharply criticized for its expenditures for such purposes.

Prime Minister Macdonald was acutely aware that the government faced a dilemma over the Indian relief issue. Macdonald and his ministers in the Indian Department decided to embark on a very delicate balancing act that was aimed at trimming departmental expenses, encouraging Indian industry, and providing natives with just enough food for their survival. Beginning in the summer of 1882, the Indian Department reduced Plains Indians rations between one-half to one-quarter and they withheld these stinted allowances until Indians were on the edge of starvation to 'encourage them to work.'

Despite Macdonald's 'economy measures,' relief costs remained high until 1887, when a downward trend began. The decline continued until 1896, when it levelled off in the $150,000 to $200,000 per year range (fig 10). Although politicians continued to regard relief payments as a serious drain on the treasury, the level of aid offered remained grossly inadequate. Indian buffalo hunters had to eat gophers and prairie dogs to survive. Some starved. It was the prospect of continued deprivation that led some of the Plains Indians to take part in the 1885 rebellion.[31]

suppliers

Over time MPs showed less concern about the drain on the treasury and the philosophical issues that government relief programs raised. Instead they became more interested in deciding who should benefit from the lucrative supply-contracting business generated by the assistance program. In the beginning the I.G. Baker Company of Fort Benton, Montana, and the Hudson's Bay Company were the two principal beneficiaries.[32] The American company supplied most of the relief in the southern Alberta and southwestern Saskatchewan territory, while the Hudson's Bay Company provided it in the Saskatchewan River valley and in Manitoba. These two companies also obtained most of the contracts for the triennial clothing allowances and for the agricultural equipment promised in the treaties. In addition, they supplied most of the needs of the North West Mounted Police. Between them, I.G. Baker and the Hudson's Bay Company received from $500,000 to $1 million worth of government contracts per year by the early 1880s.[33] This was a small bonanza that the Hudson's Bay Company directors had not anticipated in 1871. It was a godsend in the height of the depression and helped soften the blow of slumping fur sales and the slow pace of settlement which deprived the company of the volume of land sales and saleshop business they had expected in the 1870s and early 1880s. Smith's impatience with Commissioner Grahame's reluctance to go after the government contracting business aggressively is understandable in this context.

From the outset opposition MPs complained that I.G. Baker and the Hudson's Bay Company were foreign companies, and, therefore, Canadians (i.e., businessmen from their electoral ridings) were not profiting from the development of the northwest. On 9 May 1883 one MP stated in the House of Commons that 'It is scarcely in accordance with the National Policy, that $450,000 should be paid to Messrs Baker & Co of Fort Benton, U.S.'[34] Another member of the house asked Macdonald: 'Where does the Hon gentleman draw his inspiration from in permitting a Yankee firm to obtain $462,000 for supplies, which could have been obtained from our own dealers?' The prime minister sarcastically replied: 'The inspiration from which I drew ... was the greatest of all monarchs—the monarch of necessity.'[35] He went on to point out that the government did not exclude any Canadian firms from bidding for the supply contracts; I.G. Baker and the Hudson's Bay Company were simply the lowest bidders, and they had good delivery records.[36] Macdonald's replies did not silence the opposition, and members continued to push for changes in contracting procedures. In the summer of 1885 opposition MPs argued that the practice of letting government contracts 'en bloc' effectively eliminated Canadian firms, because potential suppliers had to tender for the entire range of goods that the Indian Department and the North West Mounted Police required; even worse, the suppliers had to deliver their goods at over 200 points of consumption. Small merchants and specialty manufacturers lacked the financial resources and expertise to meet these terms. One MP concluded the attack on Macdonald on this issue by observing: 'I can assure him it is not a pleasant thing for our merchants and manufacturers, who are contributors to the construction of this railway to find half a million or three quarters of a million dollars going to a foreign company, who are monopolizing the business of that country, when our own people are excluded. For my part I am not satisfied with the explanation of the premier at all.[37]

The prime minister acknowledged that block contracting and delivery requirements did pose problems for eastern Canadian firms, but he also made the barbed observation that he knew Canadian industrialists would welcome having the government encumbered in their interests. However, he noted that the House could not have the government assume the delivery costs if it was truly concerned about expenditures.[38]

This acrimonious debate dragged on until the government changed the contracting procedures for the benefit of Canadian firms. By 1888 it abandoned block tendering, so that small firms could furnish a narrow range of goods. However, government suppliers were still expected to deliver their merchandise to the various reserves.[39] Firms operated by loyal Tories were the immediate beneficiaries of the change in policy, while I.G. Baker suffered the most. The role of the American company was replaced primarily by ranchers in southern Alberta, who supplied most of the beef issued as relief, and the Montreal-based Ogilvie milling company became the major source of flour. The Hudson's Bay Company was not seriously hurt by the changes. It bought the Canadian interests of I.G. Baker in 1891, and it continued to be the major supply contractor in the prairie and parkland areas.[40]

In the woodlands of the northwest, which lay outside the boundaries of Treaties 3, 5, and 6, the government was reluctant to provide aid to native peoples because of the heavy relief expenditures that it had to shoulder in the prairies at that time. Also, officials feared that giving assistance beyond these boundaries would lead non-treaty Indians to think they had the same rights as treaty Indians. For this reason, when disease and food shortages did occur, forcing the government's hand, the Indian Department tried to mask its aid by funnelling it through the Hudson's Bay Company on the understanding that the company's officers would distribute it in absolute confidence.[41]

Given that MPS opposed making any new agreements and balked at the idea of spending money on Indians who lived outside of treaty areas, Indian Department officials could respond to the needs of the non-Indians to only a limited extent. It was for this reason that the Hudson's Bay Company had to continue to offer economic assistance to Indians regardless of whether their competitors did so. Whenever there were widespread food shortages in the north, such as in the years 1878–9 when caribou, moose, and rabbit were scarce, these outlays by the company were considerable.[42]

Given this situation, some of the company's profit-sharing officers believed that it was time to shift this burden to the government by pressing for more treaties. For instance, in 1880 James Fortescue, the chief factor of the York Factory District, wrote to the Hudson's Bay Company secretary, William Armit, to say that he thought the company should encourage local Indians to ask the government for a treaty. Fortescue argued that the advantages of extending treaties to include his district would be twofold. Annuity payments would provide an additional and badly needed source of wealth for his depleted district, and the Indians' welfare needs would become the responsibility of the government. Regarding the latter point, Fortescue observed that while it was reasonable for the company to shoulder this burden when it held a trading monopoly, under competitive conditions it put the company at a disadvantage, since the opposition traders did not share any of the cost.[43] He did not mention that the other obvious benefit of transferring this obligation to the government was that the company stood to profit from potential relief contracts. In this way a traditional drain on business profits could be transformed into a revenue-generating activity. Assuming that the company's officers dispensed all the government aid, they would not suffer any loss of prestige in the eyes of the native people. In this way they would still be in a strong position to manipulate their native clients.

The issue Fortescue raised remained unresolved before the Second World War. Obviously the company's fur-trading operations would be more profitable if the government offered adequate relief to native hunters during hard times. But, the Hudson's Bay Company could not afford to ignore native needs if the government failed to act.

Beginning with Treaties 1 and 2 (the Stone Fort Treaties), government negotiators offered the Indians of the northwest the same basic terms that had been granted to their eastern brothers in the precedent-setting 1850 Robinson Treaties. These two treaties extinguished aboriginal title to the country lying between Lake Superior, Lake Huron, and the height of land. Of particular relevance here, the Robinson Treaties gave the Indians the right to hunt and fish on undeveloped crown lands lying beyond their reserves. In July of 1871 A.G. Archibald, lieutenant-governor of Manitoba, addressed the Indians who had assembled at Lower Fort Garry (the 'Stone Fort') to discuss the proposed treaty, and he assured them: 'When you have made your treaty you will still be free to hunt over much of the land included in the treaty. Much of it is rocky and unfit for cultivation. Till these lands are needed for use you will be free to hunt over them, and make all the use of them you have made in the past.'[44] *Treaty promises*

According to Alexander Morris, who served as the lieutenant-governor of the North-West Territories between 1872 and 1876 and as the government's chief negotiator in Treaties 3–6, the restrictions on Indian hunting were primarily intended to minimize the possibilities of conflict by preventing native people from transgressing on cleared farm land. For instance, during the discussions leading up to the signing of Treaty 6, Morris told the assembled Cree and Ojibwa: 'you want to be at liberty to hunt as before. I told you we did not want to take that means of living from you, you have it the same as before, only this, if a man, whether Indian or Hudson Bay, had a good field of grain, you would not destroy it with your hunt.'[45] Later he added: 'I want the Indians to understand that all that has been offered is a gift, and they still have the same mode of living as before.'[46] Carrying the point still farther, Morris concluded: 'I see them [Indians of Treaties 3–5] receiving money from the Queen's Commissioners to purchase clothing for their children; at the same time I see them retaining their old mode of living with the Queen's gift in addition.'[47]

In essence Morris repeatedly told the Indians they were surrendering nothing of real consequence; they were 'merely' consenting to live on reserves (to be surveyed later) and agreeing not to damage farm lands while going about their normal activities. In return for these 'minor concessions' they would receive presents and gain a new source of income from annuities. This bargaining strategy worked. Even at the time, however, some politicians warned of the dangers inherent in such an approach. On 18 April 1877 MP John Schultz pointed out to the House of Commons that the treaty commissioners were convincing the Indian to 'part with his birth right for a mere trifle. The reserve question not being fixed, the Indian is under the impression that the country is still practically his for hunting purposes. This answers very well till the necessities of colonization force him on to the reserve.'[48]

When the Indians demanded to have their hunting and fishing rights preserved, they were not thinking only in terms of mere legal guarantees. They wanted the government to protect wildlife against the unbridled slaughter by white miners, loggers, settlers, and trappers that was beginning to take place along the frontiers of white settlement to the northwest of Lake Superior and in the western parkland belt. For instance, during Treaty 3 negotiations they expressed the desire that measures be taken to protect their fisheries from destruction.[49] While discussing the terms for Treaty 6, Indians asked for a law banning the use of poisons for hunting and trapping purposes. They said that white hunters were having a devastating impact on game by employing baits laced with strychnine.[50] During these same discussions, one famous Indian spokesman, Big Bear, demanded that measures be taken to protect the buffalo.[51] Morris responded to Big Bear by saying that the North-West Council was considering framing a law for that purpose. He added that everyone, including Indians, would have to obey it.[52]

Morris's reply highlights the major dilemma that Indians, politicians, and the courts alike would face in attempting to preserve native hunting and fishing rights and protect wildlife also. The ambiguity of the hunting and fishing rights clauses of the treaties suggests that insufficient thought was given to this problem. For instance, Treaty 3 provided:

Her Majesty further agrees with her said Indians, that they, the said Indians, shall have the right to pursue their avocations of hunting and fishing throughout the tract surrendered as hereinafter described, subject to such regulations as may from time to time be made by her Government of her Dominion of Canada, and saving and excepting such tracts as may from time to time be required or taken up for settlement, mining, lumbering or other purposes.[53]

Later treaties (4–7) used this same wording. In Treaty 8 it was altered to read 'usual vocations.'[54] At later dates the federal and provincial governments used these 'subject to such regulations' qualifications in the hunting rights clauses to extend conservation statutes to Indians as well as to the general population. The problem for the natives, however, is that judges generally have taken the position that the treaties protected subsistence hunting and fishing rights – the native 'avocations' – but not their commercial interests.[55] This perspective ignores the Indians' historical circumstances. At the time treaties were signed, the commercial and subsistence sectors of Indian hunting economies were interdependent. For many native groups this was a two-century-old reality by the time of Confederation.[56]

In the late nineteenth century the passage of game laws did not cause any serious hardships for native peoples. In 1893 the Ontario government (the northwestern boundary of the province lay to the southeast of the Albany and English rivers) passed the Game Protection Act and the following year the federal government approved the Unorganized Territories Game Preservation Act. These acts provided for the establishment of closed seasons for birds, big game, and fur-bearers; the banning of 'unsportsmanlike' practices such as poisoned baits, running deer with dogs, and the use of snares to kill animals other than fur-bearers; and the provision for game guardians, or wardens, for enforcement.[57] Most of the provisions of these pioneering pieces of legislation did not apply to Indians, so their treaty rights (those of the Robinson Treaties and Treaties 1–7) were not seriously impaired. As more white hunters and trappers entered the northwest, however, the need arose for more restrictive legislation. Conservationists and politicians granted the Indians fewer exemptions. For example, 1906 amendments to the Unorganized Territories Game Preservation Act (retitled the Northwest Game Act) placed a temporary ban on beaver trapping which affected Indian trappers. This law caused hardship, since it deprived them of one of their key sources of income, food, and clothing. Eventually the courts disallowed the revised act because it violated Treaties 2, 4, 6, and 7 by imposing a complete ban on the hunting of certain species.[58]

It is clear that the period between 1870 and the completion of the Canadian Pacific Railway in 1885 was very important in that it was the time when the groundwork was laid for government involvement in the native and fur trade economies. The government's response to the plight of native people in the northwest in the 1870s and 1880s served to highlight the limitations of the paternalism of the state in the late nineteenth century in comparison with that of the Hudson's Bay Company in the earlier mercantile age. In the rush to obtain Indian land as cheaply as possible without bloodshed commitments were made with little thought about what the magnitude of these financial undertakings might be. Faced with the need to impose restraint during a time of economic crises and precluded by law from curtailing annuity and other treaty allowances, senior government officials decided to stint relief and run the Indian Department on a shoe-string. Being short staffed with poorly qualified personnel, the Ottawa bureaucracy was unable to respond quickly to agents in the field, who were acutely aware of the desperate needs of the Indians.[59]

Making matters worse, Ottawa officials had no contact with Indians and they had no vested interests in their well-being. On the contrary, their self-interests were best served by catering to their political masters. For them it was easier to yield to political pressures in the capital city than to give priority to the needs of the Indians whenever there was a conflict between the two.

The manner in which Deputy Superintendent-General of Indian Affairs Lawrence Vankoughnet ran his department between 1874 and 1893 illustrates the problems the Indians had to contend with. Vankoughnet's family was of Loyalist background and had close ties with Prime Minister Macdonald. Vankoughnet was devoted to Macdonald and always deferred to his wishes. Apparently he was an archetypal Victorian in terms of his narrow-mindedness and earnestness. Vankoughnet was completely unsympathetic to Indians who were unwilling to take up farming; he gave top priority to keeping the Indian Department's budgets to the bare minimum, even refusing to allow his agents free access to the telegraph in times of crisis; and he exercised absolute control over all major decisions by refusing to delegate any real authority.[60]

Given the political agenda of the day and Vankoughnet's management style, Indian agents had to operate under adverse circumstances. They had to confront Indians' suffering on a daily basis but lacked the freedom of action they needed to deal with the problems. Furthermore, agents had virtually no chance of bringing about changes in current government Indian policies. This led some of them to resign in protest in the 1880s.[61] Decidedly the position of the Indian agents vis-à-vis their native clientele was different from that of the Hudson's Bay Company officers before 1870. From the beginning the governor and committee had given these men the right to adjust general company policies to meet local conditions whenever it served the interests of the company and its native customers to do so.[62] The kinship bonds that had developed over the years between many of the Hudson's Bay Company's men and the native people served to make these men highly responsive to the needs of their clientele. By guaranteeing 'loyal natives' that they would be looked after in hard times, the Hudson's Bay Company hoped to achieve one of its basic objectives, that of sustaining a cheap native labour force in the bush. This had been a basic company strategy since the days of Governor George Simpson.[63] While the Hudson's Bay Company held a monopoly, Indians had little choice but to remain 'faithful.' Under these circumstances there is no doubt that the company paternalism of the pre-Confederation era better served their survival needs than did the state paternalism that the Canadian government reluctantly began to develop during this period of transition. At this time some company men, most notably Chief Factor Fortescue, hoped the company could get the state to underwrite the social costs of the trade without losing any of its influence over the native peoples by having its officers act as agents for the government. But this was not to be. Gradually the state took over direct control of economic assistance programs. This was one of the ways in which the authority and power of Hudson's Bay Company's officers began to be undermined in the eyes of the native peoples.

3

The fur trade in transition, 1886–1913

Through the opening up of new railway lines to Port Nelson, to Athabasca Landing and the Peace River country, giving access of free traders to a wide area that has hitherto been the exclusive domain of the Hudson's Bay Company ... the 'Ancient and Honorable Company' has come to the realization that it must reorganize and expand its widespread system of fur trading. (Winnipeg Free Press, 24 October 1913)

Between 1886 and 1913 prosperity returned, and Canada was transformed from being predominantly a rural agricultural country in 1885 to an urban industrial one at the close of the First World War. A great deal has been written about the ways the wheat boom on the prairies fuelled the nation's development at this time.[1] The expansion of the agricultural and industrial sectors of the economy meant that fur exports, one of the traditional staples, declined in relative importance. However, the fur trade did not go into decline as is commonly thought. Rather, it boomed. The rapidly expanding economies of northwestern Europe and North America led to a long-term increase in the demand for furs of all types.[2] This trend pushed fur prices up sharply between 1895 and 1911, since the stocks of luxury furs were no longer adequate to meet mushrooming demand.[3] As a result, fur garment manufacturers began searching for cheaper substitutes, while growing numbers of fur buyers and traders, many of whom were Americans, were drawn into the Canadian north seeking new sources of supply. Taking advantage of the railway and telegraph, these newcomers seriously challenged the Hudson's Bay Company, and they began to change the character of the industry as the *Winnipeg Free Press* story cited above shows.

Until the First World War London was the pre-eminent world fur market. Within that market the Hudson's Bay Company was the key player, and it continued to handle the bulk of Canadian furs entering international trade. For these reasons the company's fur sales figures provide us with the best general picture of Canadian production and prices before the war.[4] Canadian government sources, federal and provincial, are more important afterwards, given that the Hudson's Bay Company's market share dwindled substantially.

In 1927 Harold Innis noted that the volume of furs sold at the Hudson's Bay Company's London auctions before the First World War was not strongly affected by business cycles except for the first few years after Confederation, when markets sagged following the Vienna crash. In 1881, almost fifteen years before the depression ended (fig 9), recovery began. By 1884 sales volumes surpassed the 1874 peak by nearly 30,000 skins. Subsequently, 1886, 1893, 1896, 1902, 1905, and 1911 were high points in the cycle. Low points occurred in 1895, 1898, and 1908.

A closer examination of this general trend reveals that muskrat sales were the driving force. Except for 1870, muskrat accounted for over 50 per cent of the total number of pelts sold every year before 1912. In peak years, muskrat sales dwarfed those of all other furs combined by an even wider margin (table 4). In the forty-one-year period ending in 1911 muskrat accounted for over 69 per cent of all of the pelts sold.

The overwhelming dominance of muskrat between Confederation and the First World War highlights one of the fundamental ways the fur trade of the late nineteenth and early twentieth centuries differed from that of the earlier period, particularly that before 1840. Beaver had been the staple fur during the first 150 years of the Hudson's Bay Company's operations. It was a high-value fur. Of importance to native people, in the early years beaver trapping provided a relatively stable income because the normal population cycles of this animal are not as pronounced as those of most other species. In contrast, those of muskrat are among the most extreme. Compounding the problem for the trapper, muskrat remained one of the furs of the lowest relative value. This meant that muskrat-oriented economies offered only a marginal and very uncertain rate of return to trappers. Furthermore, the absolute gain from general price increases was small, given the low base price for muskrat at the beginning of the period.

Figure 11 shows the relative changes in muskrat sales volumes and prices at the Hudson's Bay Company's London auctions between 1870 and 1911. The graph decidedly indicates that sales volumes fluctuated

TABLE 4
Composition of Hudson's Bay Company sales, 1870–1910

Rank order	Fur species	1870	1871	1872	1873	1874	1875	1876	1877	1878	1879	Total	Ten-year average
1	Muskrat	232,251	443,999	704,789	767,896	671,982	523,802	583,319	437,121	486,030	499,727	5,350,916	535,092
2	Beaver	124,000	175,000	165,000	149,000	118,000	147,000	127,000	116,000	151,000	135,000	1,407,000	140,700
3	Marten	52,308	55,453	60,455	66,841	66,750	131,170	83,439	81,174	74,703	55,734	728,027	72,803
4	Mink	27,708	31,985	39,266	44,740	60,429	72,273	79,214	79,060	84,244	62,590	581,509	58,151
5	Lynx	37,447	15,686	7,942	5,123	7,106	11,250	18,774	30,508	42,834	27,345	204,015	20,402
6	Otter, land	10,973	13,105	13,787	11,263	9,010	13,088	11,524	9,926	11,753	13,101	117,530	11,753
7	Fox, red	13,058	6,546	7,736	8,339	7,428	8,973	9,838	11,233	16,791	13,038	102,980	10,298
8	Seal, hair	9,917	15,740	5,433	9,862	3,259	14,099	3,620	7,564	7,636	6,626	83,756	8,376
9	Bear, brown	8,420	8,589	1,869	8,172	7,431	7,120	7,804	7,543	7,415	7,796	72,159	7,216
10	Fox, white	4,629	1,805	2,806	7,325	5,315	6,058	4,323	5,299	24,402	5,958	67,920	6,792
11	Fisher	7,959	6,743	7,072	3,639	3,539	3,558	3,263	3,338	5,461	6,132	50,704	5,070
12	Ermine	2,223	3,106	2,958	4,012	4,477	4,732	6,360	5,338	5,838	4,956	44,000	4,400
13	Skunk	9,606	3,286	2,621	1,759	1,322	2,077	2,828	3,928	6,933	8,395	42,755	4,276
14	Seal, fur	688	7,944	13,620	2,073	2,354	2,131	2,718	1,588	1,779	2,782	37,677	3,768
15	Wolf	5,856	5,399	2,802	6,413	3,724	3,074	2,083	1,865	2,975	2,590	36,781	3,678
16	Fox, cross	3,436	2,592	2,090	2,315	1,645	2,212	2,455	3,550	4,201	3,493	27,989	2,799
17	Raccoon	1,696	3,341	4,011	3,636	3,151	7,241	2,149	1,042	514	613	27,394	2,739
18	Wolverine	1,421	1,848	1,656	2,095	1,765	1,351	1,286	1,136	1,794	1,997	16,349	1,635
19	Fox, silver	914	696	559	694	416	795	687	971	1063	914	7,709	771
20	Otter, sea	89	107	66	99	96	134	47	127	47	26	838	84
21	Fox, blue	48	15	36	90	60	69	58	48	239	60	723	72
22	Musk ox	0	4	44	7	54	11	9	127	118	235	609	61
23	Wild cat	68	82	46	24	28	189	83	40	10	10	580	58

Rank order	Fur species	1880	1881	1882	1883	1884	1885	1886	1887	1888	1889	Total	Ten-year average
1	Muskrat	478,078	828,034	1,029,296	1,069,183	1,083,067	817,003	347,050	380,132	344,878	223,614	6,600,335	660,034
2	Beaver	120,000	121,000	116,000	105,000	104,000	120,000	103,000	84,000	103,000	83,000	1,059,000	105,900
3	Marten	46,273	46,030	52,631	62,711	71,116	78,981	79,027	51,151	73,259	64,558	625,737	62,574
4	Mink	35,072	36,160	45,600	47,508	52,290	110,824	76,503	64,303	83,023	43,748	595,031	59,503
5	Lynx	17,834	15,386	9,443	7,599	8,061	27,187	51,511	74,050	78,773	33,899	323,743	32,374
6	Skunk	7,927	6,818	5,407	7,178	6,474	12,647	21,249	11,009	16,390	11,344	106,443	10,644
7	Fox, red	12,401	9,126	6,035	5,869	4,696	10,090	11,526	11,830	17,238	14,503	103,314	10,331
8	Otter, land	8,313	10,177	10,191	11,992	9,248	12,260	10,875	8,326	11,613	8,771	101,766	10,177
9	Bear, brown	5,951	8,531	8,021	11,188	5,515	10,765	8,386	8,279	10,080	9,606	86,322	8,632
10	Fox, white	2,311	4,362	5,722	5,886	6,461	2,801	3,280	4,152	13,170	9,551	57,696	5,770
11	Fisher	4,216	5,059	5,143	4,640	3,820	4,200	4,041	4,510	6,165	5,408	47,202	4,720
12	Ermine	2,324	3,695	4,561	5,112	3,912	7,042	4,780	4,166	3,933	3,592	43,117	4,312
13	Seal, hair	4,174	4,287	5,442	3,888	2,713	1,590	6,965	1,279	2,590	672	33,600	3,360
14	Fox, cross	3,289	3,224	2,244	1,762	1,489	2,192	3,237	3,221	3,877	2,935	27,470	2,747
15	Wolf	4,707	3,136	1,459	2,121	1,580	1,848	1,344	1,180	4,793	3,404	25,572	2,557
16	Wolverine	1,777	2,471	1,614	1,883	1,583	1,528	1,203	1,245	2,452	2,031	17,787	1,779
17	Seal, fur	3,308	3,085	5,005	652	560	13	2,077	1,846	179	737	17,462	1,746
18	Fox, silver	830	912	668	506	336	622	874	836	954	639	7,177	718
19	Musk ox	567	655	564	368	235	316	395	222	514	505	4,341	434
20	Raccoon	88	22	77	7	26	139	124	325	250	217	1,275	128
21	Fox, blue	24	50	55	37	76	18	18	35	73	77	463	46
22	Otter, sea	88	22	77	7	26	35	10	10	11	11	297	30
23	Wild cat	2	24	6	19	10	24	10		33	18	146	15
24	Bear, white							45			52	97	10
25	Bear, black											0	0

TABLE 4 (continued)

Rank order	Fur species	1890	1891	1892	1893	1894	1895	1896	1897	1898	1899	Total	Ten-year average
1	Muskrat	322,160	574,742	806,103	934,646	648,687	674,811	813,159	551,716	568,934	701,487	6,596,445	659,645
2	Marten	73,123	65,146	73,850	100,257	110,015	107,002	103,329	95,911	85,284	67,738	881,655	88,166
3	Mink	35,396	29,479	42,264	58,171	50,815	51,285	70,229	76,365	70,407	41,839	526,250	52,625
4	Beaver	64,000	64,000	57,000	56,000	47,000	44,000	51,000	50,000	44,000	36,000	513,000	51,300
5	Lynx	18,886	11,529	8,352	8,660	12,902	20,331	36,853	56,407	39,437	26,761	240,118	24,012
6	Fox, red	12,058	14,134	11,256	11,964	16,031	13,087	20,311	24,676	25,691	20,399	169,607	16,961
7	Seal, fur	482	279	932	8,491	37,129	36,577	783	39,133	21,177	8,821	153,804	15,380
8	Skunk	10,814	12,665	10,646	9,214	6,841	8,885	13,664	18,842	16,755	9,874	118,200	11,820
9	Otter, land	9,298	8,193	9,798	8,671	7,474	7,512	8,919	9,346	9,690	10,016	88,917	8,892
10	Bear, black	0	8,960	11,414	9,683	7,727	8,620	8,467	9,318	9,166	8,993	82,348	8,235
11	Ermine	5,697	5,417	5,516	9,120	9,096	7,250	9,302	8,340	7,704	9,786	77,228	7,723
12	Fox, white	2,893	3,725	9,626	4,708	3,231	4,948	6,681	3,498	3,228	6,681	49,219	4,922
13	Fisher	6,557	5,683	5,208	4,828	4,044	3,631	4,169	4,805	5,247	4,964	49,136	4,914
14	Fox, cross	2,908	2,518	2,766	2,673	3,025	3,208	5,044	6,963	6,507	5,358	40,970	4,097
15	Wolf	2,532	4,286	1,725	1,577	2,086	1,498	2,655	3,980	7,655	3,575	31,569	3,157
16	Seal, hair	2,151	2,545	2,604	2,599	2,508	2,183	1,817	4,765	2,698	2,791	26,661	2,666
17	Bear, brown	11,719	1,411	1,875	1,390	1,107	1,190	1,090	1,030	972	910	22,694	2,269
18	Raccoon	153	172	171	194	218	743	575	1,642	6,466	2,916	13,250	1,325
19	Wolverine	2,243	1,416	1,147	1,017	889	652	579	822	1,064	904	10,733	1,073
20	Fox, silver	649	565	665	615	617	682	981	1,398	1,250	1,018	8,440	844
21	Musk ox	ND	1,358	1,935	888	1,187	761	494	326	340	453	7,742	774
22	Bear, white	ND	83	130	90	134	81	128	77	141	130	994	99
23	Fox, blue	25	38	83	51	34	69	67	44	46	61	518	52
24	Wild cat	ND	14	13	13	7	29	15	50	32	27	192	19
25	Otter, sea	15	9	6	8	11	1	0	3	2	1	56	6

Rank order	Fur species	1900	1901	1902	1903	1904	1905	1906	1907	1908	1909	1910	Total	Eleven-year average
1	Muskrat	767,741	928,199	1,650,214	1,488,287	924,439	1,056,253	695,070	407,472	172,418	302,195	749,142	9,141,430	831,039
2	Marten	64,446	55,777	57,131	79,147	52,639	35,752	45,441	47,494	34,874	23,640	28,979	525,320	52,532
3	Mink	45,978	47,813	57,620	66,549	54,673	55,996	60,053	39,169	21,534	17,857	21,788	489,030	44,457
4	Beaver	44,000	41,000	44,000	48,000	34,000	30,000	54,000	35,000	30,000	34,000	39,000	433,000	39,364
5	Ermine	14,075	11,664	16,374	33,883	15,902	12,670	21,704	25,633	27,821	26,872	34,281	240,879	21,898
6	Lynx	15,185	4,473	5,781	9,117	19,267	36,116	58,850	61,478	36,301	9,704	3,410	259,682	23,607
7	Otter, land	9,799	9,190	8,711	10,296	6,463	4,892	10,580	7,726	6,137	6,361	5,487	85,642	7,786
8	Fox, red	11,533	9,446	6,992	6,235	6,216	7,215	12,204	12,736	7,537	3,641	3,396	83,151	7,559
9	Fox, white	3,623	2,929	8,515	10,751	5,579	4,690	6,394	11,459	6,785	2,068	4,803	67,596	6,145
10	Skunk	11,012	6,172	5,749	5,207	5,427	6,090	9,129	11,581	5,235	1,591	1,613	68,806	6,255
11	Bear, black	9,137	7,829	7,087	6,445	6,085	4,614	5,041	4,177	4,100	4,042	4,579	63,136	5,740
12	Seal, fur	21,620	9,039	8,352	5,832	6,532	35	50	65				51,525	4,684
13	Fisher	5,042	3,454	3,716	3,235	2,590	2,095	3,020	4,022	4,701	3,600	2,525	38,000	3,455
14	Fox, cross	3,742	1,534	1,460	1,974	2,212	2,396	5,011	5,457	3,194	1,782	1,380	30,142	2,740
15	Wolf	3,104	2,643	1,366	1,805	1,972	1,246	1,707	2,799	4,510	3,858	3,149	28,159	2,560
16	Raccoon	13,544	9,177	1,973	1,024	718	404	281	602	243	141	266	28,373	2,579
17	Seal, hair	4,158	2,599	3,061	2,509	1,124	762	3,706	1,152	1,522	1,766	1,517	23,876	2,171
18	Wolverine	923	776	635	695	627	412	504	730	894	763	807	7,766	706
19	Bear, brown	897	778	788	726	640	463	495	435	388	397	453	6,460	587
20	Fox, silver	608	325	283	493	422	491	942	1067	663	397	281	5,972	543
21	Musk ox	516	574	274	256	333	100	92	45	113	107	76	2,486	226
22	Bear, white	118	58	170	96	55	54	149	138	60	93	71	1,062	97
23	Fox, blue	19	24	68	90	43	17	44	89	64	14	28	500	45
24	Wild cat	67	41	5	4	5	0	0	2	0	1	0	127	12
25	Otter, sea	6	1	0	1	0	0	0	0	0	0	0	8	1

SOURCE: Jones, *Fur Farming*, and GD HBCA PAM A 104/Box 13

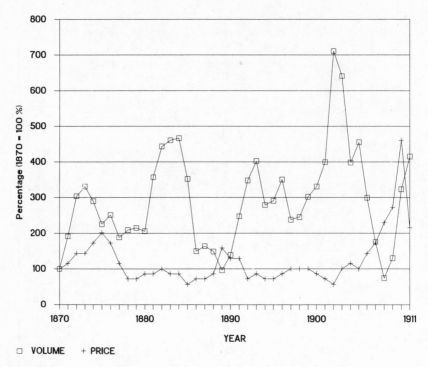

□ VOLUME   + PRICE

Figure 11
Hudson's Bay Company muskrat sales: changes in volume and price,
1870–1911

much more widely than did price. Sharp declines in numbers seem to
have influenced prices considerably, pushing them upward, whereas
sales peaks drove prices downward, but by smaller margins. It is reasonable to suppose that supply was the key determinant in price,
considering that in many areas of the north, most notably, 'muskrat
country,' the native people had few alternative trapping opportunities.
Being largely dependent on muskrat to earn the income they needed
to sustain their current lifestyles, natives actively had to trap the animal
regardless of current market conditions.

From 1870 until 1890 beaver ranked second in terms of volume.
Thereafter it declined in relative importance as the number of pelts sold
diminished. While sales headed downward, prices advanced between
1878 and the eve of the First World War (fig. 12). There were two

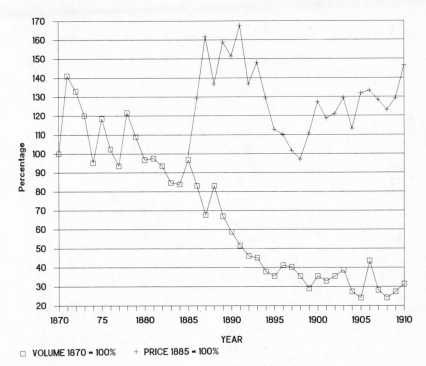

□ VOLUME 1870 = 100%   + PRICE 1885 = 100%

Figure 12
Hudson's Bay Company beaver sales: changes in volume and price,
1870–1910

primary reasons for these contrasting trends. Heightened demand
caused depletion of beaver stocks. By the end of the century beaver
were in sharp decline in many quarters. The stock of beaver pelts that
were available at the Hudson's Bay Company's London auctions was
further reduced by competitors, who were beginning to deflect significant numbers of Canadian pelts to other outlets after 1885.

Marten ranked third behind beaver, accounting for almost 7 per cent
of total sales. The trading picture for this species is very different from
that of beaver (fig. 13). Sales figures suggest that marten supplies were
adequate to meet demand until the turn of the century. Also, in contrast
to the beaver's life pattern, an eight to ten-year cycle is apparent. After
a sharp drop in prices between 1872 and 1879, stability was maintained
until 1892, when an upswing began which continued to the end of the

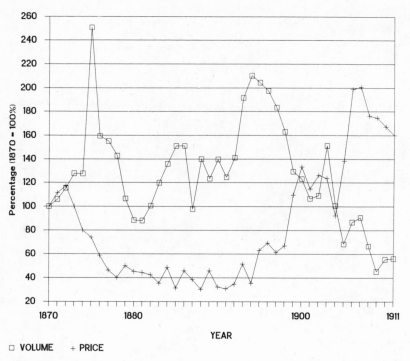

Figure 13
Hudson's Bay Company marten sales: changes in volume and price,
1870–1911

period. Considering that the sales volumes slumped throughout this period, it is likely that heavy trapping pressure was taking a toll on the resource. Also, the Hudson's Bay Company's competitors made a concerted effort to siphon off a larger share of the output of this valuable species, thereby contributing to the long-term trends noted.

Mink sales accounted for roughly 5 per cent of the aggregate volume before 1912 and ranked fourth in terms of total turnover. A seven- to twelve-year cycle is apparent in figure 14 with peaks following those of marten by two to three years.[5] Before 1900 mink prices appear to have reacted to the short-term cyclical swings of supply with a narrow range of movement. At the turn of the century, however, mink prices began an upward spiral, paralleling the movement in sales volumes between 1899 and 1903. Thereafter prices continued to rise, but sales

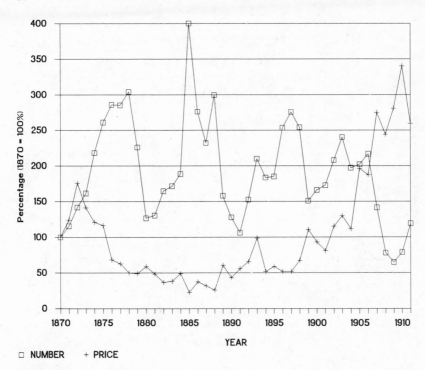

Figure 14
Hudson's Bay Company mink sales: changes in volume and price,
1870–1911

declined. From these trends it appears increased demand triggered the
price advance that began around 1900; afterwards, declining supplies
reinforced it.

Lynx followed mink in importance. The marked cyclic fluctuations
of lynx populations have drawn much attention. Few species exhibit
greater regularity (fig. 15). The primary prey of lynx is hare and it is
the population of the latter that determines that of the former. Both
moved in nine- to ten-year cycles. Between 1870 and 1911 five complete
lynx cycles took place. No general trend is evident. Prices tended to
move in opposite directions from those of supply until 1900 (fig. 16).
Thereafter, prices moved upward through the entire fifth cycle. Once
again it appears that demand was growing at a rate that exceeded the
supply.

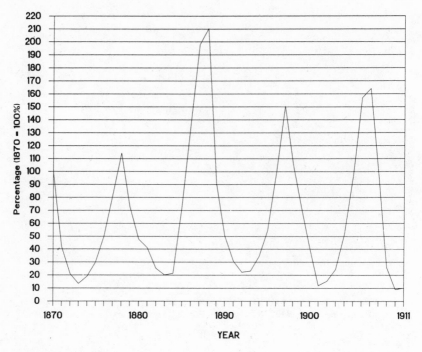

Figure 15
Hudson's Bay Company lynx sales: changes in volume, 1870–1911

Ermine sales are of particular interest. The fur of this member of the weasel family was of very low value, and it was not of any importance in the early trade. The Hudson's Bay Company does not even list it on its fur inventories in the eighteenth century; before 1875 ermine did not rank among the top ten furs in terms of volume. Thereafter it increased in significance very rapidly. In the first decade of this century it ranked fifth (table 4). Considering that price movements paralleled those of volume, it appears that increased demand was chiefly responsible for the changes (figs 17 and 18).

Collectively these furs – muskrat, beaver, marten, mink, lynx, red fox, and ermine – comprised 95 per cent of the Hudson's Bay Company's fur sales between 1870 and 1911. Unfortunately, data are not readily available to ascertain what the total value of the company's sales of these various furs were. However, if average prices are used to estimate the values, beaver decidedly was the most important, fol-

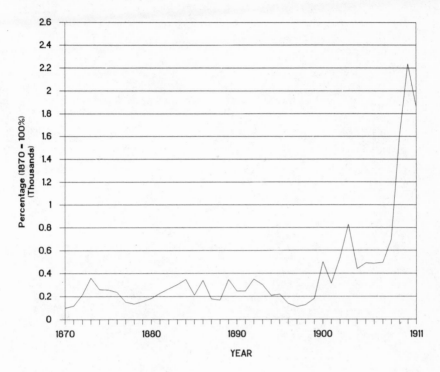

Figure 16
Hudson's Bay Company lynx sales: changes in price, 1870–1911

Changes in fur market

lowed by marten, white fox, lynx, muskrat, mink, fisher, red fox, silver
fox, and ermine. In aggregate, these furs earned nearly £12 million in
the forty-one year period.

This discussion shows that by the first two decades of this century
the complexion of the fur market had changed substantially. The
decreasing supplies of prime furs and the growing demand for them
meant that garment manufacturers sought cheaper alternative types
of pelts. So, furs previously of little value grew in importance, and
fur manufacturers prepared and used them in new ways. The best
examples are mink, muskrat, and ermine.[6] In the early nineteenth
century mink was worth only fifty cents a skin, and garment makers
used it mostly as coat lining material.[7] As mink became a fashionable
fur, they substituted muskrat for this purpose. Shortly after coats of seal
fur became hot fashion items in the late nineteenth century, hunters

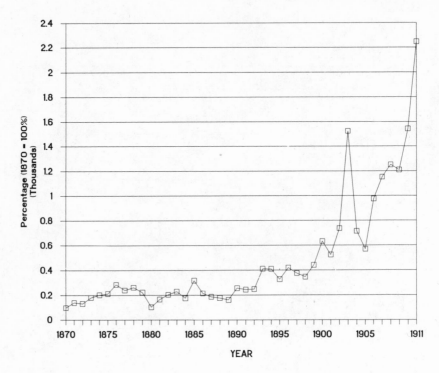

Figure 17
Hudson's Bay Company ermine sales: changes in volume, 1870–1911

decimated the herds and the price of seal pelts soared. In response,
fur dyers and dressers in Leipzig, Germany, perfected methods for
shearing and dyeing muskrat in order to produce imitation seal. It was
usually marketed as 'Hudson Bay seal.'[8] As bleaching and dyeing
techniques improved, manufacturers could process a greater array of
cheap raw furs into high quality imitations of premium natural furs.
Some of the most important of these are listed in table 5.

As early as 1887 the marketing of certain furs under many different
names created so much confusion that the London Chamber of Commerce banned the use of unauthorized names to market furs in
England; violators were subject to prosecution under the Merchandise
Marks Act of 1887. The chamber permitted manufacturers to use the
following trade terms: seal muskrat for muskrat, seal otter for pulled
natural otter, imitation or mock fox for white fox, beaver possum for

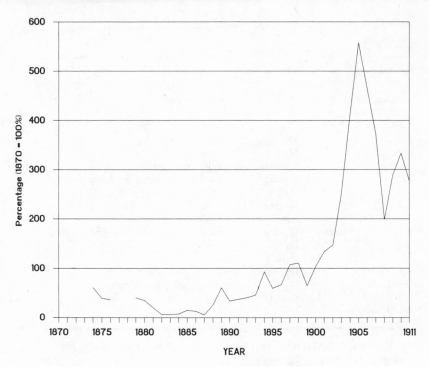

Figure 18
Hudson's Bay Company ermine sales: changes in price, 1870–1911

pulled natural opossum, and sable mink for dyed mink. Despite these steps, the problem remained, and it was the subject of frequent commentary in British trade journals.[9] In Canada and the United States similar efforts were made, also with only limited success. Of importance to the Canadian fur trade, the expansion of fur-dyeing activities popularized types of pelts that previously were mostly utility furs. Muskrat, squirrel, skunk, and raccoon serve as good examples. These furs became very fashionable early in this century.

In 1870 the Hudson's Bay Company still dominated the collection of Canadian furs. In most areas of the north it held a virtual monopoly on the business. Traditionally buyers from continental Europe bought the bulk of the company's furs in London at the autumn and spring auctions. Leipzig buyers were particularly important to the trade. Before the First World War this German city ranked second only to

TABLE 5
Fur imitations

Natural fur	Process	Marketed as
American sable	Dyeing	Russian sable
Fitch	Dyeing	Sable
Goal	Dyeing	Bear
Hare	Dyeing	Sable or fox
Mink	Dyeing	Sable
Muskrat	Dyeing	Mink or sable
Muskrat	Dyeing	Seal, electric seal, Red River seal and Hudson Bay seal
Nutria	Dyeing and pulling	Seal, electric seal, Red River seal and Hudson Bay seal
American opossum	Dyeing	Marten, sable; red, blue and silver fox
Otter	Dyeing and pulling	Seal
Raccoon	Dyeing	Alaska bear, silver bear
Skunk	Dyeing	Alaska sable, black marten
White hare	Dyeing	Fox
White rabbit	Dyeing	Ermine

SOURCE: Jones, *Fur Farming* and E. Austin, 'Color Index of Dyed Furs,' *Fur Trade Review* (January 1928), 64–72

London as a fur-marketing centre. It had been an important market since the Middle Ages, and it became the leading world centre for fur dying and processing by the turn of this century. For this reason the Leipzig market was different from that of London in that a much higher portion of the turnover consisted of dyed and treated furs. The London and Leipzig markets complemented each other because of their different orientations.[10] Of relevance here, Leipzig dealers bought a substantial share of their North American raw fur in London.

The growth of the North American fur market beginning in the late nineteenth century acted as a catalyst for changes in the international marketing system. In 1870 there were fewer than 200 furriers in the United States, and their gross product was worth only $8.9 million; by 1900 there were over 1,000 furriers producing goods valued at more than $55 million. Reflecting this development, between 1870 and 1900 the United States became a net importer of furs for the first time.[11] In Canada, fur garment manufacturing and sales also expanded, but the domestic industry, concentrated in Montreal and Toronto, remained small compared with that of the United States.

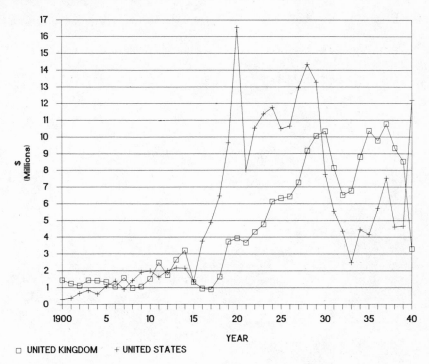

Figure 19
Value of Canadian fur exports, 1900–40: United Kingdom and United States

Initially, most American fur imports came from London, but a substantial portion of this traffic originated in Canada, especially the imports of beaver and mink. This fact encouraged Americans to take an active role in the Canadian fur trade beginning in the last quarter of the nineteenth century. The fur export data for Canada before the First World War indicate the extent of their success. Figure 19 shows that between 1868 and 1907 the annual value rose from just under $500,000 to $2.6 million. Shipments to England accounted for most of this growth during the first twenty years. Exports stagnated between 1889 and 1900, apparently because of supply shortages, before they surged forward again between 1901 and 1907.[12] This time it was shipments to the United States that accounted for most of the growth. Figure 20 shows that the English market continued to decline in importance until 1917.[13]

While the expanding North American fur market was fuelling inter-

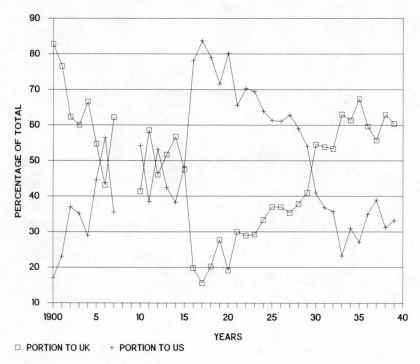

YEARS

□ PORTION TO UK   + PORTION TO US

Figure 20
Canadian fur exports, 1900–40

Changes in the fur trade business

national competition for Canadian furs, improvements in communication and transportation systems made it possible to conduct the fur-buying business in innovative ways. Some of these innovations enabled small operators seriously to challenge the Hudson's Bay Company in its traditional territory (fig. 21).

telegraph & cash buying

Of great importance, the establishment of telegraph service broke the Hudson's Bay Company's monopoly of market information. Local newspapers published wire releases of the latest sales in London and elsewhere. One of the earliest to do so was *The Commercial* published in Winnipeg. Raw-fur dealers located in urban centres in Canada and the United States used the telegraph to keep in close contact with the buying agents they dispatched to towns located along the railway lines. As early as 1886 agents from Montreal, Toronto, Winnipeg, and Minneapolis were active in the vicinity of Edmonton. Most of them reached the area by taking the train to Calgary, where they connected with stagecoach lines running to Edmonton.[14] These men included Battleford and Prince Albert on their buying circuits. Cash-buying agents who represented eastern firms came to be known as 'live wire travellers' because they depended on the telegraph to keep in close contact with their home offices for advice regarding which furs to buy and how much to pay for them.[15] These buyers also obtained money by wire when necessary. Thus, the telegraph made extensive cash fur buying a feasibility in the north for the first time by facilitating rudimentary electronic banking.

By the turn of the century most of the leading American, British, and German fur-dealing houses had resident agents, or branch offices, located in the major Canadian cities situated along the southern margins of the boreal forest area, such as Sudbury, Winnipeg, and Edmonton. The Hudson's Bay Company responded by establishing cash fur-purchasing agencies in leading urban centres. The directors intended that agencies collect those furs that the company's inland trading posts lost to opponents. The strategy backfired. The Hudson's Bay Company's fur-purchasing agencies actually helped many of these smaller operators undercut its own trading operations by providing them with quick cash for their collections. An added problem in the late nineteenth century was that many of the furs bought at the agencies were not 'prime collections'; in other words, they were not bought directly from the collector who had obtained them from the trapper. Instead, too many of the furs the company's purchasing agencies bought were 'stale,' being more than a season old. Often stale furs had been resold several times before the company's agents acquired them.

The integration of transportation and telegraph systems made it possible for a variety of new types of businesses to develop rapidly in the 1870s and 1880s. One of the most important of these were the mail-order fur-buying companies – or the direct receivers, as they were called in the industry.[16] Operators who conducted this type of business placed advertisements in local newspapers or they sent out flyers which listed the prices that they were currently paying for furs.[17] One of the earliest mail-order buyers for which there is a record is G.W. Goernfeld of Hamilton, Ontario, who was active in the Edmonton market by 1886. He placed an advertisement in the *Edmonton Bulletin* announcing that he would pay the highest cash price for furs and skins. Goernfeld said he would send price lists on request.[18] In January of the same year F. Ossenbrugge of Toronto placed an ad in the

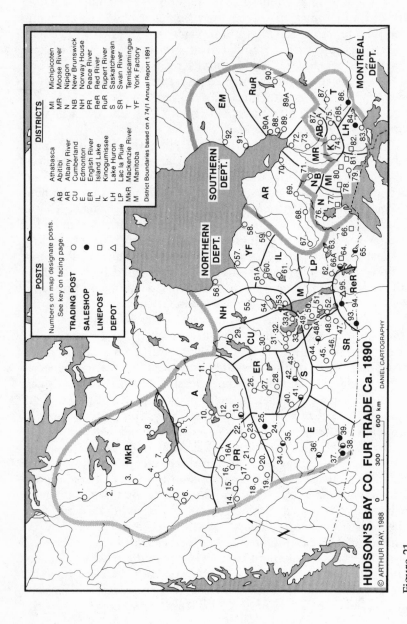

HUDSON'S BAY CO. FUR TRADE Ca. 1890

POSTS

Numbers on map designate posts.
See key on facing page.

TRADING POST	○
SALESHOP	●
LINEPOST	□
DEPOT	△

DISTRICTS

A	Athabasca	MI	Michipicoten
AB	Abitibi	MR	Moose River
AR	Albany River	N	Nipigon
CU	Cumberland	NB	New Brunswick
E	Edmonton	NH	Norway House
ER	English River	PR	Peace River
IL	Island Lake	ReR	Red River
K	Kinogumissee	RuR	Rupert River
LH	Lake Huron	S	Saskatchewan
LP	Lac la Pluie	SR	Swan River
M	Mackenzie River	T	Temiscamingue
MkR	Manitoba	YF	York Factory

District Boundaries based on A 74/1 Annual Report 1891

© ARTHUR RAY 1988   0   300   600 km

DANIEL CARTOGRAPHY

Figure 21
Hudson's Bay Company fur trade, ca 1890

Commercial announcing 'A full line of Native Skins and Furs Always on hand ... Highest Prices paid.'[19] A.B. Shubert of Chicago became one of the largest mail-order fur-buying houses to operate in western Canada. The Canadian branch of this company, A.B. Shubert, Ltd, maintained headquarters in Winnipeg.[20]

During the trapping season direct-receiving houses sent market quotations to their regular customers as often as once or twice a month if markets were unsteady. The shippers had to accept a house's system of grading and valuation. Normally a small shipping charge was added. In a sellers' market receiving houses often reduced or eliminated shipping charges altogether.[21] Trappers and independent fur-buying agents who disposed of their furs through the direct-receiving services of fur manufacturers avoided paying sales commissions, and, on large shipments, they usually did not have to pay transportation costs.

Consignment fur selling was another very significant innovation. As early as 1888 Stennett, Gemmell & Company of Winnipeg advertised in the *Commercial* that they were acting as agents for the sale of raw furs on commission. The firm offered to provide shippers with price lists showing '3 leading markets of interest' during the season and 'would keep you informed of each and every change that occurs in various markets in the prices of raw furs throughout the year, which information should insure you from making a loss.'[22] Commissions and shipping charges were deducted from the proceeds of the sales. The consignment and mail-order houses were a boon to trappers and small independent traders because they made it easier for them to dispose of their returns quickly, which reduced the amount of capital needed to conduct their business. It also meant that it was easy for newcomers to enter the business, and they did so in growing numbers.

Shortly after Joseph Wrigley succeeded James Grahame as trade commissioner, he realized that he needed to tighten the management of the fur trade department in order to streamline operations so that the company could meet these new challengers. But before he could accomplish this task, it was imperative that he obtain accurate information about the business affairs of the various districts. Accordingly, Wrigley undertook a tour of inspection of the prairie and parkland posts in August of 1885 and of the Western Department (British Columbia) in October. In addition to making these and subsequent visits himself, it was clear to him that a regular system of examination was sorely needed. With this objective in mind he convinced the governor and committee to make a number of changes in the current assessment scheme. Henceforth key trading posts and districts were to be inspected on a regular rather than on an occasional basis.[23] Wrigley replaced the rank of inspecting chief factor with that of inspecting officer to reduce the friction that had developed between the inspectors and district managers. This had become a problem under the old system because inspecting chief factors were assigned the responsibility for specific districts and they made their recommendations to these subordinate officers.[24] Wrigley established his scheme along the lines used by banks, whereby the inspectors could visit any post and reported directly to the commissioner. He assessed their information and recommendations, and, before taking corrective actions, he held discussions with the appropriate district managers to obtain their opinions and advice.[25]

Between 1886 and 1892 Hudson's Bay Company inspectors travelled throughout much of the old northern and southern departments and their reports provide us with a clear idea of the extent to which the subarctic fur trade was changing and the ways in which the Hudson's Bay Company tried to cope with the trends. At the time the inspectors began their work it had become common practice for mass merchandisers to use the rate of inventory turnover, or 'stock-turn' as it was called, as one of the key measures of performance. Although this concept apparently was not used in North America before 1870, the Hudson's Bay Company was applying it by 1880.[26] Apart from the fact that it was becoming a common business practice to do so, the economic depression of the 1870s forced the directors to manage their investments more carefully. In 1876 the governor and committee informed the stockholders that under these trying circumstances the company's capital was stretched to the limits.[27] Obviously one way of maximizing the company's limited resources involved identifying those posts and districts where stock-turns were unsatisfactory, so that inventories could be trimmed to reasonable levels.

It appears that the earliest surviving set of stock-turn figures are those for the districts of the Northern Department for 1880 (table 6). Considering that these calculations were made just before the completion of the Canadian Pacific Railway, they probably were fairly typical of those of the older mercantile fur trade. These data show that the inventories were cleared about once a year under the best circumstances and once every seven years in the worst. Wrigley moved quickly to address this problem. In November of 1885 he encouraged district managers to abandon the practice of indenting a year or two

TABLE 6
Hudson's Bay Company return on capital in the Northern Department, 1880–92

District/Post	Fur returns $	Capital[d] $	Gain/Loss $	Per cent	Capital turnover[b]
Northern Department, 1880					
Saskatchewan	28,000	200,000	19,000	10	86
Swan River	15,344	30,000	3,000	10	23
Lac la Pluie	35,000	60,000	5,300	9	21
Norway House	37,000	60,000	6,200	10	19
Severn	6,561	6,000	2,922	49	11
Trout Lake	10,664	11,000	6,402	58	12
Churchill	9,698	14,000	5,682	41	17
York Factory[c]	7,909	105,000	(6,450)	(6)	159
Total	150,176	486,000	42,056		
Average	18,772	60,750	5,257	9	44
Lac la Pluie, 1886					
Seine River	1,000	NA	NA	NA	NA
Lac Seul	14,280	11,556	NA	NA	10
Trout Lake	7,461	NA	4,992	NA	NA
Rat Portage	NA	43,808	4,893	11	NA
Whitefish Lake	1,649	2,453	379	15	18
Northwest Angle	2,232	2,745	378	14	15
Whitedog	4,349	5,042	812	16	14
Wabagoon	3,172	5,738	(305)	(5)	22
Hungry Hall	953	2,248	57	3	28
Total	35,096	73,590	11,206		
Average	3,900	9,199	1,401	15	18
Red River, 1887					
Manitou Post[d]	23,190	10,487	568	5	5
Portage la Prairie[d]	15,816	9,363	(3)	(0)	7
Tobogan	9,500	11,500	1,954	17	15
Red River Indian Settlement	822	NA	491	NA	NA
Dog Head Reserve	2,215	NA	667	NA	NA
Broken Head Reserve	82	NA	(68)	NA	NA
Total	51,625	31,350	3,609		
Average	8,604	10,450	1,203	7	15
Nipigon District, 1888					
Red Rock	7,000	6,000	NA	NA	10
White River-Michipicoten					
White River	13,000	8,964	NA	NA	8

TABLE 6 – continued

District/Post	Fur returns $	Capital[a] $	Gain/Loss $	Per cent	Capital turnover[b]
English River, 1890					
Green Lake	4,249	11,600	(761)	(7)	33
Isle à la Crosse	11,023	43,879	(2,550)	(6)	48
Souris River	1,550	2,300	91	4	18
Portage la Loche	2,802	8,723	(1,183)	(14)	37
Total	19,624	66,502	(4,403)		
Average	4,906	16,626	(1,101)	(5)	34
Athabasca, 1892					
Ft Vermilion	21,922	21,845	6,797	31	12
Ft Smith	5,542	7,180	(205)	(3)	16
Ft Resolution	11,779	11,162	1,913	17	11
Ft Chipewyan	15,499	19,916	4,509	23	15
Ft McMurray	4,493	6,918	(248)	(4)	18
Total	59,235	67,021	12,766		
Average	4,384	4,369	1,359	13	15

[a]Cash and the value of inventories
[b]Number of months
[c]The large capital investment here reflects the fact that this post supplied other districts.
[d]Most of the returns were from the saleshop.
SOURCE: Inspection Reports, 1880–92, HBCA PAM D 25/1–12

in advance in favour of a semi-annual plan if it was possible to do so. By taking this action Wrigley managed to reduce the Northern Department indent for 1886 by £13,342 over the previous year.[28]

Although this initial saving was impressive, the inspection reports filed between 1886 and 1890 revealed that, apart from the saleshops and posts adjacent to the railways, the Hudson's Bay Company still managed only a relatively slow turnover – once every twelve to forty-eight months (table 6). Not surprisingly, the remote English River District had the poorest showing in this respect, but even the Athabasca posts had a stock-turn of at least a year in spite of the transportation improvements that the company had made in that quarter after 1870. The sluggish stock-turns suggest that more aggressive approaches to trading were needed or inventories had to be slashed.

In addition to stock-turn, gross margin (income from sales minus the

gross margin

cost of goods) was the other major indicator of business performance that merchants used in the late nineteenth century.[29] In the 1880s the Hudson's Bay Company managers used a somewhat similar yardstick. They compared the gain or loss on a post's fur returns (the inventory value less market value) with the capital investment (inventory plus cash).[30] At first glance the profit margins look very respectable. In the late 1880s and the early 1890s the rates of return ranged from a high of 31 per cent at Fort Vermilion in the Peace River District to a low of minus 14 per cent at Portage la Loche in the English River District (table 6). The problem is that the results are very misleading, given the way the company assessed post fur returns. Valuation tariffs were drawn up using the average London price for each variety of fur. This meant, for example, that if a trader bought premium beaver pelts for more than the average price, he was credited with a loss even if the company actually sold those pelts for a profit in London. Conversely, if he obtained low-grade skins below the average selling price, he was credited with a profit even though the company probably had to dispose of them at a loss.[31]

This accounting procedure was an outgrowth of the era of company monopoly when traders bought on averages. According to this scheme, a trader obtained a trapper's entire collection by offering him a single price that took into account the varieties and grades of furs that it included. However, this strategy and the business practices that developed in association with it became anachronisms as the trade became highly competitive and opponents targeted their buying to the most valuable furs.

The fact that the company still determined fur profits and losses by average valuations in the 1880s and 1890s probably explains why profit levels do not seem to be related to the intensity of competition. For instance, some of the best gains were made in the highly exposed Athabasca District and some of the poorest results were obtained in the relatively remote English River District.

If the spatial pattern of profits and losses is unclear at this time for these reasons, the inspection reports do provide useful insights into the changing geography of the fur trade (fig. 22). They make it clear that the territories adjacent to and south of the Canadian Pacific Railway in northern Ontario were being overrun by competitors. The same was true of the lands in Manitoba and the Northwest Territories traversed by steamboat lines and wagon roads. The primary outfitting centres for the opposition were the cities and towns of Mattawa, Sudbury, Fort

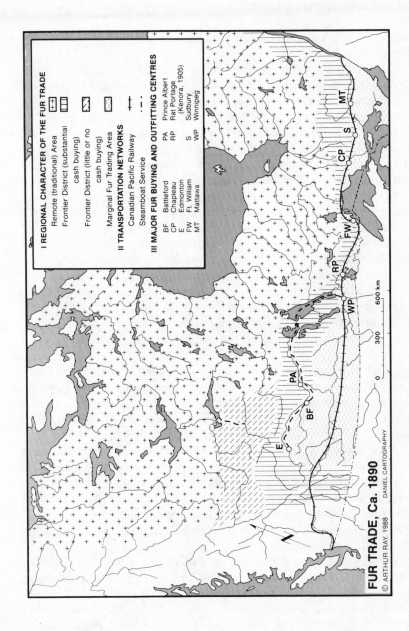

Figure 22
Fur trade, ca 1890

William, Rat Portage (Kenora after 1905), Winnipeg, Prince Albert, and Edmonton.

To secure as many furs as possible from Indian and white trappers, competing traders and fur buyers used a variety of old and new tactics. As in the past, the Hudson's Bay Company kept in close contact with native groups throughout the hunting / trapping season by using 'flying posts' and trippers. In many areas the company provided small 'independent' traders (often natives) with outfits of goods at preferential rates. The practice usually involved retaining one reliable native from among a group of related hunters in the hope that these men would keep their hunting camps 'cleaned up' of furs. By using Indian middlemen in this way, the company sought to protect the credit it had extended in outfits by making sure that the hunters' furs did not fall into the hands of rival traders during the trapping season. The company bought the collections of its native 'agents' at higher prices than it paid to trappers. Opponents resorted to all the same tactics.

Wherever the struggle for furs was intense, cash fur buying became a significant component of the business. This meant that the Hudson's Bay Company had to overhaul some of its operating procedures. Previously the company had paid the Indians more for their furs when they took them in barter than they did when they bought them with cash. This was done partly to encourage Indians to opt for the traditional mode of exchange which was more profitable for the company. Too often this strategy did not work because Indians appreciated the advantages that they obtained by selling their furs for cash whenever it was possible to do so. For instance, when Sudbury began to develop as a mining centre, it also became an important locus for retailers and cash fur buyers. Indians started to frequent the city to take advantage of its competitive market which offered better terms than they could obtain at nearby Hudson's Bay Company trading posts.[32] By the turn of the century Indians frequented a number of other towns and cities in northern Ontario; most important were Chapleau, Red Rock, Port Arthur, and Rat Portage.[33]

Some Hudson's Bay Company post managers adopted innovative tactics in an attempt to deal with this problem. In the Timiskaming area they developed a 'special order' trade whereby Indians were allowed to place advance orders for goods. When these arrived, the traders charged only a very small advance over the company's cost-landed price (the prime cost of the merchandise plus transportation charges to the point of sale). Apparently 'special order' trading mostly involved staple items such as flour. Company inspectors disliked this practice; they believed it enabled Indians and others to estimate the company's profit margin on merchandise sales.[34] Rather than having district and post managers find local solutions to general problems, inspectors Edward K. Beeston (formerly the chief accountant in the commissioner's office) and Richard Hardisty (previously an officer in the Athabasca and Saskatchewan districts) believed that the company needed to develop general policies. Accordingly, they made several suggestions that were intended to bring fur-pricing strategies in line with new conditions. At the time the company used two price schedules. One set the maximum prices to be paid for furs in barter transactions, and the other established them for cash purchases. To stop the flow of too many good furs to the opposition, Beeston and Hardisty recommended reducing the differential between the two tariffs by raising the cash standard. Also, they recommended rating the 'Made Beaver' equal to one dollar. The Made Beaver was the principal unit of value ('Made Marten' was also used in districts where this fur was important) in the traditional fur trade, and it was equivalent to a prime winter beaver pelt. Finally, the two inspectors called for the abandonment of the long-standing company custom of offering the same prices for credit/barter and ready/barter transactions. Beeston and Hardisty noted that this practice encouraged Indians to take a large share of their 'prompt trade' to the opposition. To stop them doing so, the inspectors wanted the company to give the Indians more for their ready/barter business.[35]

In order to become more price competitive and to expand cash fur purchasing it was essential to make a concerted effort to keep district and post managers abreast of current fur market conditions. Beeston and Hardisty, echoing a complaint raised by Wrigley previously,[36] noted that the opposition usually had more up-to-date information about external markets than the Hudson's Bay Company's men did. The post and outpost managers often received market news more slowly than their rivals because information had to filter downward through the company's cumbersome hierarchy. This meant post managers often bought furs at prices that reflected only local competitive situations. The true price-setters tended to be the 'live wire travellers,' whose overhead costs were usually at least 15 per cent lower than those of the Hudson's Bay Company.

By buying very close to their profit margins, these competitors set prices the company could not meet. None the less, company officers attempted to do so, and Beeston and Hardisty said that because of this prices varied from place to place along the Canadian Pacific Railway line 'for no apparent reason'[37] (table 7). On rising markets the company could still turn a profit on this reckless approach to fur buying, thanks to the length of time it took to get the furs to market; however, as Wrigley noted, when prices were falling, such as during the depression of the 1870s and 1880s, it suffered heavy losses.[38] To reduce the risks of fur buying Beeston and Hardisty recommended that: 'some method be adopted by which posts paying cash for furs be advised periodically of the prices they should not exceed.'[39] Wrigley had made a similar suggestion previously, but the governor and committee overruled him because they believed that the spring auction served as the only reliable guide for setting fur-purchasing prices.[40]

The inspectors also advocated reorganizing the districts of the old Southern Department. Beeston and Hardisty noted that the three districts of Michipicoten, New Brunswick, and Nipigon had been created when the Southern Department was supplied by water routes from James Bay (fig 22). However, following the completion of the Canadian Pacific Railway, the flow of traffic had been reorientated in an east-west direction towards Winnipeg and Montreal rather than towards Moose Factory.[41] The inspectors described the resulting administrative problems as follows:

The present arrangement is undoubtedly unsatisfactory. The officer in charge of the Michipicoten District is stationed at the extreme east of his district, while the officer in charge of Lake Huron has little to the west of him. We therefore suggest that all these Districts be reconstructed and formed into two districts called Lake Huron and Lake Superior, the headquarters of the former being Sudbury and the latter with head quarters at Red Rock pending the establishment of Fort William or Port Arthur.[42]

Also, Beeston and Hardisty thought that there were serious problems with the chain of command. Over the years the district managers routinely delegated responsibilities to men located in the outlying subdistricts. This practice weakened the authority of the district headquarters. In order to tighten the administrative control Hardisty and Beeston wanted the subdistrict system to be eliminated.[43]

On 15 January 1889 Wrigley issued an important circular to the district managers which touched on some of the issues the inspectors had raised in their 1888 reports. The managers were ordered to make 'every effort' to 'maintain the system of barter by means of Made Beaver and Made Marten.' Having convinced the governor and committee of the need for local flexibility in fur-buying tariffs, Wrigley was able to authorize district managers to frame their own tariffs to meet local competition within certain limits. These were as follows. They could not sell goods for less than the local cost-landed price (the valuation tariff) plus 10 per cent. Furthermore, the commissioner warned them to regard this as the lowest price. Unless competition was extreme, he expected them to charge enough to cover those district expenses that were not included in the cost-landed calculations.[44]

The commissioner also informed the district managers that whenever the traders under their command bought furs for cash, they were not allowed to pay higher prices than those specified in the valuation tariff unless they obtained the manager's prior approval.[45] As we have seen, this tariff was a very crude price schedule, and it did not take into account transportation costs or other expenses. When district managers did authorize paying higher prices than those the company specified, they were supposed to instruct their traders to increase merchandise prices accordingly.[46] Regarding the fur-purchasing tariff, after a great deal of lobbying Wrigley persuaded the governor and committee to adopt a varying rate that was adjusted periodically during the course of the year to reflect trends in North American and European markets. Although the committee members had relented on this issue by not basing their calculations solely on the company's auctions, the manner in which they applied the floating standard was not entirely satisfactory to Wrigley. He favoured vigorous buying at the low end of the market and a cautious approach on the high end; the company tended to do the opposite.[47]

On 8 June 1898, nearly a decade later, Commissioner C.C. Chipman called a meeting of district managers from the North-West Territories at Athabasca Landing to discuss his and the governor and committee's plans to make additional alterations in business procedures. Chipman, a Nova Scotian and former public servant, had replaced Wrigley in 1891.[48] With his appointment the governor and committee reverted to the initial arrangement whereby the saleshops, land department, and fur department were placed under the direction of a single commissioner. Chipman was a close ally of Governor Donald A. Smith, and the two worked in concert to manage company affairs. The 1898 meeting had been called because Chipman and the governor and committee were aware of the fact that the north, particularly the Athabasca,

TABLE 7
Hudson's Bay Company fur-purchasing tariffs: Northern Department, 1888–9

FUR	Price Range	Abitibi	Timisca-mingue	La Cloche	Red Rock	Lac Seul	Rat Portage	Wabi-goon	Savanne	Pine Portage	Ft Francis
Bear	Low	8.00				1.00	2.00	10.00	4.00	20.00	1.00
	High	10.00				12.00	15.00	18.00	15.00	25.00	30.00
	Average		10.00	15.00	4.25						
Beaver (lb)	Low	2.75				1.00	1.00	10.00	2.50	2.50	1.00
	High	3.00				3.00	5.00	18.00	4.50	5.00	9.00
	Average		3.00	3.00	4.29						
Castorum	Low	2.00	3.00						1.50		
	High	5.00							2.00		
	Average										
Fisher	Low	4.00				2.00	4.00	4.00	3.50	7.00	1.00
	High	6.00				5.00	5.00	7.00	7.00	9.00	2.00
	Average		4.00	4.00	5.16						8.00
Fox red	Low					0.50	0.50	0.50		0.50	0.50
	High					1.00	1.00	1.00		1.00	1.75
	Average		1.25	1.00	1.50						
cross	Low	3.00				1.50	2.00	3.00	1.50*	4.00	1.50
	High	4.00				7.00	10.00	7.00		10.00	20.00
	Average		5.00	3.00	6.00						
silver	Low	35.00				5.00	15.00	40.00	45.00	50.00	10.00
	High	40.00				40.00	45.00	75.00	50.00	60.00	50.00
	Average				38.33						

Species		1	2	3	4	5	6	7	8	9
Lynx	Low	1.75				0.50	1.50	0.50	2.00	1.00
	High	2.00				1.00	2.00	2.50	3.00	5.00
	Average		1.50							
Marten	Low	1.00	1.50	2.00		0.50	1.50	1.50	1.75	0.75
	High	1.25				1.50	2.00	2.00	2.00	2.50
	Average		0.80	1.30						
Mink	Low		1.00			0.10	0.75		0.50	
	High					0.75	1.00		0.75	
	Average	0.50	0.40	0.63				1.00		
Muskrat	Low					0.05				
	High					0.08		1.00		
	Average		0.40	0.40		0.50				
Otter	Low	7.00	8.00			3.00	4.00	5.00	8.00	2.00
	High	9.00				6.00	7.00	8.00	9.00	10.00
	Average		8.00	9.22				8.00	10.00	10.00
Skunk	Low	0.40	0.50					0.50	0.50	0.50
	High									
	Average					0.50		0.50		
Wenusk	Low	0.40	0.10							
	High									
	Average							0.50		

All figures are in dollars.

SOURCE: Inspection Reports, 1880–92, HBCA PAM D 25/1–12

Mackenzie River, and Peace River areas, was changing rapidly, as many white prospectors, trappers, and traders were drawn into the region, owing to the excitement created by the Klondike Goldrush. In particular, company officials anticipated the conclusion of Treaty 8 which was needed to keep the peace between natives and whites. In his call for a meeting Chipman instructed the managers to bring statements showing the cost-landed and selling prices of goods in their respective districts; a complete list of Indian advances for Outfit 1897; a list of all officers and servants employed; a statement of the costs of shipping goods between posts within their respective districts; and a list of all buildings at each post, including a full description of their current condition, recommended repairs, and cost estimates. The district managers were also told to prepare recommendations for the future conduct and control of the business of the district under their charge.[49]

Later, when recounting the meeting to Company Secretary William Ware, Chipman wrote that the proceeding began with a lengthy discussion of the need to overhaul the tariffs again and to change the way the company calculated post profits and losses. Since cash tariffs were being used (along with barter tariffs) in all the western districts except Mackenzie River, Chipman wanted to introduce cash purchasing into the latter district before company opponents did so. Proposing to take the lead in this way marked a major departure from the company's position in 1889. However, Chief Factor Camsell, who was in charge of the district, expressed reservations, noting that 'at present the tariff in Mackenzie River District is entirely upon the old lines of the *Made Beaver* system and that so far no effect from the introduction of the cash tariff had been felt.'[50] At length the assembled officers decided to exempt Mackenzie River from making any change for the moment, but all agreed that the time had arrived when it was advisable and desirable to adopt the cash tariff entirely in the districts of Athabasca, Peace River, English River, and Cumberland.[51] In the Edmonton District it was extensively used already. The managers decided to exempt Fort Resolution in the Athabasca District and transferred it to the Mackenzie River District. Likewise they permitted Lac du Brochet and Pelican Narrows of the Cumberland District to operate along traditional lines, because the trade of these posts was 'somewhat of a different character' from that of the rest of the area.[52] In reality, with the exception of Edmonton, few of the districts in question moved entirely to cash fur buying before the First World War. But movement in that direction was beginning.

At the 1898 meeting the district heads drew up a general price schedule for trade goods to be used as the basis for the substitution of a cash tariff for the Made Beaver one, recognizing that future revisions would be made as the need arose. Furthermore, they acknowledged the need to allow some deviation from the list for remote posts, because they 'should have at least such prices as would fully cover the extra cost of transport to them, and that prices should as far as possible be regulated by those obtaining in adjacent posts.'[53]

It became clear from the discussions that the widespread introduction of cash fur buying would not be enough to place the company on a competitive footing. The procedures used to establish fur-buying prices and to credit post managers for their results had to be overhauled, a goal Wrigley tried but failed to achieve. Purchasing prices were still set in relation to current London prices (averaging all grades of a given species together) from which the company deducted 20 per cent to cover shipping, warehousing, officers' profits, and other costs.[54] At the urging of the commissioner the officers decided to draw up a graded purchasing tariff which included detailed descriptions of each class of fur. They expected post managers to buy their furs in reference to this guide.[55] The revised schedule raised prices by cutting the allowance for shipping and warehousing fur returns by 10 per cent.[56] By making this alteration, the company hoped to eliminate the widespread practice of giving bonuses or gratuities to its native clients for their collections of furs.[57] The officers had resorted to this tactic to meet their competition and the bonuses were hidden fur-purchasing costs. Chipman was convinced that many managers registered profits in their account books when their posts actually suffered operating losses, because these bonuses were not taken into consideration. The commissioner firmly believed that trading bonuses would not be needed if the company had a more competitive pricing structure. When making this suggestion he stressed that it was not his intention to eliminate those gratuities that were paid on the arrival or departure of Indians, at regales, and at New Year 'according to the old custom of the country.'[58]

When Chipman sent the revised 1898 tariff to Secretary Ware, he asked to have the London office break down future sales results into the same categories, so that his office staff could keep price lists up to date with London markets and thereby maximize the chances of buying furs at a profit. By taking these actions, the commissioner also hoped to bring the fur-grading practices used at the trading posts in line with those used at the company's London warehouse – the world standard. Chipman was unsuccessful, however, and disputes between the Fur Trade Department and the London warehouse over grading practices continued into the 1930s. Post managers often were irritated by the fact that the London graders applied stricter measures. The result was that the company's traders received less credit for their returns than they thought they should. Worse, the demanding London standard put the post managers at a competitive disadvantage in the north. Their rivals sold their furs in markets where less stringent grading practices ruled.

Besides making these adjustments to the fur purchasing system, Chipman, like his predecessor, wanted the company to scrap the old scheme for valuing post returns so that traders received credit for their collections according to what they fetched at the London auctions.[59] While often crediting traders with profits for furs the company sold at a net loss, the commissioner noted that the current system encouraged post managers to go after inferior furs.[60] The company needed to give them every incentive to seek aggressively the best pelts rather than merely concentrate on obtaining maximum volume.

Strangely, the governor and committee were slow to respond to Chipman's recommendations. The directors waited until the outfit year of 1913–14 to end the practice of allowing post managers to make a 'fictitious profit from mediocre furs' when they adopted a modified version of the kind of scheme Chipman had suggested. Under the new arrangement the company credited post managers for their furs, using the autumn sale prices in London as the guide. Under this new arrangement, the company carried a post's unsold furs on inventory at cost.[61] But this new scheme was not entirely satisfactory, and district managers voiced objections to it as late as the 1930s. At a district managers' conference held in 1931 they pointed out that autumn sales figures included 'stale' furs which therefore devalued 'fresh' winter collections. This fact discouraged the company's traders from meeting their local competition.[62]

The decision at the turn of the century to expand cash fur-buying activities was not solely a response to more extensive cash purchasing by opponents. By making this move senior company officials were trying to address the perennial problem of debt collection. They thought that bad-debt losses were unreasonably high and were getting out of control in some districts (fig. 23). The officers discussed this subject at length at the 1898 meeting at Athabasca Landing. According to Chipman, everyone present agreed that the abolishment of Indian fur and treaty debts (advances against annuity income) was very desir-

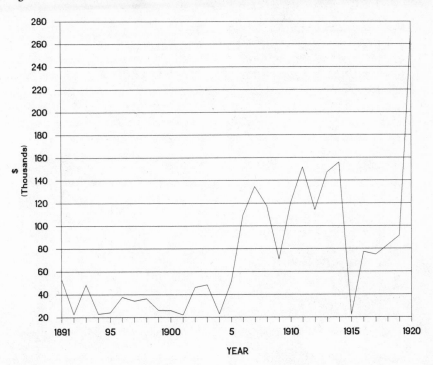

Figure 23
Outstanding Indian debts: Hudson's Bay Company, 1891–1920

able.[63] However, this was a very old refrain. Over the long course of the company's history senior officials had repeatedly attempted without success to eliminate or curtail sharply the debt system. Credit was too central a feature of the business. Not only did Indians depend on receiving it, but they believed the company had an obligation to provide it. Credit represented a kind of reciprocal obligation which was very compatible with Indian notions of mutual trust (balanced and general reciprocity), and as long as competitors extended credit, the Hudson's Bay Company had no choice but to do likewise.

In reality, the bad-debt problem never was as serious as it seemed to those in the commissioner's office. When it was viewed (as most traders did) as an inevitable expense of collecting furs, the cost was very low. As figure 24 shows, the ratio of uncollected Indian debt was below 6 per cent of the value of returns in the late nineteenth century.

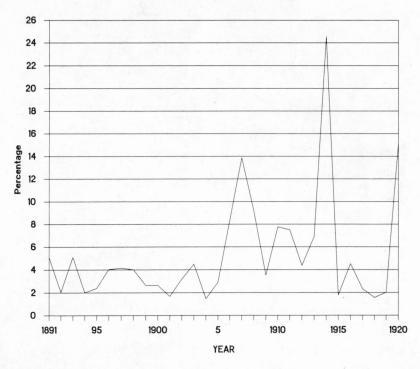

Figure 24
Ratio of Indian debts to fur returns: Hudson's Bay Company, 1891–1920

Furthermore, the ratio was in decline between 1891 and 1901. The true cost to the company was even less than these data suggest, given that advances were given in goods valued at their full cost-landed prices. In the late 1880s these prices still included gross profit margins of 100 per cent or more. As many company traders pointed out, this meant that the real losses to the company were not as great as the accounts showed. Furthermore, contrary to the statements of the commissioner, native people were, on the whole, very credit worthy. Although the company's officers said that competitors did 'demoralize' and 'unsettle' the minds of some of the native hunters and trappers by encouraging them to default on their obligations, most native hunters did not do so. In any event, competition was strongest when fur prices were rising, so that the inflated value of the company's returns provided some compensation. The ratio of unpaid debt to returns declined on rising markets and increased on falling ones.

accounting sys. made Indians look unreliable

The manner in which the company treated delinquent accounts also served to present a distorted picture of the true credit worthiness of Indians. In 1887 it adopted the practice of writing off 'bad debts' at an accelerated rate. According to this scheme, credits issued to native people in the form of goods were discounted 25 per cent from their cost-landed value when first entered in the debt books. If a debt was still outstanding after the close of the outfit in which it was issued, it was discounted another 25 per cent and regarded as 'doubtful.' After one year, the company wrote it off altogether.[64] Whenever native people paid their debts after they had been written off, a common occurrence, the company registered the payment as an 'extraordinary gain' in the post balance sheet in the outfit year in which the Indian paid it.[65] For this reason Indians often were not officially credited for settling old accounts. In other words, the accounting system was not set up to accommodate the business of native people, who often could not settle their affairs within the company's business (outfit) year. This discrepancy made them appear to be unworthy of receiving credit to those who were unfamiliar with the way the trading system worked.

It was for these various reasons that Chipman's 1899 orders to curtail sharply advances to Indians was no more successful than similar commands from his predecessors had been. The traders largely ignored the instruction to reduce them in the Timiskaming area and to eliminate them entirely in the Lac la Pluie, Lake Superior, and Lake Huron districts.[66] It seems that it was only in the Peace River District that they made a concerted effort to bring credit trading to an end. There traders achieved some short-term success even though the Indians resisted.[67] After only a slight reduction in credit losses was made in the department as a whole, the bad debts began to mount again after 1902 (fig. 23).

In 1903 the commissioner made yet another effort to trim these expenses by adopting the credit policy used in the saleshops. He gave post managers the authority to provide up to $100 of debt per customer. For amounts between $100 and $500 they had to obtain the approval of the district manager. Only the commissioner's office could authorize advances for more than $500.[68] This new policy did not work, and losses rose sharply between 1904 and 1914. The new controls failed for several reasons. Fur harvests were poor in 1905–6 and Indians needed help. Also, the Russian-Japanese war of 1904–5 hurt the industry by driving fur markets downward. Lower fur prices reduced Indian purchasing power. The resulting upward trend in the Indians' debt load led senior company officials to renew their calls for the elimination of credit trading altogether. Once again post and district managers steadfastly refused to comply. One of them ridiculed the company's proposal by quoting to the commissioner an Indian's reaction to the proposal: 'I have a good dog and when furs are scarce I do not kill that dog, but I keep him and feed him as I know that he will be useful to me again when furs are plentiful.'[69]

Generally district and post managers always resisted efforts to restrict credit. One of the accountants in the commissioner's office explained why. 'The abolition of Indian debts was looked upon by those who had not tried it as likely to drive away the Indians and cause a great loss of trade to the Company, while it would build up the opposition traders who continued to give debt and would endeavor to poison the minds of the Indians towards the Company.'[70] With considerable justification, company traders also believed that the unevenness of competition precluded the uniform application of any policy dealing with this aspect of the business.[71] The problem for the company was that post managers had a variety of clever ways to circumvent whatever rules and regulations were in force. For instance, they kept unofficial debt records, known as 'vest pocket' or 'purgatory' ledgers to record unauthorized lines of credit.[72] These were kept hidden away in case district managers or inspectors arrived unexpectedly to make an audit. Traders cleared their books of those 'purgatory accounts' which were outstanding at the end of the year by charging the goods given out to 'sick and destitute accounts' or by crediting Indians more for their furs than they were worth. We shall never know how much uncollected debt was hidden in this fashion or the extent to which the unreported amounts compensate for the fact that the official record tended to exaggerate the picture.

Strangely, as late as the turn of the century, the Hudson's Bay Company made no concerted effort to anticipate changing consumer demand in the north, and it took no significant steps to modernize invoicing and retailing practices. Mostly the company continued to offer the high-quality staple lines for which it was famous rather than taking the lead and experimenting with new lines of merchandise. It was the opposition traders who led the way. These small merchants obtained their outfits mostly from dry-goods wholesalers in cities, primarily Sudbury, Kenora, Winnipeg, Prince Albert, and Edmonton. They introduced what were termed 'fancy goods' or 'treaty goods' for the annuity business. Generally speaking, these articles were cheaper than the company's traditional staples and of lower quality. Popularized by treaty trade, Indians came to demand 'fancy goods' in addition to the old staples. Also, a steadily growing number of white visitors wanted to buy new articles, such as printed cottons, cheap clothing, fancy dress goods, straw hats, and playing cards. Sales of these items to the newcomers whetted the Indians' appetite for them.[73] The company's traders who managed posts on or near major transportation routes attempted to keep pace with these demands by ordering new lines of merchandise through looking at samples brought to them by travelling salesmen and forwarding their orders to the company's buyers. In the late 1880s this practice was widespread in northern Ontario in those districts traversed by the Canadian Pacific Railway line.[74]

Conducting the business this way created serious problems. In order to fill the indents of the post managers the company had to place many small orders with a variety of suppliers and manufacturers. This meant that the Hudson's Bay Company did not receive the volume discounts it should have, and it forfeited a considerable competitive advantage as a result. There were other problems. Many of the post managers did not fill out their requisitions in sufficient detail, and their invoices often took so long to be processed that the goods were no longer available.

Very early in his brief term of office, Wrigley attempted to bring some order to the company's indenting system. He set aside part of the new Winnipeg store to serve as the supply depot for the Northern Department. According to his scheme, the depot was supposed to furnish the district managers with samples and patterns to guide them in placing their orders. Managers who supervised nearby districts were encouraged to visit Winnipeg to select their goods. Before the Winnipeg depot was permitted to process the indents of the various districts, the respective managers were expected to submit their orders to the commissioner and the Canadian subcommittee for approval.[75] Following a tour of inspection of present-day northern Ontario in 1888 and 1889, Inspectors Beeston and Hardisty made a number of suggestions for improvements for this region which paralleled Wrigley's reforms for the Northern Department. For instance, the two inspectors recommended that post managers be required to deal only with salesmen who represented reputable firms and who carried letters of authorization issued by the commissioner. They proposed that the indents the managers placed should be sent to the appropriate district head for his approval before being forwarded to the depot. In addition, Beeston and Hardisty advocated sending post managers, particularly those in charge of line posts, to Winnipeg or Montreal, where they could see the range of items that were available and obtain some familiarity with current retail trends and marketing procedures.[76] The two men also advocated having the company increase the assortment of newer lines of merchandise which were in demand, although they did not specify exactly what goods should be imported.[77]

It appears that Wrigley's reforms were not effective, nor were the inspectors' recommendations acted upon immediately. It was not until the 1898 meeting at Athabasca Landing that the officers agreed that the district managers should assume the responsibility for filling out requisitions.[78] Fifteen years later, Norman H. Bacon, who took over as commissioner in 1913, tightened controls even more. Bacon did not think it was a good idea to leave requisitioning entirely in the hands of district managers. Rather, he decided to take a more active role. Beginning in 1913, he required district managers to justify their orders to the commissioner's office. Bacon also concluded that line post managers and men in charge of frontier districts were not successfully meeting the competition for the new 'white trade,' so he experimented with bringing them in to Winnipeg in the way Wrigley, Beeston, and Hardisty had recommended nearly twenty-five years earlier. In addition, he sent two buyers out to meet with the managers.[79]

It is astounding that the company's managers took so long to make even these minor changes in merchandising practices within the Fur Trade Department, given that retail sales were increasingly important to the department as a source of revenue. This was a consequence of the fact that escalating competition for furs by cash buyers was cutting deeply into the profit margins on furs. For example, the 1909 annual report of the Fur Trade Department showed that the 'apparent' gross profit from operations was $992,949. Of this amount $56,754 (6 per cent) was derived from fur and $936,195 (94 per cent) from goods sales. Regarding these figures Commissioner R.E. Hall, who served between 1910 and 1913, remarked: 'the importance of holding and increasing the volume and profits of the merchandise needs no further illustrations.'[80] None the less, in his short term of office Hall was no more innovative in this area than his predecessors had been.

By the eve of the First World War Hudson's Bay Company officials came to regard all areas lying within fifty miles of major transportation routes as 'frontier districts.' They considered lands lying beyond the fifty-mile zone as being 'inland' or 'remote' territories. The company still ruled remote areas, where barter trading along traditional lines was the norm. The Canadian Pacific Railway – or the 'line' as it was known locally – marked the frontier in northern Ontario until construction of the Canadian Northern (1899–1915) and National Transcontinental railways (1903–13). In the late 1880s company men regarded the region to the south of the Canadian Pacific Railway as lying beyond the 'traditional fur trade area.'[81] Farther west, the great lakes of Manitoba, the Saskatchewan River, the Athabasca River, and the Peace River marked the frontier, because of the steamboat service that was available.

The Hudson's Bay Company attempted to shield its remote districts from the worst effects of competition and modernization by aggressive actions on the frontier. For this purpose it maintained 'line posts' at key points along the railways. The line posts served the needs of white customers (trappers, prospectors, miners, loggers, railway workers, and others) and offered stiff competition against fur-trading rivals. Reflecting their dual purpose, line posts included a saleshop where substantial cash business was conducted.

The company's spatial strategy was an old one. The directors were willing to run heavy losses at the frontier in order to drain the resources of competitors, making it difficult for them to expand into the lucrative inland districts. But the policy was not successful. The problem was that native people were too sensitive to price differentials, and they were willing to go great distances to obtain better prices. The traders pointed out repeatedly that: 'travel, as you are aware, is not an object to an Indian.' As early as 1891 James Fortescue reported that as far away as Moose Factory Indian hunters: 'keep back their best fur, and threatened to carry it all to the lines if their demands are not granted.' Fortescue added: 'It is tantamount to a system of strike, or coercion.'[82] Indeed, in 1886 Indian boat brigademen from this post did go on strike for wages that were comparable with those being paid at the 'line.'[83] Clearly anything that the Hudson's Bay Company did to reinforce price differentials between remote and frontier posts merely served to attract Indians from farther afield, given their response to these differences and their attitudes toward travel. Nearly forty years later this characteristic continued to be a problem. In 1933 the district manager of Saskatchewan, R.A. Talbot, thought the solution lay in 'educating' the Indians. According to Talbot: 'At posts in proximity to line Posts, an effort should be made to discourage the Indians travelling out a matter of 40 to 80 miles to line posts to secure commodities at lower prices than exist at these interior posts ... Efforts should be made to prove to the Indian that his time is of some value, a fact that he does not at present take into consideration at all.'[84] This recommendation is of particular interest, given that in the old days the Hudson's Bay Company depended on the Indians not to take travel time into account.

While the Hudson's Bay Company was struggling with countless small operators all along the expanding southern frontier, a new and formidable opponent appeared in its traditional heartland when the Revillon Frères of Paris launched a spirited fight for a share of the northern fur trade. The Revillon family had been active in fur retailing in Paris since 1723. In the late nineteenth century Victor Revillon revolutionized the business by marketing fur garments as articles of fashion and by using drapery shops as outlets. By taking these initiatives, he broadened the market to include middle-class buyers. Equally important, he accelerated the turnover of fur garments, because consumers became preoccupied with keeping abreast of fashion trends. Initially the Revillons bought raw furs through wholesalers. By the late 1800s the firm became active as a raw-fur wholesaler buying in the Leipzig and London markets. By the turn of this century the Revillons opened an agency in New York to handle raw and dressed furs. Shortly thereafter they decided to secure a sizeable portion of their raw furs directly at the source in order to avoid paying substantial commissions to agents and brokers. In 1899 they opened a small warehouse in Edmonton where they purchased furs for cash.[85] In 1903 the Revillons bought an established fur-trading business in the Peace River country from Colonel J.K. Cornwall (known as 'Peace River Jim') and his partner, Fletcher Bredin.[86] Two years later they established a general wholesale business in Edmonton to supply small retailers, government agencies, and their own expanding network of western posts.[87]

In 1902 the Revillons took the first steps to establish themselves in eastern Canada when they sent a small trading party overland from the Canadian Pacific Railway to James Bay. The following year the Revillons dispatched the steamship *El Dorado* from Quebec City and they mounted another overland expedition from the railway. Their intention was to make a grand entry into the Moose River area by land and sea to impress the native people. Instead, the Revillons suffered a humiliating and costly disaster.[88] The *El Dorado* was not well suited to the shoal waters of James Bay, and it ran aground at a loss of $120,000.[89] Despite this severe set-back, the overland party did establish a camp on the mainland at Moosonee. A short while later the Revillons made this new settlement the centre of their operations in James Bay.

name changes

By 1903 the Revillons operated twenty-three establishments from coast to coast. In the same year, the Frenchmen chartered a private company, the Revillon Canada Far Northern Company. They changed the firm's name to Revillon Brothers and reorganized it as a joint-stock company a year later. Finally, in 1912 they restyled it as the Revillon Trading Company and operated under the name Revillon Frères.[90]

The Revillons established a fur-buying operation along lines that were similar to those of the Hudson's Bay Company. In remote districts beyond the frontier regions the firm attempted to obtain most of its furs through barter. In 1901 the Revillons imported $45,000 worth of stock for that purpose. In 1902 the amount was increased to $400,000, and by 1903 it totalled over $700,000.[91] Obviously the Revillon brothers had forged a formidable organization in the north very quickly. By the outbreak of the First World War they were seriously challenging the Hudson's Bay Company in the remote James Bay area and in the Athabasca River / Peace River country.

Clearly the Hudson's Bay Company was under attack in most of its traditional trading preserve on the eve of the First World War. Small competitors were swarming over all those tracts of land that railway and steamboat lines had made accessible. The powerful Revillon Frères organization had established itself in the cradle of the London-based company's operations. Yet despite the heavy inroads that opponents were making in the Athabasca and Lake Superior areas, these districts were still among the Hudson's Bay Company's leading producers, ranking first and third, respectively (fig. 25). These two districts, along with second-ranking Saskatchewan and fourth-ranking Mackenzie River, accounted for over 50 per cent of the skins the company obtained in Canada. However, the distribution of profits (fig. 25) shows a different pattern. The two leading contributors were the remote districts of James Bay and Nelson River, followed by the highly exposed districts of Lake Superior and Athabasca; these four accounted for over 60 per cent of the total. The strong showing of James Bay and Nelson River was the result of the high gross profit margins they were able to maintain on goods, while that of the Superior and Athabasca districts came from the high volumes of merchandise sales generated at line posts.

The Hudson's Bay Company's merchandise sales records for 1911 (table 6) provide some additional clues about the changing nature of the northern economy by indicating the share of the business that was generated by the fur trade and by the saleshops. In five areas of the country, all secluded districts, over 70 per cent of the turnover was

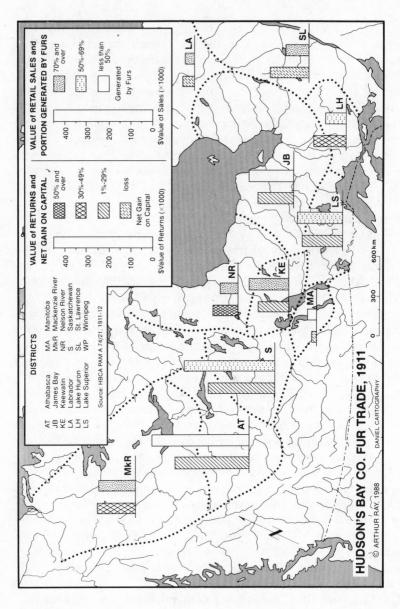

Figure 25
Hudson's Bay Company fur trade, 1911

generated by bartering furs. Included were the Mackenzie River, Kee-watin, and Nelson River districts. Saskatchewan, Lake Superior, and Lake Huron ranged between 50 and 69 per cent. Bartering furs accounted for less than 50 per cent of the volume in the remaining territories. Somewhat surprising is the fact that the districts of James Bay and Athabasca fall into this category along with Manitoba.

When surveying the scene just before the outbreak of the First World War, senior Hudson's Bay Company officials concluded that it was no longer possible to conduct a traditional fur trade throughout most of the Subarctic. For this reason and with the objective of gaining a larger share of the increasingly lucrative trade in arctic fox, in 1913 the directors decided to embark on a major expansion program in the Arctic. The company's announcement captured the imagination of a *Winnipeg Free Press* reporter, who wrote that 'the company will make [a] last stand against civilization at the Arctic Ocean.'[92] The outbreak of war shortly thereafter forced the company to mothball this plan until 1919.

4
The turning point:
the impact of the First World War
on the northern fur trade

*To this day the Indians have not forgiven the Company for what happened
at the beginning of the war, and I think any experienced trader will agree
that the Hudson's Bay Company never fully regained their old-time prestige
with the Indians.*
(Philip Godsell, ca 1930)[1]

The First World War caused major disruptions to international trade.
In the fur industry the interruptions offered a golden opportunity
for merchants in North American cities to challenge the traditional
dominance of their counterparts in Europe, particularly those in London and Leipzig. They wasted no time in doing so. The restructuring
of the international fur-marketing system that resulted had a major
impact on the industry in the Canadian north. It served to unleash a
tidal wave of competing buyers who flooded the north with cash,
shaking the foundations of the old order. The Hudson's Bay Company's very cautious and sluggish response to wartime economic conditions enabled new opponents to entrench themselves. These
newcomers deflected an increasing portion of Canadian furs directly
to the United States markets, as the export data reveal (fig. 20). Despite
efforts to dislodge the interlopers after the war, the company never
was able to regain undisputed control of the business.

Although producers had an increasing array of outlets through
which to dispose of their furs, auctions continued to play a pivotal role
in the marketing system. A large proportion of the returns that fur-
buying agents, mail-order, and direct-receiving houses collected they

eventually disposed of at public auctions. Not surprisingly, many of the leading fur dealers and brokerage houses invested in auction companies. The auctions, especially the large ones, served several important functions. They made it easier for brokers to obtain the assortments of the different types and grades of furs that their clients (dyers and garment manufacturers) needed. Often this process involved buying portions of many different fur lots. Besides simplifying local fur purchasing, the major auctions established regional and world prices. The continuing importance and increasing profitability of the auctions provided the incentive for a growing number of firms to compete for the business. In the ensuing struggle these competitors diverted a greater share of production away from the Hudson's Bay Company's sales. Some of it went to other London rivals; an even larger portion went to the sales floors of new contenders located in the United States and Canada. *Lampson Co*

By the outbreak of the First World War the most important London rival of the Hudson's Bay Company was C.M. Lampson & Company. Curtis M. Lampson established this firm in London in 1830.[2] Lampson came to the city from the United States originally to serve as an emissary of John Jacob Astor, founder of the American Fur Company. He remained in London and built up a firm of his own. Beginning in 1885, his company began to streamline fur auction procedures by arranging show bundles that were precise mathematical samples (normally 10 per cent) of lots containing as many as 20,000 skins. Also, Lampson initiated the practice of printing sales catalogues that listed the grades of the various lots.[3] These innovations, which the industry as a whole eventually adopted, expedited the sale of large quantities of fur, thereby lowering transaction costs. The company also forged close links with Canadian and American dealers in order to draw furs to its auctions. In 1873 C.M. Lampson & Company opened an agency in New York, represented by James Tinker. Tinker retired in 1878 and Alfred Fraser replaced him. Upon his arrival, Fraser organized Alfred Fraser Incorporated, and this company represented Lampson & Company until 1936.[4] Of particular importance, Lampson & Company was very successful in its effort to build a consignment business that handled large quantities of North American furs. By the late 1880s Lampson's auctions provided an important outlet for Canadian fur buyers, so important that Canadian newspapers began to report the results of these sales along with those of the Hudson's Bay Company.[5]

A.W. Nesbitt, organized in 1913, quickly became another leading *Nesbitt* London auction house that handled large quantities of North American furs, ranking third behind the Hudson's Bay Company and C.M. Lampson & Company.[6] F. Huth's firm was another newcomer. Founded in 1809, this fur company did not become involved in the London auction business until 1911. After opening a branch in New York in 1923, Huth became a leading dealer in North American furs.[7] Other fur auction houses were active in London on the eve of the First World War, but most of them specialized in African, Asian, Australian, and South American hides and pelts.[8]

The First World War had an immediate and major impact on the world fur-marketing system when the Board of Trade of the British government temporarily suspended auctions in London during the autumn of 1914. In response, the governor and committee of the Hudson's Bay Company ordered their traders not to buy furs from the Indians during the winter of 1914–15. They believed that the market would collapse once sales resumed. This policy explains the abrupt decline in the value of Canadian fur exports in 1914 (fig. 20). Still wary in the spring of 1915, the committee approved the resumption of fur purchasing and sales, but only on a very limited scale compared with pre-war days. Meanwhile, in the United States high levels of employment in wartime industries served to increase the demand, while the supply fell because of the diminished flow of furs from Europe. Fur prices surged upward as a result, encouraging large numbers of American buyers to rush into the Canadian north, where they discovered, to their great delight, that the Hudson's Bay Company men were temporarily barred from competing against them. Norman H. Bacon, who had become the Hudson's Bay Company's commissioner in 1913, recommended that counter-measures be taken immediately. He pleaded with the London directors to reverse their disastrous wartime sales policy. Bacon wanted the authority at least to sell company furs in the United States so that he could conduct buying activities more vigorously in Canada. By not taking these steps, the Hudson's Bay Company risked letting the Americans establish themselves in Canada. Furthermore, the company was missing a lucrative opportunity by not taking advantage of the buoyant North American market.[9] Also, selling in North America would reduce inventory times and thereby lessen speculative risks.[10]

The unwillingness of the governor and committee to give Bacon the freedom of action he needed to conduct a vigorous trade served to emphasize one of the basic underlying problems that plagued the company's fur-buying and selling operations. The directors' primary

interests lay elsewhere, given the changing character of the company.
By the outbreak of the war fur-trading operations ranked third, in
terms of gross income, behind land and retail sales. As land sales soared
during the wheat boom years, the company made unprecedented
profits, and stockholders received dividends of between 25 and 40 per
cent on their shares between 1905 and 1913.[11] These windfall profits
made the company's directors so complacent and out of touch with
Canadian realities during this time that even the saleshops languished.
Only in 1910 did the company begin to awaken again, when plans
were laid to build a chain of modern department stores. Blueprints
were drawn up between 1910 and 1912, and store construction began
in Calgary and Vancouver in 1913.[12] So, on the eve of the war the
governor and committee were absorbed with retail operations. To
make matters worse from Bacon's perspective, the outbreak of war
created an even more attractive business opportunity for the company,
when on 9 October 1914 the governor and committee concluded an
agreement with the French government which made the company
overseas purchasing agent for France for the duration of the war.[13] This
role involved creating overseas subsidiaries and agencies, arranging
credits for the French government, organizing steamship service, as
well as purchasing and transporting foodstuffs, fuel, lumber, and muni-
tions. In the end the company handled more than 13 million tons of
cargo under this contract.[14]

Given these circumstances, the governor and committee were not
prepared to devote their energies to the conduct of the fur trade
under the extremely volatile circumstances of the time, nor were they
prepared to give their commissioner complete freedom to do so. With
respect to the fur trade, it appears that the governor and committee's
only major concern involved preserving London's future as the world
entrepôt for furs. They believed that selling Hudson's Bay Company
furs in United States markets would undermine that objective, and it
was for this reason that they were not sympathetic to Bacon's proposal.
Bacon firmly believed, with very good reason, that the governor and
committee's decision did not make good business sense. He continued
to pressure them to change their policy. Eventually, the committee
members relented somewhat and authorized limited sales in the United
States beginning in June of 1916.[15] But this reluctant action was short
lived. In the winter of 1917 the London committee reverted to its
former policy by ordering the suspension of fur sales in Canada and
the United States despite the record prices the company was receiv-

ing.[16] Bacon was furious and he resigned 3 October 1918.[17] It would not be until 1924 that the directors authorized a resumption of fur sales in Canada, but even then they set a strict limit of $250,000 per season. Furthermore, these sales were intended only to dispose of furs purchased with cash.[18]

North American fur merchants quickly took advantage of the opportunity to challenge the Hudson's Bay Company. Their struggle to gain the ascendancy added fuel to the inflationary pressures created by the war. New York and St Louis fur dealers were first off the mark. In 1916 the New York Fur Auction Sales Corporation was incorporated as a joint-stock company.[19] Most of the investors were fur dealers who bought and sold lots on the exchange.[20] London furriers promptly complained about the 'Teutonic Flavour' of the organization, charging that Leipzig fur merchants were backing the scheme with the intention of diverting to New York furs that normally went to the German city. Definitely Leipzig firms were well represented in the new auction company. The first president of the New York company was Charles S. Porter, who represented G. Gaudig & Blum of Leipzig. One vice-president, David Steiner, worked for Joseph Steiner Brothers of New York and Leipzig, and the other vice-president, O.G. Becker, came from Becker Brothers Company of Chicago, New York and Leipzig. The treasurer, Edward Spear, was associated with the New York branch of Theodore Thorer Company of Leipzig.[21]

British sensitivity over this issue was understandable. Apart from the international political issues involved, London dealers risked losing a lucrative business to New York. They estimated that on the eve of the war, annually $15 million worth of furs were sent from New York to London for sale. This represented commissions of roughly $750,000 per year. Although the United States government later seized the assets of the German firms operating in the country, the New York Fur Auction Sales Company continued to conduct highly profitable operations during the war.[22] Somewhat ironically, in 1919, Norman Bacon, the disgruntled former Hudson's Bay Company Fur Trade Commissioner, became president of the organization, serving in that capacity until 1921.[23]

In 1916, the same year that fur auctions began in New York, leading fur dealers in St Louis established the International Fur Exchange by joining the St Louis-based wholesale fur concern of F.C. Taylor Fur Company, established in 1871, with that of Funsten Brothers & Company, established in 1881. In their struggle for market supremacy, the

St Louis merchants gained a critical advantage over New York. In 1913, Colonel P.B. Fouke of Funsten Brothers secured the exclusive right to market all United States government Alaskan seal skins and other furs.[24] Previously these commodities had been sold in London. The auctions of United States government furs provided the foundation upon which the International Fur Exchange built its business. In 1918 the company handled sales in excess of $32 million. One year later the International Fur Exchange claimed that it conducted what was 'probably the largest business in the world for the wholesale purchase and sale of raw furs.'[25] That same year the company was reorganized, and an additional $2,925,000 in cash was raised to expand operations.[26] The organizers encouraged companies and individuals who regularly dealt with the International Fur Exchange to buy shares in the new corporation[27] and sent a prospectus to the Hudson's Bay Company.

In Canada only one major auction house was established before the end of the First World War. This was the firm of Little Brothers of Vancouver, founded in 1915. However, other cities, notably Edmonton, Prince Albert, Winnipeg, Toronto, and Montreal, already had been important regional fur-buying centres for many years.[28] A substantial portion of the furs sold in these cities, particular those of the western prairies, were put to tender by dry-goods wholesalers whose customers consigned furs to them in payment of their accounts.[29]

In spite of the early beginning on the west coast, Montreal became the dominant fur auction centre. Here, a group of nationally prominent businessmen organized the Canadian Fur Auction Sales Company Ltd in 1920 with an initial capital investment of $5 million. It was their intention to make Montreal the 'St Louis of Canada.'[30] The subscribers included Lord Shaughnessy, chairman of the board of directors of the Canadian Pacific Railway; Sir Herbert Holt of Holt Renfrew and Company and president of the Royal Bank of Canada and the Montreal Light, Heat and Power Company; Lorne C. Webster, director of the Merchants' Bank of Canada; P. Cowans of the Montreal stock brokerage firm, McDougall & Cowans; J.W. McConnell, president of the St Lawrence Sugar Refinery; and W.A. Black, vice-president of Ogilvie Flour Mills Company. In addition, several prominent Montreal fur dealers, including Holt Renfrew and Company, held interests in the concern.[31] The organizers of the new company did not intend to limit themselves to the consignment business. They also planned to buy furs and engage in fur-dyeing activities. The first auction took place in the Rose Room of the Windsor Hotel on 22 March 1920; it was a resounding success, exceeding all expectations. The new Montreal company sold a total of $5,093,120 worth of furs, many pelts at prices that exceeded those obtained at the most recent auctions in St Louis and New York.[32]

During the inflationary period the auction business became ever more lucrative; prices soared and sales volumes skyrocketed. In 1918 the International Exchange Corporation of St Louis earned a gross income of about $1.2 million from commissions. Just before the market crashed late in 1920, the February sale in St Louis disposed of more than $27 million worth of fur.[33] With commissions averaging 5 per cent of sales, this one event generated a gross revenue for the auction house of about $1.35 million. Profits of this magnitude lured others into the business, raising competition to a frenzied pitch.[34] Auction houses waged the struggle in a variety of ways. Most spectacular were the perks that they offered to the buyers and agents who attended the sales. For example, on 11 October 1919 the New York Fur Auction Sales Corporation held a formal dinner for 800 buyers at the Hotel Pennsylvania. The company provided live entertainment and a fur fashion show.[35]

By 1920 London and North American auction houses had been so successful in building up their consignment business that they forced the Hudson's Bay Company to abandon its 250-year-old policy of selling only 'house' furs (those owned by the company). Accordingly, in 1921 the company announced that it would offer a consignment service.[36] During the summer of 1922 Frank C. Ingrams, secretary of the Hudson's Bay Company, arrived in New York to promote the new venture.[37]

In the scramble for furs between 1914 and 1920, buying became highly speculative and was financed largely by the lavish use of credit. When the inflationary bubble burst late in 1920, overextended buyers suffered heavy losses as market values plummeted below the prices shippers and buying agents had paid for their furs. A panic hit the industry and many fur auction companies faced financial ruin in 1921. The International Fur Exchange of St Louis was one of those hardest hit by the collapse. On 26 March 1921 its debts totalled $18,050,604; the organization was bankrupt.[38] The New York Fur Auction Sales Company was also in difficulty, as were many raw-fur dealers throughout the United States and Canada.[39] In 1921 the Hudson's Bay Company reported that United States banks lost over $10 million because of bankruptcies in the industry.[40] Company officials blamed the problem on the reckless use of credit in the North America. Although speculation and the problems that it generated undoubtedly were most strongly felt in the United States, the British market was not immune, and creditors forced the liquidation of A.W. Nesbitt in 1920.[41]

Meanwhile, during the war the mushrooming demand for furs, the international and interurban struggle for increased shares of Canadian output, and the liberal extension of credit by banks, auction houses, and leading fur-buying agencies all served to set off a short burst of unprecedented competition in the Canadian north. Large and small operators entered the fray. Nowhere was the struggle more intensive than in the fur-rich Athabasca-Mackenzie district. Here all the major players were active.

One of the most important newcomers to appear on the scene was J.H. Bryan. According to the veteran Colonel J.K. Cornwall, Bryan arrived in the Edmonton area shortly before 1914, when he operated as a small cash buyer. Cornwall claimed that Bryan had no prior experience with the industry, either through association or by experience, but he compensated for these shortcomings by being industrious, sober, and a good listener. Supposedly Bryan obtained his education quickly from other traders who spoke freely when drinking.[42] He also had the advantage of learning on a rising market.   *Lamson + Hubbard*

Following his initial fur-buying tour Bryan ventured to New York where he made important business connections and obtained substantial financial backing. He returned to Fort Chipewyan and began to build a string of posts in the Athabasca-Mackenzie district. Between 1915 and 1917 Bryan established operations at Fort Chipewyan, Fond du Lac, Fort Resolution, and Fort Rae. In 1918 he expanded to Fort Simpson, Fort Nelson, and Fort Norman.[43] The same year he convinced Lamson and Hubbard Corporation of Boston to invest over $1.5 million in a Canadian operation. The Boston company bought his posts and retained Bryan as manager.[44] At the time Lamson and Hubbard (incorporated in 1882) was one of the largest raw-fur-dealing companies in the United States. After a reorganization of the company in 1918, they registered their Canadian operations in Edmonton under the name Lamson and Hubbard Canadian Company Ltd (hereinafter Lamson and Hubbard).[45]

With considerable fanfare, Lamson and Hubbard immediately launched an expansion program. Following the lead of the Hudson's Bay Company, heavy investments were made in the development of a major transportation system in the Athabasca-Mackenzie region for the purposes of carrying the company's own cargo and that of the general public. Lamson and Hubbard wanted to develop the same capacity as that of its London-based rival. Accordingly, in the spring of 1919 Lamson and Hubbard began the construction of a stern-wheeler for use between Fort Smith and Fort McPherson. Besides this large craft, a steam tug and tow barges were built for the Liard River; they introduced two large gas boats on Lake Athabasca and Great Slave Lake and purchased a steamer for operations between Fort McMurray and Fort Fitzgerald.[46] In addition, the company invested nearly $27,700 to import from San Francisco two caterpillar tractors and eight three-ton iron trailers for use on the Fort Smith portage.[47] Also they employed two gas-powered tugs and forty to fifty scows of ten- to twenty-ton capacity to haul cargo between this portage and the end of steel.[48] As early as the summer of 1919 Lamson and Hubbard shipped 450 tons of trade merchandise into the Athabasca-Mackenzie region. Clearly the Hudson's Bay Company faced a formidable new rival in the area.

The Northern Trading Company of Edmonton became the third-leading contender in the region. The early history of this company is not entirely clear. What is known is that in 1913 the Northern Trading Company bought the firm of Hislop and Nagle which had been active throughout the Mackenzie River valley as early as 1882.[49] After this merger Colonel Cornwall developed a close association with the Northern Trading Company, eventually becoming one of the driving forces behind it. Cornwall first came to northern Alberta during the Klondike Goldrush. He stayed behind in the Peace River area, where he joined forces with Fletcher Bredin and built a string of small trading posts. In 1903 Cornwall and his partner sold their operation to Revillon Frères and immediately thereafter he turned his energies towards building the Northern Transportation Company. In 1904 his first steamer, the *Midnight Sun*, was operating on the Lesser Slave Lake River.[50] The Northern Transportation Company expanded operations rapidly thereafter.[51] By 1911 the Northern Trading Company shipped large outfits into the Mackenzie District using the colonel's riverboat service.[52] In order to challenge effectively the Hudson's Bay Company and Lamson and Hubbard, in 1918 the Northern Trading Company obtained financial backing from A.W. Nesbitt of London and concluded a fur-marketing arrangement with this firm.[53]

The struggle for dominance of the Athabasca-Mackenzie riverboat business and fur trade under wartime conditions affected the local industry in many different ways. Most important, favourable transportation rates served to open the area to small fur buyers. Consequently, cash fur buying became widespread for the first time. According to

Colonel Cornwall, before 1914 these cash transactions were of only minor significance beyond the immediate hinterland of Edmonton.[54] The outbreak of war and the Hudson's Bay Company's reactions to wartime market conditions in London set the stage for a major, if temporary, shift in business practices. When the governor and committee ordered their men not to buy furs during the winter of 1914–15, they also informed them that they were not to extend the usual lines of credit to the Indians. When Commissioner Bacon prepared to carry out the latter order, his close adviser, Nathaniel MacKenzie, a veteran trader, warned him not to do so. MacKenzie pointed out that 'it was to the past loyalty of these Indians and their forefathers that the Company owed its prosperity, and that the line of policy embarked upon could not help but be looked upon by the natives as a flagrant breach of trust.'[55] He added: 'that by the time word reached many of the posts much of the debt would already have been given out. Why not,' he counselled, 'instead of appealing to the Indian Department to come to the aid of its charges, set an example to other panic-stricken firms with a "business as usual" slogan?'[56]

Writing about this episode at a later date, Hudson's Bay Company trader Philip Godsell observed: 'MacKenzie knew that, orders or no orders, many of the older traders would ignore them to a certain point and risk dismissal rather than see the Indians stuck. Again he argued that Indian debt, instead of being entirely cut out, should be confined to necessities, and that prevailing panic fur values be disregarded and the Indians be paid sufficient for the skins to enable them to get along until the worst of the crisis was over.'[57]

MacKenzie's assessment was accurate. When Bacon subsequently ignored his advice and set about carrying out the order: 'many of the post managers risked dismissal by giving out a little debt.'[58] But, as Godsell recorded: 'usually ... it was not shown as such in the books but was entered in a "Purgatory Ledger" and never saw the light of day. Others spent much of their own earnings in doing what they could to alleviate the Indians' distress.'[59] We shall never know the extent to which the credit reductions Bacon appears to have achieved (fig. 23) were offset by these clandestine actions of the older officers. Besides taking these extreme actions, the governor and committee set the 1914–15 purchasing tariff 83 per cent below the March market prices to permit modest fur buying in the hope of retaining Indian loyalty. Naturally, the competition obtained most of the fur. The company's volume dropped 50 per cent below that of the previous year.[60]

This was not just a temporary set-back. By all accounts the company's officers suffered permanent damage to their prestige in the eyes of the Indians. According to Godsell: 'the opposition traders ... took the fullest possible advantage of this situation, especially when the Indians visited them and asked for twine and gunpowder in debt.' On these occasions: 'Why,' they asked, 'do you not go to the Company's traders and remind them of the promises they always made the Indians to come to the rescue whenever they were stuck? When these traders first came amongst you they only had a small ship and enough goods to build a small post! Now they are everywhere. Did they not make this money out of the Indians?'[61] Godsell complained that 'it was logical propaganda and it was driven home with emphasis. Hardly ever did we refuse debt without having this, and other things the traders were supposed to have said, dinned into our ears.' He added: 'I think any experienced trader will agree that the Hudson's Bay Company never fully regained their old-time prestige with the Indians.'[62]

Bryan, with his Boston and New York financial backing, was one of the men who led the assault when the company faltered. He mounted a major cash-buying operation in the Athabasca-Mackenzie area. Colonel Cornwall reported: 'Bryan found the North ready for his cash. Prices had been down – low, in fact, no value was attached to fur. Some Hudson's Bay men acted as his agents, took his cash and were satisfied to let him take the fur. Some other traders did the same. They also sold him their fur. He had agents everywhere and trusted his money in a most reckless manner to every Tom, Dick and Harry who laid claim to fur buying. He secured a great deal of fur. He took it East and sold it at an unheard of profit.'[63] With fur prices shooting upward on the North American markets, it was possible to get away with this reckless approach to the business.

When Lamson and Hubbard bought control of Bryan's business in 1918, they expanded their cash-purchasing operations. The Hudson's Bay Company, the Northern Trading Company, and the 'lesser operators' did likewise. Many years later Colonel Cornwall reflected on this development: 'It is not hard to imagine what virgin soil the cash buyer had to work with. He proceeded to cultivate it, advised the Indians to take cash, disregard his debt, posing as a saviour and a friend of the trapper, illustrating his arguments by paying more in cash than the trapper could get in trade at the Posts.'[64] He added: 'The cash buyer failed to advise the trapper that he had been staked months previously, that he had been carried over the lean years when fur was scarce, that no cash buyer came when fur was down, and a dozen more good and sufficient reasons.'[65]

In the bidding war Lamson and Hubbard and Northern Trading Company tended to be 'price setters' and the Hudson's Bay Company a 'price taker.'[66] Cash buyers from these three concerns, and 'lesser operators' combed the entire district, but they were most active in the Athabasca area. On the eve of the First World War one-third of the Hudson's Bay Company's Athabasca returns were bought with cash in Edmonton.[67] Beyond this city, Fort McMurray was the most important centre for cash buying. Hudson's Bay Company records indicated that in 1920 prices were very high there because cash buyers arrived from Edmonton on every train.[68] Even well beyond Fort McMurray cash buying was highly competitive. In 1920 Hudson's Bay Company officials complained that at Fort Simpson the 'practise of bidding on furs' was driving cash prices upward. According to company inspector T.P. O'Kelly: 'the practise is certainly open to criticism. Beginning with the white trappers, it has extended to the Indians and if continued, will result in estranging their loyalty to the company.'[69] Although cash trading generally did serve to undermine the traditional customer loyalties of the Indians, some of the Hudson's Bay Company post managers devised innovative ways of taking advantage of the new development. For instance, in 1919–20 Americans from the Yukon area visited the hinterland of Fort McPherson and bought large quantities of fur for cash. Regarding the reaction of the Fort McPherson post manager to this development, O'Kelly noted: 'McPherson had resorted to an ingenious method of receiving cash deposits from the Indians and allowing them 5%. In this way, some of the money paid out by the Yukon traders was collected by the Company and used for purchasing furs. Providing the Post has the goods desired by the Indians, most of the credit will be taken out in trade.'[70]

By 1920 the prices Indians were obtaining for their furs (in cash and goods) had risen to the point where they had much more purchasing power than they needed to satisfy their demand for goods even though their consumption of 'store foods' was increasing. Some of them responded by curtailing their output.[71] Others continued to collect furs, and many situations developed in which the traders found themselves in debt to the Indians. For example, in 1920 the Hudson's Bay Company traders owed their hunters $16,000 at Fort Nelson, $4,100 at Fort Simpson, $3,000 at Fort Liard, and from $2,000 to $3,000 at the other posts on the lower Mackenzie River.[72]

The Hudson's Bay Company traders handled Indian credit balances in a variety of ways. At most posts the Indians' surplus furs were put on account, and the trappers subsequently drew against their deposit.

TABLE 8
Hudson's Bay Company fur trade of the
Mackenzie River District, outfit 1918

Year	Cash	Credit	Barter	Total
1917	$38,594	$137,782	$ 71,937	$248,313
1918	$48,342	$198,837	$103,957	$351,136

SOURCE: 'Mackenzie District Report,' LOCI, HBCA
PAM A 92/19/5

However, this led to confusion in the records because bookkeepers often treated these transactions as credit trade. In other words, they treated Indian debt and credit purchases the same way in the accounts. In British Columbia they used a different procedure. There the company gave Indians tokens or script. This was the common practice in the trade before 1870. In 1918 the Hudson's Bay Company adopted this as a general policy.[73] However, this arrangement proved to be unsatisfactory to many Indian bands. For example, in the 1920s Indians living in northern Ontario demanded payment in cash for that portion of their returns that exceeded their debts and purchases. They wanted the money so that they could deal with competing merchants who offered better prices or carried goods that the company did not stock.[74]

Although cash trading became an integral aspect of the business, barter continued to account for most of the traffic in fur. For example, the Hudson's Bay Company's 1918 annual report for the Mackenzie River District showed that cash purchases accounted for under 16 per cent of the turnover in 1917 and just below 14 per cent in 1918 (table 8). No doubt this is a conservative picture. Cash buying was probably more important to the opposition, given that the district report stated the Hudson's Bay Company was losing its share of this trade.[75]

Although credit barter remained a key component of the business during this highly competitive period, debt losses during the war were lower than those of the preceding decade for several reasons. The sharp drop in 1914 (fig. 23) was the direct consequence of the governor and committee's order not to buy furs during the winter of 1914–15. That order included the instruction not to give credit. This combined action also explains why the debt/return ratio tripled during the same year. Indians were unable to dispose of most of their collections to the company (fig. 24).

As soon as the directors lifted their trading restrictions in 1915, the officers made a concerted effort to regain their native clients. They extended credit liberally once again. Table 8 shows that credit/barter transactions accounted for over 50 per cent of the Hudson's Bay Company's sales in the Mackenzie River district in 1917 and 1918. This represented a major retreat from the no-credit policy of 1914. The commissioner urged district managers to keep a tight reign on credit, but post managers usually claimed that it was necessary to exceed the limits they had been given because their opponents were issuing debt very liberally.[76] Not surprisingly, the amount of credit that had to be written off increased, but it remained well below the levels of the immediate pre-war years. Also, the debt loss/returns ratio remained low during the war.

As in earlier years the debt load varied greatly among the districts. The James Bay District shouldered the biggest burden. In 1918 this district had debt losses of roughly $50,728, or 61 per cent of the total, and in 1919 they amounted to $31,380 or 34 per cent. The reason for the discrepancy was that the region suffered from severe depletion of fur and game and its native residents had become heavily dependent on a single resource – fox. Poor fox years created havoc.

The efforts of competing traders to curry the favour of Indians through competitive merchandising posed another set of problems for the Hudson's Bay Company. Fur prices rose more rapidly than did those for merchandise, resulting in a sharp increase in the consumer demand of native people. This development aggravated an old problem – the company's transportation capacity could not be expanded rapidly in the short term. Transportation constraints were particularly severe at the outer limits of the network where the all-important outposts were located.[77] Apart from the considerations of cost, wartime manpower and supply shortages made it impossible to enlarge substantially the cargo capacity. Accordingly, Commissioner Bacon did not favour price cutting as a strategy to win Indian favour.[78] A partial solution involved importing more high-priced and low-bulk 'fancy goods.' This was a favourite tactic of many of the company's opponents.

As in the previous eras of competition, camp trading, tripping, and the operation of outposts became commonplace as everyone made a concerted effort to carry the trade to the native people. The difficulty was that this practice also increased the demand for labour at the very time when enlistments in the armed services and conscription reduced the number of experienced traders who were available. The newer firms, most notably the Northern Trading Company and Lamson and Hubbard, tried to obtain some of the men they needed by luring them away from the Hudson's Bay Company. As an enticement, and to reward employees for their efforts, these rival firms paid men according to the results they obtained. The company's officers had no such incentives, since the company had abandoned the profit-sharing plan for officers in 1893.[79] To meet this new challenge the Hudson's Bay Company introduced a bonus scheme for its men. Besides providing incentives, bonuses were used to supplement the wages of older men, who resented the fact that the company often had to pay new recruits higher salaries in the fiercely competitive labour market.[80] Despite these measures the company still faced labour shortages and it had to recruit natives to manage their outposts, run tripping operations, and engage in camp trading. Competition for these men was keen. At the end of the war trippers received $8 per day, not including provisions and food for their dog teams. These high wages of course added considerably to the cost of collecting furs.[81]

Native managers

More problematic for the Hudson's Bay Company, by 1919 'native' (mixed-blood) men managed a high proportion of its outposts. For instance, natives directed nearly all twenty-nine of the Hudson's Bay Company's Mackenzie River District outposts. There were serious drawbacks to employing natives in this capacity. Louis Romanet, acting manager of the Mackenzie River District, said they were 'keen' but paid no attention to costs.[82] There were several reasons. Most native men were illiterate and they had been given no training in simple bookkeeping. Even more troublesome, they extended credit too liberally to their kinfolk, and often they paid them too much for their furs. For these various reasons, employing native outpost managers added to the costs of buying furs.

The general trends outlined above had a differential impact on the north. The Athabasca-Mackenzie region was one of the areas that was most strongly affected; for as indicated, all the major players engaged in a fierce contest for the riches of the district. Between 1917 and 1922 the Hudson's Bay Company estimated the annual shares of the local 'primary fur trade' that various competitors were securing in the Mackenzie River District. These were the furs that the company obtained directly from trappers, in contrast to 'secondary trade' which came through the hands of other traders. In the lower Mackenzie River valley below Great Slave Lake the Hudson's Bay Company's share ranged from 40 to 75 per cent.[83] Lamson and Hubbard and Northern

Trading Company were the only significant opponents in this area except at Fort McPherson and Arctic Red River, where Aklavik merchants drew away some of the business. In the upper Mackenzie River area the Hudson's Bay Company's portion was as low as 29 per cent in 1922, and many more rival traders operated. At Fort Chipewyan, for instance, the company faced twenty-seven opponents.

By the close of the war the volume of 'secondary trading' in the two districts was substantial. For example, in 1918 Revillon Frères of Edmonton bought the Northern Trading Company's entire collection of white fox and marten for $125,000.[84] At Fort Chipewyan in 1920 trader Colin Fraser sold 75 per cent of his winter collection to Lamson and Hubbard for $40,000. The same year Fraser sold his entire spring returns to the latter company for an unspecified amount.[85] In 1920 most of the Hudson's Bay Company's Athabasca returns were bought in Edmonton from other traders and dealers.[86]

Another important wartime development in the region was the appearance of white trappers in significant numbers for the first time. At least one of the major competing firms, Lamson and Hubbard, was instrumental in bringing about this change, because it brought in these trappers specifically to break the native monopoly and increase output.[87] By doing so the company contributed to a problem that already was becoming acute in many areas; for as fur prices rose, increasing numbers of miners, prospectors, and loggers became involved in trapping and trading on a part-time basis. In fact, when prices peaked in 1920, many miners abandoned their diggings in the quest for fur.[88] The problem was that most of these newcomers were interested only in making quick profits. Thus, they were ruthless hunters and trappers, and they contributed in a substantial way to resource depletion. Louis Romanet regarded them as the scourge of north because of the harmful impact they had on the environment.[89] Also, they proved to be economic trend-setters for local native people in terms of consumer-spending and fur-selling practices (preferring to deal in cash). They were particularly important in this regard after the First World War.

Outside the Athabasca-Mackenzie region, the construction of the second transcontinental railway system, beginning in 1910, had more impact on the northern fur trade than any other development that took place between 1885 and the end of the First World War. East of Lake Nipigon the construction of the main line and various feeders had the effect of shifting the 'frontier trading district' of Ontario northward some 100 to 300 kilometres and west of the lake up to fifty kilometres.

In Manitoba construction of the Hudson Bay Railway continued, and rail service extended beyond The Pas toward the lower Nelson River by the end of the war. Beyond Manitoba railways reached through the North Saskatchewan River valley, and one small feeder line extended from Prince Albert northwestward to Big River. The reason this phase of railway construction was so important was that it made all the southern portions of Old Rupert's Land readily accessible to small fur buyers with limited means just as wartime price inflation began.

The small operators were not the only newcomers to cash in on the wartime bonanza. In 1919 Sir Herbert Holt obtained the backing of a syndicate of 'prominent Montreal businessmen,' and he reorganized Holt, Renfrew and Company which already had retail fur outlets in Quebec City, Montreal, Toronto, and Winnipeg. The company made an offering of $2 million worth of stock equally divided among common and preferred shares and a $225,000 bond issue. Holt intended to use the capital he raised to expand retail activities, to secure a larger share of the company's furs directly from trappers, and to expand the company's fur-farming activities.[90] In this way the Montreal merchants took advantage of wartime opportunities to renew their challenge to the Hudson's Bay Company in the field as well as on the auction floor.

It is widely recognized that the First World War marked a major turning point in Canadian economic history. At the end of the war the American economy had developed to the point that growth was self-sustaining. In contrast, Britain suffered heavy financial losses in the war and its commercial empire began to decline. As the United States economy expanded, Americans began to invest heavily in Canada. It is estimated that in 1900 British capital accounted for 85 per cent of the total foreign investments in Canada and that from the United States 14 per cent. These were the days when Britain was the great exporter of capital. By 1920 British investments stood at 53 per cent and those of the United States at 44 per cent.[91] These heavy financial investments facilitated economic development, massive immigration, and urbanization, leading historians correctly to regard the period 1896 to 1921 as the time of the great Canadian transformation.[92] The rise of New York and St Louis and the re-emergence of Montreal as leading centres in the North American fur trade have to be understood in this context. The North American challenge to London was symptomatic of these larger economic processes.

In 1887 Commissioner Joseph Wrigley inspected posts in the northwest and met with senior officers in Winnipeg; here seen with some of them in front of the old Upper Fort Garry gate. *Row 1*, from left: Captain W.H. Adams (factor), Horace Belanger (chief factor). *Row 2*: Joseph Fortescue (chief factor), Alexander Munro (chief factor), Thomas Smith (assistant commissioner), Joseph Wrigley (commissioner), Richard Hardisty (chief factor), Lawrence Clarke (chief factor), Roderick McFarlane (chief factor). *Row 3*: Archibald McDonald (chief factor), Arthur Robertson (secretary to the commissioner), James McDougall (chief clerk), William Clark (chief factor), Colin Rankin (chief factor), Dr W.M. MacKay (chief trader), Peter W. Bell (chief factor), Murdoch Matheson (junior chief trader), M.S. Beeston, Samuel K. Parson (chief factor). *Row 4*: James H. Lawson (factor), W.J. McLean (chief trader), Cuthbert Sinclair (junior chief trader), A.R. Lillie (executive chief trader), James L. Cotter (chief trader). *Row 5*: Alex Matheson (factor)

Site plan of Norway House, 1889: district headquarters, important depot on the Hudson's Bay Company's transportation system, boat-building centre, and formerly meeting place of the Northern Department council

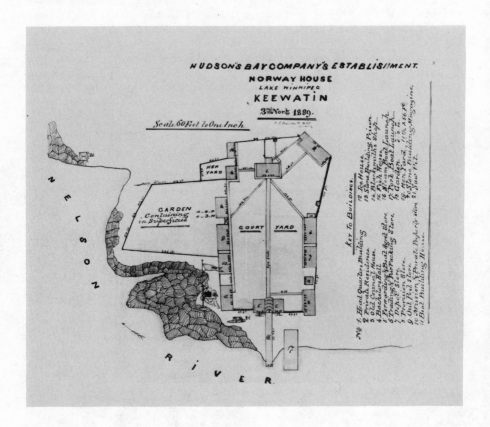

Loading the Hudson's Bay Company's *Grahame* at Fort McMurray, Alberta, 1899–1900

North-West Mounted Police post and Hudson's Bay Company's store at Grand Rapids, Athabasca River, 1899

Colonel J.K. ('Peace River Jim') Cornwall carrying mail to northern Alberta, ca 1900

Trading post of Fletcher Bredin and Colonel J.K. Cornwall at Fort St John, British Columbia, ca 1903

Two unidentified native paddlers who accompanied Governor-General Earl Grey's expedition between Norway House and York Factory, 1910 (opposite, bottom)

Fort Smith, NWT, 1913: $36,000 worth of silver fox

The Bernstein Fur Company of Toronto was one of the many fur-buying companies that took advantage of improving transportation and communications systems to advertise their fur-buying services.

Ad for 'mail-order' fur-buying firm of A.B. Shubert

Ad from the *Winnipeg Free Press*, January 1920, announcing the first sale of the Canadian Fur Auction Sales Company of Montreal

On 2 February 1920 the International Fur Exchange of St Louis, Missouri, held a $27 million sale

'Moose Works' at Moose Factory in the early twentieth century, where Métis workers and tradesmen repaired and built boats and large schooners for use in James Bay (opposite, bottom)

Launching Northern Trading Company's steamboats *Northland Pioneer* and *Northland Trader* at Bell Rock, NWT, 1922

Map of the operations of Lamson and Hubbard Canadian Company

A Lamson and Hubbard fur shipment worth $150,000, Edmonton, 1922

R.D. Ferrier of Lamson and Hubbard at Vermilion Chutes, Peace River, with the 1923–4 winter supplies for the company's small post at Little Red River

5

The international marketing of Canadian furs, 1920–1945

Between the two great wars the world economy went through the throes of boom and depression. The fur trade did not escape the buffeting. Depletion of fur stocks in boom years brought about greater government intervention for conservation purposes. Fur prices were in flux and the mix of fur output changed substantially. Meanwhile the struggle for dominance in the international fur-marketing system continued unabated. A new order emerged in the early 1930s only to be upset once again by the economic and political crises created by the Second World War. All these trends affected the position of London and the Hudson's Bay Company in the international marketing system. Its share of the business declined as a growing number of rival concerns appeared on the scene.

During the interwar years the fortunes of the fur industry roughly paralleled those of the general economy, but the extremes were greater, as is readily apparent from figure 26, which shows the movement in the weighted price (based on constant dollars) of a hypothetical bale of selected wild furs (muskrat, beaver, ermine, marten, red fox, and lynx). Figure 27 portrays the changing value of Canadian fur returns (in constant dollars) in relation to output. It is interesting that prices slumped more sharply than production during the depths of the depression (for reasons that will be discussed later), whereas during the Second World War they advanced sharply but output slumped. The very rapid growth of the fur-ranching industry was one of the most important developments to take place during this period. The values of wild and ranched fur output expressed in constant dollars

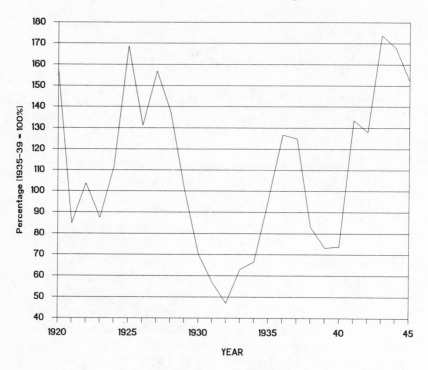

Figure 26
Changing prices, 1920–45: selected Canadian wild furs

are shown in figure 28. The depletion of fur-bearers and the the resulting steep rise in the price of some pelts, particularly mink and silver
fox, provided the stimulus for this development.

Regarding supply shortages, trapping pressures in excess of local
carrying capacities had caused significant depletion problems by the
turn of the century. This crisis led provincial and federal governments
to pass legislation aimed at conserving dwindling furbearer populations – particularly those of the two traditional staples of the fur industry in the north, beaver and muskrat. As noted earlier, the first
conservation legislation dates back to 1893 and 1894.[1] In the 1890s
conservationalists were primarily concerned with the devastating
impact that white hunters' use of poison baits was having on wildlife,
and key provisions in the acts banned the use of these baits.

After the turn of the century federal and provincial game laws

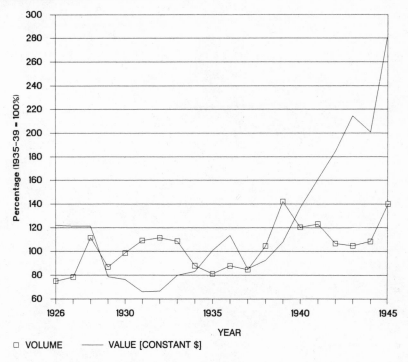

Figure 27
Canadian fur production, 1926–45: relative changes in volume and value

included this restriction, but subsequent acts concentrated on regulating production by establishing 'bag limits,' open and closed seasons, and game sanctuaries. Sometimes provincial authorities banned the trapping of certain species for extended periods spanning several years. Most often closed seasons were established for beaver and muskrat. One of the first provinces to adopt this form of legislation was British Columbia, which imposed a six-year ban on beaver trapping in 1911.[2] The province of British Columbia also took the lead in the effort to regulate access to resources by establishing the first registered trapline system in 1925.[3] Under this program licensees were given the exclusive right to trap on specific tracts of land, the objective being to minimize competition and conflict between native and white trappers over the use of different hunting territories. Other provinces were slow to follow this lead. After closing beaver and other trapping to whites

*registered
traplines*

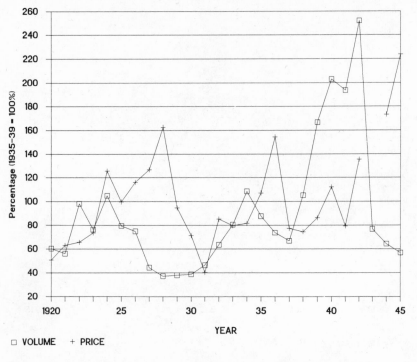

□ VOLUME + PRICE

Figure 28
Canadian wild mink production: changes in volume and price, 1920–45

in 1927, Ontario introduced registered traplines in 1935. The other provinces followed later: Alberta (1937), Manitoba (1940), Quebec (1945), Saskatchewan (1946), the Northwest Territories (1949), and the Yukon (1950).[4]

white trappers

The implementation of registered trapline systems was a direct response to the invasion of the north by white trappers. These newcomers were particularly troublesome for several reasons. Significant numbers of them moved in and out of the trapping sector of the economy during the high and low points of the business cycles. At boom times, such as that of 1919–20, they sought to skim off the profits, while in hard times, such as during the depression, they came to live off the land and earn a small cash income from trapping. In 1933 the *Fur Trade Review* reported that there were more men in the bush than ever before prospecting and trapping because jobs were scarce.[5] This observation

serves to highlight another problem. Fur trapping, often combined
with trading, served to grubstake other primary pursuits such as logging, mining, and prospecting. The growing use of the bush plane in
the 1930s opened most of the more remote areas of the north to white
trappers for the first time, breaking the Indian trapping monopolies
there.[6] In some areas, such as in northern Saskatchewan, these newcomers worked out satisfactory accommodations with local Indian
bands. In fact, the Chipewyan of Patuanak, Saskatchewan, regarded
these depression-era invaders as entertaining anomalies or *hotet'stini*
(bushmen).[7] However, in many areas the situation was very different.
Too often the white trappers came only for the short term, so they
showed little regard for game conservation, and they disrupted the
local native economies by upsetting traditional territorial allocation
systems. They were particularly disruptive in the Peace River area and
in northern Ontario.[8] Unfortunately for the natives, the establishment
of registered trapline programs to address the various problems the
white trappers created also served to legitimize their presence, thereby
further restricting native freedom to use undeveloped crown land.

The establishment of large beaver and muskrat preserves took place
mostly in the 1930s and 1940s. Usually these ventures involved the co-
operation of federal and provincial governments as well as private
companies – most notably the Hudson's Bay Company. By the late
1940s the federal Indian Affairs Branch and the company operated
eight different beaver sanctuaries which included almost the entire
area surrounding James Bay.[9] In Manitoba and Saskatchewan provincial and private muskrat preserves were set aside at several places
adjacent to the Saskatchewan River. One of these was situated near
the delta of the river, where the Manitoba government granted a
five-year lease for a 'muskrat farming' enterprise in 1933. The leased
territory encompassed 124 lakes and 241 miles of traplines in an eighty-
square-mile tract of land. In 1938 the Hudson's Bay Company obtained
a private lease from the Saskatchewan government for 300,000 acres
to establish a muskrat reserve at Cumberland Lake near the Manitoba-
Saskatchewan boundary. As part of the agreement the company
retained the right to restrict the trapping of local residents if necessary
and to prohibit it altogether for non-residents.[10]

Before the 1920s game enforcement was weak because there were
not enough police and game wardens. White and native trappers alike
disregarded the laws. Fur traders engaged in widespread smuggling
of contraband (out of season or banned) fur, particularly beaver. Some

of them got caught. For example, in 1910 R.C. Wilson, Hudson's Bay Company manager of Montizambert in northern Ontario, was convicted of having otter, beaver, and muskrat skins out of season and a Port Arthur judge fined him $6,447.58.[11] Revillon men in northern Ontario also were active smugglers who met with mixed success.[12] During the Laurier years Revillon Frères was able to have fines for dealing in contraband fur quashed on several occasions. Their legal representative at that time was on Laurier's patronage list and a representative of the prime minister had recommended him to Revillon Frères.[13] Besides the activities of these companies, white trappers, especially those evading conscription during the latter part of the First World War, flouted the law.[14]

In spite of occasional arrests, generally the application of game laws was so spotty at this time that Philip Godsell of the Hudson's Bay Company stated that smuggling, which senior company officials did not sanction, was virtually a sport in northern Ontario. Godsell himself took part, and he proudly described his technique as follows:

The transport I was operating comprised some thirty or more large canoes of the Lac Seul Freighter type, each capable of carrying thirty 'pieces,' by means of which the goods for the posts at Cat Lake and Osnaburgh were freighted over the two hundred mile stretch of lake and river between there and Lac Seul. From Osnaburgh the Albany River flowed swiftly onward past Fort Hope until it emptied into Hudson Bay at Fort Albany. What better method of avoiding detection than to disguise the fur bales as trading goods, mix them with the regular freight as far as Osnaburgh, then hire canoemen to rush them down to Fort Albany ... While the fur was going north disguised as trading goods the Game Authorities and police would be closely watching the railroad for it to be shipped, and by this method I had in mind I hoped to 'put it over' them with ease.[15]

The uneven enforcement of game laws was still a problem as late as the 1930s. It was the subject of extensive discussions at the 1931 meeting of the company's district managers in Winnipeg. According to the minutes, the managers complained that opponents used 'political influence' in their efforts to violate the game laws in Ontario and Quebec; in the prairies laws were 'very laxly enforced'; and in Keewatin there were only three game guardians, so that 'post managers have not seen a game guardian in years.'[16] The assembled managers stated that only the most northerly districts and British Columbia were largely free of contraband trading. After airing the issue, the commissioner and managers passed a resolution stating that the company could not resort to the methods of its smaller competitors, nor would it act as informants against them.[17] In spite of uneven enforcement, by the 1930s government regulations were beginning to have a significant influence on local production.[18] In this important regard the fur trade of the 1920s and 1930s differed from that of the earlier period. Natural biological cycles and shifting market forces alone no longer were the sole determinants of trends. As a good example, between 1935 and 1939 the beaver output of Ontario declined temporarily because the government imposed closed seasons on the animal during these years. In the long term more effective government conservation programs did achieve positive results.[19]

As noted, one of the most important consequences of supply shortages was that prices of certain luxury furs rose sufficiently to encourage large-scale ranching. Most noteworthy in this regard were silver fox and mink. Beginning in the 1890s, silver-fox ranching increased rapidly, and by the late 1930s ranches, mostly located on Prince Edward Island, accounted for nearly all the Canadian output.[20] Although wild mink remained important (fig. 28 and table 9), by 1938 almost 50 per cent of the total value of production came from farming operations. Most of them were located in southern Ontario within 300 miles of Toronto.[21] Ranchers made attempts to extend their operations to a variety of other species, including red fox, cross fox, blue fox (a colour phase of arctic fox), raccoon, skunk, marten, fisher, and fitch. But these various efforts had achieved only limited results by the late 1930s.[22] However, because silver fox and mink ranching was so successful, these furs accounted for a growing share of the total value of Canadian fur production (fig. 29).[23] According to Hudson's Bay Company reports, higher yields of beaver, ranched mink, and silver fox accounted for most of the 40 per cent increase in the volume of Canadian fur output between 1935 and 1945.[24] The problem for mink and silver-fox breeders was that they flooded the market, driving prices downward. None the less, ranching did offer the prospect of matching supplies to demand, and eventually ranchers organized themselves into breeders' associations for that purpose.[25] In the short term, however, the growth of the ranching industry dampened price advances for wild mink and silver fox, and it fundamentally altered the geography of production of these two species.

The demand for most other furs outpaced supplies, and the composi-

TABLE 9
Total production of leading fur-bearers,
1920–45

Species	Quantity	Average price($)
1 Muskrat	63,167,299	3.54
2 Red squirrel	31,432,880	0.34
3 Ermine	16,962,243	2.53
4 Mink (wild)	4,927,489	30.55
5 Skunk	3,492,817	3.62
6 Red fox	2,906,082	47.47
7 Beaver	2,601,433	49.07
8 Arctic fox	1,181,502	62.31
9 Marten	764,644	62.33
10 Lynx	380,445	77.36
11 River Otter	269,376	55.56
12 Fisher	110,193	141.48
Total	128,196,403	

SOURCE: Novak et al., *Furbearer Harvests in
North America*

tion of Canadian fur output changed significantly as a result. What is most striking is that utility furs of low value came to dominate production. Returns of muskrat continued to outpace those of all other furs by a wide margin (table 9). Figure 30 shows that between 1920 and 1945 production exhibited cyclical variations, but no substantial long-term trend is evident. Prices, on the other hand, advanced from 1920 to 1926, they declined markedly between 1927 and 1931, and thereafter they more than doubled. None the less, muskrat remained a fur of relatively low value. Partly this situation resulted from product substitution. As muskrat prices advanced fur dyers increasingly turned to rabbit, which became the major rival. Australia and Tasmania were the major exporting areas, but Canadian production advanced also. Table 10 lists the trade names for dyed rabbit. Mendoza beaver and sealine were the two biggest sellers; sealine competed with Hudson Bay seal (muskrat).[26]

Dyers also used hare, a close relative of rabbit, which had a more woolly textured fur.[27] After glazing (a treatment designed to give the fur a lustre and to reduce its tendency to mat and curl), shearing, and dyeing it black to resemble Alaska seal, manufacturers sold hare as

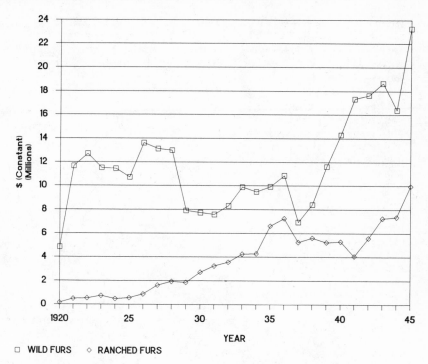

Figure 29
Value of Canadian raw fur output: wild and ranched, 1920–45

'electric seal.'[28] Arctic hare has denser and longer hair than rabbit or other species of hare and manufacturers used it to simulate arctic fox as the price of the latter rose sharply in this century. Also, dyers treated hare to look like beaver (Mendoza beaver, for instance) and seal (sealine).[29]

Red squirrel, a fur of very low value, was unimportant before the 1930s (fig. 31). Subsequently prices and production increased very rapidly, and by 1945 returns for this fur were second only to those of muskrat (table 9). Manufacturers used the lower grades of squirrel to line outer wear, the common ones to trim cloth and fur coats, and those of the highest quality to make full-length garments.

Ermine output continued the advance already noted for the period before the First World War. Between 1920 and 1945 this fur ranked third in terms of volume. When it first gained popularity in the late

Squirrel prod. increased due to need to obtain income in the face of declining pops. of other fur-bearers.

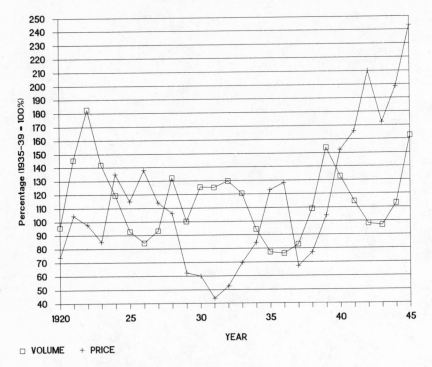

□ VOLUME   + PRICE

Figure 30
Canadian muskrat production: changes in volume and price, 1920–45

TABLE 10
Trade names for dyed rabbit[a]

Natural fur	Name for imitation
Seal	Sealine
Beaver	Beaverette, French beaver, Mendoza beaver
Nutria	Nutriette
Chinchilla	Chinchillette
Squirrel	Squirrelette

[a] The general trade name for dyed rabbit
   is Coney, even though coney is in reality
   a species of *Hyrax*.
SOURCE: Bachrach, *Fur*, 184–9

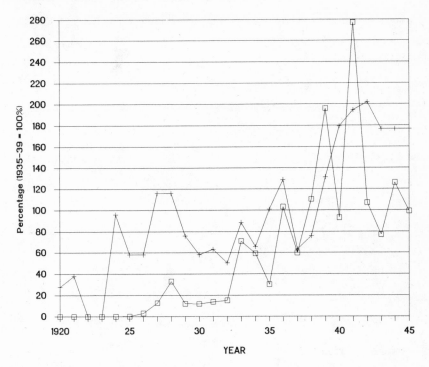

Figure 31
Canadian red squirrel production: changes in volume and price, 1920–45

nineteenth century, manufacturers used ermine mostly for making fur wraps, coats, and for trimming. In the 1920s and 1930s garment makers employed it extensively on fur-trimmed cloth coats which were the rage at that time. Figure 32 shows that ermine returns advanced nearly 50 per cent between 1920 and 1928. In contrast, prices moved upward over 150 per cent between 1920 and 1928 before plummeting in 1929. For the next ten years they changed very little. During the Second World War they increased dramatically. In spite of this price surge, however, ermine remained a low-priced fur (table 9). The flat production and price profiles for ermine during the 1930s suggest that supplies were nearly equal to demand. One of the reasons for this likely was that Canadian producers had to compete with the Russians who supplied very high-quality ermine and with dyers who produced an imitation from rabbit fur called ermeline.[30]

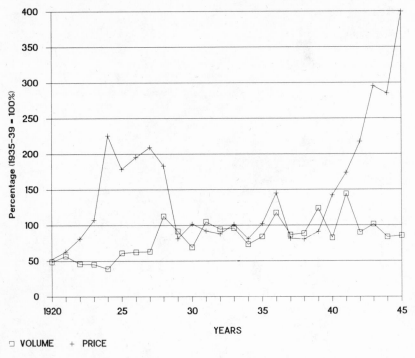

Figure 32
Canadian ermine production: changes in volume and price, 1920–45

Skunk was another utility fur that gained favour during this period (ranking fourth by volume). It became especially popular with fashion designers who liked to employ furs with sharply contrasting colours to produce geometric, zig-zag, and circular patterns.[31] Output was steady in the early 1920s, slumped with the onset of the depression, and rallied thereafter (fig. 33). Prices were relatively high throughout the 1920s, remained low during the 1930s, and rallied strongly in the early 1940s.

Red fox also became very popular in the 1920s and 1930s.[32] Garment makers fashioned this fur into scarves, and in the early 1930s the sales of red fox scarves exceeded the combined totals of those made from all other species. Sales data for this fur (fig. 34) show that prices moved upward from 1920 to 1929 before they declined sharply until 1934. Following a modest three-year rally the market renewed its downward

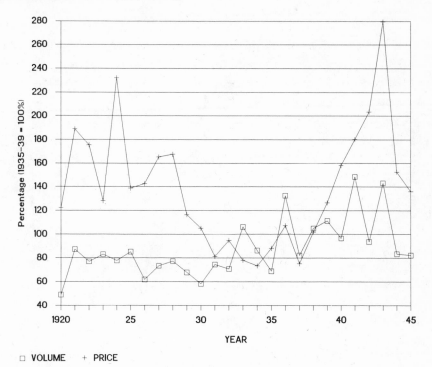

Figure 33
Canadian skunk production: changes in volume and price, 1920–45

trend again until 1940. Only a slight recovery took place during the war. Three production cycles are evident during the same time period, the peaks occurring in 1925, 1935 and 1943.

Between the wars, beaver, the traditional staple, declined to seventh place in terms of the volume of returns (table 9). Between 1921 and 1929 production dropped dramatically (over 300 per cent) while prices rose significantly during the same period (fig. 35). Obviously supplies were not adequate for the demand. This shortfall encouraged manufacturers to make imitations of beaver from rabbit and from a variety of other cheap pelts from around the world. Australian opossum, baby seal, lamb from the Mediterranean and Balkan countries, moufflon (Chinese goat), nutria (a rodent indigenous to South America), pahmi (an animal similar to the badger and native to China and northern India), and slink lamb from South America are examples.

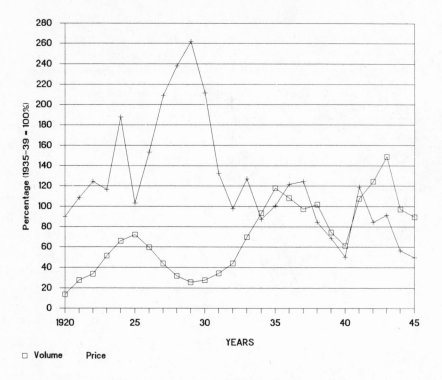

Figure 34
Canadian red fox production: changes in volume and price, 1920–45

Beginning in 1935 beaver prices and production began a ten-year rally. During this time fur dyers and processors developed new techniques to make the pelt attractive in a market that began to favour short-haired and light-weight furs instead of the long-haired ones that had been popular previously.[33] Manufacturers sheared beaver pelts to expose the soft underwool and highlight the darker fur near the centre and lighter hair towards the edges. In this way they were able to produce a natural and very attractive two-tone effect. Shearing also reduced the tendency of the fur to curl. Besides treating beaver in this manner, manufacturers shaved the leather side of the pelt to reduce its weight. First introduced in the United States, these skins, marketed as 'featherlite beaver,' became popular in Europe, beginning in Paris in 1937.[34]

The sales data for marten, the traditional luxury fur of the pre-1870

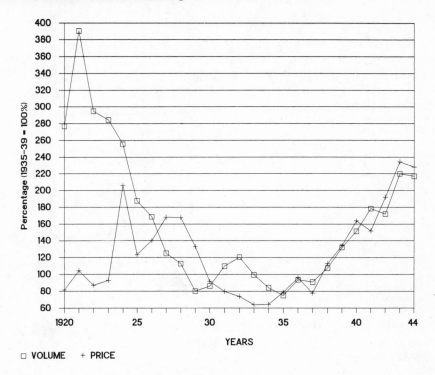

Figure 35
Canadian beaver production: changes in volume and price, 1920–44

triad, show that the volume of returns plummeted between 1921 and
1933, while prices vacillated, with no long-term trend being evident
(fig. 36). Between 1934 and 1944 prices advanced strongly, but production declined slowly, suggesting that stocks were not adequate for the
demand. A somewhat similar pattern is evident for the other long-
established luxury fur – lynx (fig. 37). Three production cycles took
place between 1920 and 1945, with the amplitudes of the peaks declining over time. Meanwhile, prices moved erratically upward over the
twenty-five-year period, suggesting that demand increasingly
exceeded supplies.

This discussion has focused on only those furs that dominated Canadian output in order to present a general picture of price and production trends between the wars. During this time the mix of Canadian
fur output changed. Four of the top five furs according to volume were

changes in the mix of Canadian fur output

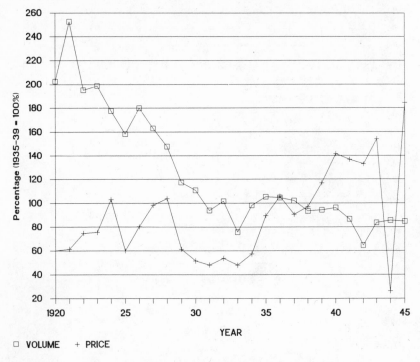

Figure 36
Canadian marten production: changes in volume and price, 1920–45

low-priced ones (table 9). This means that a larger portion of wild fur returns consisted of pelts that gave trappers a low rate of return on their efforts. Also, many low-value fur species, especially muskrat, ermine, hare, and rabbit, experience much greater population fluctuations than beaver does. This meant that trapping incomes were less stable than they had been in the earlier beaver-dominant fur trade of the pre-1840 era.

The rapid return of prosperity following the market collapse of 1920–1 made it possible for the more important auction companies to refinance their operations and for new houses to establish themselves. Because of the very rapid growth of the fur-garment-manufacturing industry that was taking place in New York City, the New York Fur Auction Sales Co. had little difficulty in securing the new financial backing that it needed to restructure.[35] In 1900 the city was only a

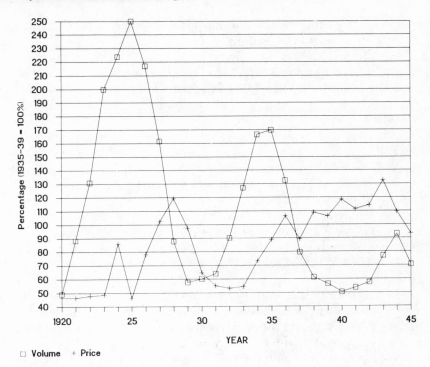

□ Volume   + Price

Figure 37
Canadian lynx production: changes in volume and price, 1920–45

minor centre when compared with London, Leipzig and Paris, but it was the world leader by the mid-1920s. In 1923 local fur garment manufacturers produced $155,267,779 worth of goods, making the industry the fifth-ranking one in the city in terms of value added. The output of the New York firms accounted for over 78 per cent of the total production for the United States. Moreover, the over 2,000 wholesale manufacturers in the city were supported by roughly fifty dressing and dyeing firms and some 500 merchants, importers, exporters, and dealers, who handled raw furs as well as dressed and dyed pelts.[36]

The St Louis dealers faced more difficulty in putting their house in order. It was not until the summer of 1922 that Colonel Fouke secured the financing he needed from New York, Chicago, and St Louis bankers to restructure the fur auctions in St Louis. Capitalized at $3 million and known as the Fur Merchants Sales Company, the new organization held its first auction in the autumn of 1922.[37] Thereafter St Louis resumed its position as a leading auction centre.

When the St Louis fur auctions collapsed temporarily after the First World War, an opportunity was presented for Winnipeg merchants to enter the business. By the time of the debacle St Louis dealers had deflected to their sales many of the Winnipeg furs that formerly were consigned to New York brokers for sale in that city or in London. As early as 1909 this business was worth $2.5 million.[38] It was Hyman Yewdall, a leading local businessman, who first moved to take advantage of St Louis's misfortune when he played a central role in organizing the Winnipeg Fur Auction Sales Ltd in 1921.[39] He obtained the backing of many of the leading dry-goods and grocery wholesalers who were operating in western Canada at that time. Included were R.J. Whitla and Company; John W. Peck and Company; Robinson, Little and Company; Greenshields Ltd; Western Grocers Ltd; Campbell Brothers and Wilthese; Congdon-Marsh Ltd; and Traders Trust.[40] Most of these firms took in considerable quantities of furs in the normal conduct of their business, and at least two of them, R.J. Whitla and John W. Peck, had been dealing in pelts since the late nineteenth century.[41] In this respect the organization of the auctions represented a natural progression in the city's commercial development.

The initial advertisements for the Winnipeg company stated that the auctions were being organized because of the crisis in St Louis and in order to make sure that Canadian trappers received full value for their catches in the future. The organizers claimed, with justification, that most of the furs shipped from Canada to St Louis or New York were mixed with southern furs in order to raise the value of the latter; this practice worked to the detriment of northern trappers by devaluing their returns.[42]

To attract business, the Winnipeg Fur Auction Sales Ltd announced that it would hold frequent sales, beginning with at least one per month during the trapping season; provide bonded warehouse service; and issue warehouse receipts that shippers could use to obtain credit from the auction house or from other sources.[43] In the aftermath of the 1920–1 market collapse the move towards more frequent sales was important because it reduced the risks of losses that shippers and their creditors had to assume whenever markets were in decline. Also, by being able to sell their collections more often, small traders needed less capital to operate.

Dealers in Edmonton watched this development in Winnipeg with considerable interest and scepticism. They did not believe Winnipeg could challenge New York or London.[44] According to reports in the *Fur Trade Review*, at the end of the war this Alberta city probably ranked second to Montreal as a fur-marketing centre. Its hinterland reached from The Pas in the east to interior British Columbia on the west and from the Arctic coast to the American border. In 1920 this vast hinterland yielded approximately $4–5 million worth of raw fur every year. Yet, at the end of the First World War there were no large auction houses in Edmonton. There was, however, a 'fur selling scheme' operated by the Edmonton Raw Fur Merchants Association in order to provide member trappers and operators with a means of disposing of their furs locally. The association provided free warehouse accommodation for members and a selling service that was free of commission charges. Sales were by private treaty.[45]

In spite of the availability of the local marketing service, many of the small Edmonton dealers, and nearly all the large ones, were in the habit of marketing their collections in London (mostly through Nesbitts), New York, and St Louis, where better prices usually prevailed. Some were beginning to sell in Montreal also. Therefore, liquidation of Nesbitt in 1920 and the disruption of the St Louis market were unsettling in Edmonton, and it was partly for this reason that Yewdall's activities in Winnipeg were closely followed. Initially the larger Edmonton dealers doubted that he would be successful, so they planned to continue to ship most of their furs to New York and London. In the latter market, the firm of Delaitte, Plender and Griffths Company had replaced Nesbitts.[46]

During its first year of operations, the Winnipeg Fur Auction Sales Company did much better than its sceptics had predicted, turning over more than $1 million worth of furs. More important, the prices obtained in Winnipeg were 10 per cent higher on average than those realized at the most recent New York and Montreal sales, because nearly all the furs sold were prime-quality northern Canadian skins.[47] Based on this initial success, Yewdall was able to convince the larger trading companies to use his company's services. In 1922 he announced that he had concluded marketing agreements with Lamson and Hubbard Canadian Company and the Northern Trading Company. According to the terms, the two companies agreed to market their entire 1922 collections at the Winnipeg Fur Auction Sales Company's auctions.[48]

Their initial success made Yewdall and his associates optimistic that soon Winnipeg would outdistance Montreal and become the pre-eminent Canadian auction centre. Although this prediction was not to materialize, in the prosperous days of the 1920s the sales volumes increased steadily. Max Finkelstein, 'the dean of the Winnipeg fur trade,' estimated that the city turned over $4.5 million in furs in 1929, just as the depression began to take hold (this was 10 per cent below the level of 1928).[49]

Despite this strong beginning, by 1930 the Winnipeg Fur Auction Sales Company was in severe financial trouble. Partly, the company's problems were the result of the five-year struggle it had waged against the Hudson's Bay Company for control of the Northern Trading Company (discussed below), and partly it was the result of the gathering depression. Like many other businesses, when the market collapsed in 1929 the Winnipeg Fur Sales Company found itself in the vulnerable position of having extended liberal credit to smaller dealers who collectively held large stocks of fur. Yewdall and his associates considered forcing these dealers to sell their inventories, but there was no market for them. The Winnipeg Fur Auction Company had to back off.[50] The future of the Winnipeg auctions looked very bleak.

At this juncture one of the leading local fur brokers, C.G. Wilson, took over the net assets of the Winnipeg Fur Auction Sales Company. Wilson had begun his career as an apprentice clerk with the Hudson's Bay Company. In 1915 he resigned as a district manager headquartered in Montreal and joined the armed services. In 1923 he arrived in Winnipeg to open an office for the New York Fur Sales Corporation, which was expanding the Canadian aspect of its business.[51] Beginning in 1928, he established his own fur brokerage firm next door to the Winnipeg Fur Auction Sales Company. Wilson combined the two firms as the Dominion Fur Auction Company, Ltd.[52] The new organization met with considerable initial success. In 1931 it declared a dividend of 50 per cent, but the company decided not to distribute it to the stockholders in order to maintain its cash position.[53]

Although the economic outlook was bleak in 1930, some veteran fur men remained so optimistic that they undertook new business ventures. One of these was George Soudack of Winnipeg. Soudack began in the business as a trapper before establishing a brokerage firm in Winnipeg about 1915. By 1930 he had branches in Fort William, Edmonton, Regina, and Vancouver.[54] In that year Soudack announced the formation of Soudack Fur Auctions Ltd with a capitalization of $50,000. He planned to conduct regular weekly and monthly sales by auction, and he had raised enough capital to make advance payments for furs.[55]

Subsequently the two Winnipeg houses competed very aggressively to expand their respective sales of northwestern Canadian furs. They extended credit very liberally to steady clients. Regular consignment sellers received advances against their fur shipments of as much as 100 per cent, and they were not required to put up their furs as collateral.[56] In order to minimize the risk of loss on liberally extended credit the auction houses took advantage of the latest improvements in commercial and short-wave radio to provide their preferred clients with the most current market information available by sending them coded radio and telegraph messages. They used commercial radio to broadcast commercials, fur market reviews (twice weekly), and entertainment programs to the Northwest Territories, northern Alberta, Saskatchewan, Manitoba, and northwestern Ontario.[57]

The successes that North American companies achieved in building highly lucrative consignment sales organizations encouraged the Hudson's Bay Company to make a concerted effort to increase its share of this business by corporate take-overs. At the time the company was merely following a well-established trend considering that the period between 1924 and 1929 was the heyday of corporate take-overs in North America.[58] In 1928 the company arranged to purchase C.M. Lampson & Company, which was still one of the leading consignment sellers of Canadian furs – particularly ranched furs. The take-over agreement specified that Lampson's would be converted from a partnership to a stock-holding company in which the Hudson's Bay Company bought 30 per cent of the shares at the outset. It was committed to buying the remaining stock over a fifteen-year period.[59] In April of 1936 the *Fur Trade Review* of New York announced that C.M. Lampson & Company had taken over the New York fur department of the financially troubled Fred'k Huth & Company of London and New York.[60] Huth was a major New York outlet for Canadian ranched fur.[61] In June the Hudson's Bay Company amalgamated these three concerns to form Lampson, Fraser and Huth, Incorporated.[62] This became the company's consignment sales organization (by auction or by private treaty) in the United States and Canada on the eve of the Second World War.

In the prairie provinces provincial governments became involved in fur marketing mostly to serve the needs of part-time trappers. The Alberta government was the first off the mark. Beginning in 1915 the Department of Agriculture conducted fur auctions in response to the persistent demands of small trappers, who believed that they could obtain better prices by this means than by shipping their furs to collecting houses.[63] The reason that the Department of Agriculture held these sales was that many farmers in central and northern Alberta trapped to supplement their incomes.[64] The link between frontier farming and fur trapping was so strong that the Hudson's Bay Company complained that 80 per cent of Alberta's fur dealers were country storekeepers who obtained their pelts from farmers and schoolboys.[65] Travelling buyers visited these merchant-dealers to collect their furs, paying them in cash. In turn, the storekeepers used their earnings from fur money to help pay for their merchandise inventories. When the depression struck, farmers and homesteaders, merchants, and small buyers were more anxious than ever to maximize their earnings from trapping. This is why they pressured the Alberta government to expand its auction service. After William Lavine and Frederick Swartz organized Edmonton Fur Auction Sales Ltd in 1935, the government curtailed its activity.[66]

In 1931 the Saskatchewan government entered the business, when it conducted the first major fur auction ever held in the province. The purpose of this and later sales was to help provide relief to destitute native people. Indians from the Stoney Rapids and Pelican Rapids reserves, for example, had been given special permission take beaver in their homelands, which by then were closed to trapping for conservation purposes. The closure had left them destitute. The Stoney Rapids and Pelican Rapids Indians sold their beaver to police and to other authorized government agents, who gave them 'chits' to spend at the nearest trading post or store.[67] These furs were then sold at the government's auctions in Regina.

Although the Manitoba government did not become directly involved in raw-fur selling, it did exert an influence on the local business none the less. The government sold the output obtained from the province's large muskrat reserves at the public auctions held in Winnipeg. Given the strong market for muskrat during this period, the government's business gave a major boost to the local auction houses. The Montreal Fur Auction Company wanted to secure some of this traffic, but the government refused to sell out of the province, preferring instead to promote the local economy.[68]

The European drift towards war in the 1930s sent shock waves throughout the international fur-marketing system. In the long term New York benefited most from the turmoil. Between the end of the First World War and the early 1930s Leipzig gained in strength as a world marketing centre because the city's fur dyers and processors continued to be the leading innovators. An added advantage was that the Leipzig auctions handled large quantities of Russian furs, ranking second only to London. These exports were very important to the Soviet government in the 1920s, since they provided an important source for the foreign currency needed to finance economic development.[69] The Soviet Union was the largest fur producer / exporter in the world during this decade.[70] The Leipzig auctions obtained a sizeable share of this business because German dealers had invested heavily in the Russian fur trade at the end of the Franco-Prussian war.[71] With these advantages the city's fur industry flourished in the 1920s despite Germany's economic difficulties.

Tragically, the fur manufacturers and merchants of this German city were the first to suffer from the political upheavals that swept Europe beginning in the early 1930s. Jews owned most of the firms. The Nazis began to persecute them in 1933. Leaders of the international fur trade community were quick to express their outrage, those from London and New York leading the way. On 29 March 1933 members of the London fur trade met at the Hudson's Bay Company's Beaver House to discuss the issue. It was the largest meeting the industry had ever held. Mr Reginald Groner, president of the British Fur Trade Alliance, opened the meeting by pointing out that 'whilst all Jewry must be affected by the happening in Germany, the Fur Trade was especially concerned because so many of its members there had not only ties of friendship and business, but blood relationships with the German people.'[72] Subsequently, the assembly passed resolutions expressing sympathy with the German Jews and pledging support for all efforts to pressure German authorities to put an end to their persecution. On 10 May 1933 a rally of some 100,000 people was held in New York to protest the Nazi actions. Members of the fur-trading associations and unions took an active part.[73] On 29 June 1933 twenty-six fur associations and fur clubs operating in New York joined the National Council of Fur Trade Organizations established to help German Jewry. On 25 July this council arranged a boycott of German firms.[74]

These were genuine expressions of humanitarian concern about the plight of German Jews. However, there were also worries about what kind of long-term economic impact the flight of Leipzig fur dealers, manufacturers, and skilled workers would have on the future of the industry. London and New York businessmen were particularly anxious to attract these refugees. At first most of these displaced Jews settled in Paris. This prompted an editorial in the *British Fur Trade* in September of 1933 which began as follows:

'Which is it to be?' is a question that arises as a result of the exodus of leading German fur men from Leipzig. It is a question which is exercising the mind of the German fur trader. It is also a question which, I think, should exercise the minds of the authorities in our own trade here. For the moment German fur men seem to prefer Paris as the seat of their future activities ... because the French Government is offering greater facilities for their settlement than is the case with our own Home Office.[75]

The editorialist went on to point out that unless London was able to gain its share of these immigrants: 'ten years hence and the French fur Trade will be able to look upon the misfortune that has beset German Jewry as one of the factors which have raised it to a premier position in the European Fur Trade.'[76] He concluded by reminding his readers how the London business had benefited from the persecution of the Huguenots centuries earlier.

His fears never materialized. Even before France was overrun by the German armies, many of the refugee fur men had moved on to London and New York, where they were safer and their business prospects were better. Initially the English city was the major beneficiary, obtaining 80 per cent of the business relocations. These were worth nearly $50 million annually. Between 1933 and 1937 the value of German fur imports and exports declined by 50 per cent, while those of London doubled (a gain of £15 million).[77] Although the migration strengthened London's position as a marketing centre on the eve of hostilities, the war subsequently undermined it, shifting the advantage to New York.

As it had when the First World War broke out, in July 1940 the British government placed an embargo on the importation of furs into the country.[78] Through the Board of Trade, the domestic industry was also shackled by the rationing for clothing (through coupon restrictions) and by a 100 per cent purchase tax on furs.[79] The board took these actions largely to boost morale. Government officials were anxious that the wealthy not be able to obtain luxury goods during wartime austerity. Because of these measures the value of the British fur trade in 1943 was only 8 per cent of what it had been in 1940.[80] For the duration of the war, the Board of Trade turned a deaf ear to all arguments put forward by the industry for any relaxation of restrictions.

Because they remained convinced that any liberalization of fur sales might have a negative impact on the general public's attitude toward austerity measures, board members even rejected out of hand the calls to permit the manufacture of cheap fur garments from domestic rabbit. One of the reasons why the industry's leaders made no headway was that none of them was ever appointed to the board. Industries that were represented fared much better.[81]

The Hudson's Bay Company responded very differently to the political and economic circumstances created by the Second World War than it did to those of the First World War. This time company officials made a concerted effort to conduct the fur trade as vigorously as possible with little regard for long-term nationalistic considerations. In his testimony before the Board of Trade in 1943, company spokesman Norman R. Beynes stated that one of the reasons the company had built up its operations in New York in the late 1930s was to have in place a 'shadow organization' in the event that war broke out in Europe.[82] In this way the company sought to avoid the mistake it had made during the First World War.

In 1943 the London Board of Trade began to consider the post-war future of the fur industry in England. It sent a circular to fur firms asking them to respond to a series of questions aimed at helping the board develop a policy that would promote the post-war reconstruction of the industry. In their replies, industry representatives stressed that the traditional entrepôt function of London had been critical for the general growth of the British fur trade. They argued that it was essential that the Hudson's Bay Company move back to London from New York in order to rebuild this aspect of the business.[83] However, Beynes stated that the company would not return to London unless the wartime trading restrictions were eliminated as soon as hostilities ended. Otherwise, he claimed that the Hudson's Bay Company would direct its energies towards sustaining New York as the new entrepôt of the industry.

The Board of Trade took the position that it was willing to lift the wartime restrictions only if the industry could demonstrate its ability to generate a positive long-term flow of foreign currency. Business leaders were able to meet this condition, and on 22 January 1945 the Board of Trade responded by taking some of the measures that were needed to rebuild the business in London. For example, the purchase tax on furs was reduced.[84] The *Economist* applauded this move and encouraged the board to take additional steps to strengthen the British industry, noting that the entrepôt aspect of the business traditionally earned more United States dollars than any other product listed separately in trade returns except for alcohol.[85] Taking this fact into account, the government promptly lifted the fur embargo in November of 1945. As promised, the Hudson's Bay Company moved back to London. Its first sales were held in February 1946. Once again the British fur industry began the struggle to regain what it had lost to the Americans under wartime conditions.

6

The struggle for dominance in the Canadian north during the 1920s

A great revolution has taken place within our Fur Trade Departments during the past few years. The Fur Trade of the world is also undergoing rapid and marked change. It is our business to recognize these changes, to grasp their significance for ourselves and to organize and act accordingly.
(Hudson's Bay Company governor, 1934)[1]

In the immediate aftermath of the First World War the Hudson's Bay Company took stock of its position in the Canadian fur trade and then made a concerted struggle to regain the ground it had lost. In the 1920s the main thrust of company's effort was directed towards an expansion program in the western Arctic (which will not be discussed here) and take-over challenges. The latter involved only the larger opponents. Generally the company's strategy did not achieve the desired results.

The Hudson's Bay Company district managers' reports filed just after the 1920–1 depression made clear the extent to which the fur trade had changed and the problems the company faced in attempting to make a come-back (fig. 38). Some of these problems were of a short-term nature; others reflected the new realities of northern life and the international fur-marketing system. These latter troubles persisted.

Figure 39 shows the distribution of fur returns and merchandise sales in the Fur Trade Department in 1922. The newly combined Athabasca-Mackenzie District was the leading district in terms of returns (17 per cent of the total) and retail sales (nearly one-third of the total). The Lake Superior District ranked third as a fur producer, yielding 11 per cent of the total, and second in merchandise, accounting for almost 20

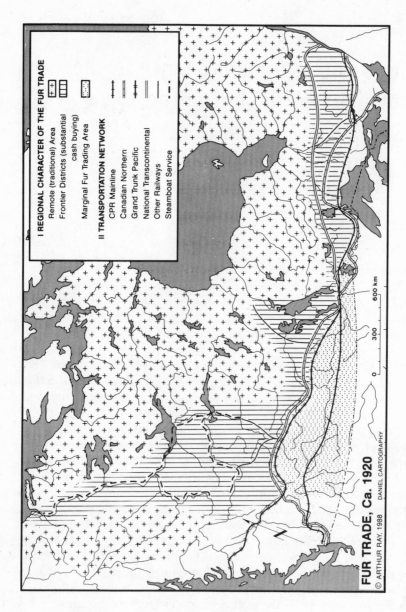

Figure 38
Fur trade, ca 1920

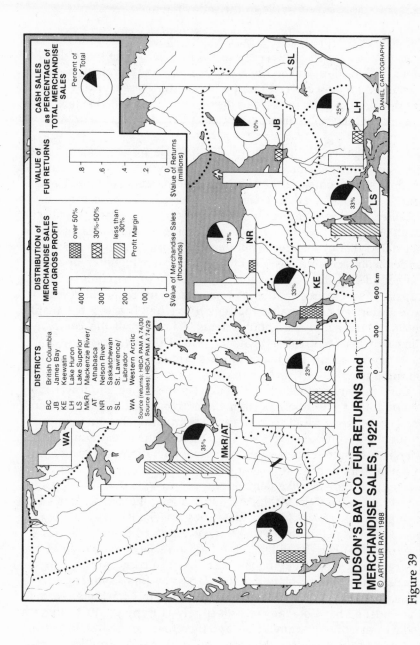

Figure 39

Hudson's Bay Company fur returns and merchandise sales, 1922

per cent of the goods sold. Figure 39 also shows the portion of those sales that were cash transactions in 1922. In five of the seven districts of the old Northern and Southern departments these types of exchange accounted for between one-quarter to one-third of the turnover. In all the districts the gross profit margins on merchandise had fallen below 100 per cent (fig. 39). This represented a marked departure from previous eras.

In the Mackenzie River valley the struggle for supremacy in the fur trade remained predominantly a three-way battle between the Hudson's Bay Company, the Northern Trading Company, and Lamson and Hubbard (fig. 40 and table 11). Collectively these three firms obtained over two-thirds of the fur returns in 1922. A large number of small operators shared the remainder. Acting District Manager Romanet stated that in 1922 three-quarters of the posts in the district were under 'frontier conditions' – in other words, were highly competitive.[2] He added that this was not the consequence of the region's having superior fur resources; rather, it was on account of the oil boom that was underway and because the region was highly accessible, thanks to its superior transportation systems.[3] The sites of the company's forts had become 'real settlements' where prospectors, clergy, and government agents lived, and tourists visited. Romanet claimed that all these people were also fur traders.

Cash fur-buying took place throughout the region, but it was most important in the southern portion. Buyers congregated at Fort McMurray because they could reach it easily from Edmonton by train. Most of them were Jewish buyers who belonged to the Edmonton Raw Fur Merchants Association. Besides these frequent visitors, every merchant in town dealt in furs.[4] Romanet stated that little bartering was done; whites and Indians alike demanded cash. In 1923 they sold $113,000 worth of furs at Fort McMurray. Of this amount the Hudson's Bay Company's share was $28,000, McMurray merchants obtained $60,000, and buyers from Edmonton took $25,000. Apparently in the Mackenzie region below Fort Providence the Hudson's Bay Company did not engage in any cash buying. Instead, the company returned to the practice of issuing drafts for credit balances on furs. Company traders issued $20,000 worth of these in 1923.[5] White trappers, referred to in the Hudson's Bay Company records simply as 'trappers' (to distinguish them from natives), wanted cash, and therefore they sold an increasing portion of their returns 'outside' the territory, in Fort McMurray, Edmonton, or to agents of the Winnipeg Fur Auction Company. These

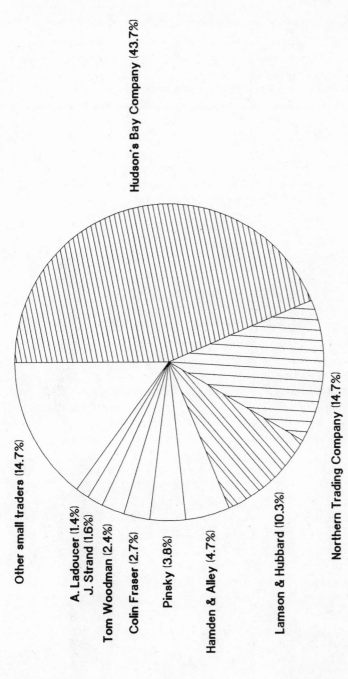

Hudson's Bay Company (43.7%)

Other small traders (14.7%)

A. Ladoucer (1.4%)
J. Strand (1.6%)

Tom Woodman (2.4%)

Colin Fraser (2.7%)

Pinsky (3.8%)

Hamden & Alley (4.7%)

Lamson & Hubbard (10.3%)

Northern Trading Company (14.7%)

Figure 40
Mackenzie River District: estimated shares of fur returns, 1922

TABLE 11
Hudson's Bay Company fur trade, 1922: Mackenzie River District

District/Post Mackenzie	Competitors	External links	Share of furs (per cent)	Nature of competition
Ft McPherson	Lamson and Hubbard	Lamson and Hubbard, Boston	15	
	Aklavik merchants	Settlement of Aklavik	5	
	Hudson's Bay Co.	London	85	
Arctic Red River	Northern Trading Co.	Winnipeg Fur Auctions	39	Liberal credit and prices for goods
	Aklavik merchants	Settlement of Aklavik	11	
	Hudson's Bay Co.	London	60	
Good Hope	Lamson and Hubbard	Lamson and Hubbard, Boston	ND	Prices for goods and 'personalities'
	Northern Trading Co.	Winnipeg Fur Auctions	ND	
	Hudson's Bay Co.	London	ND	
Norman	Northern Trading Co.	Winnipeg Fur Auctions	ND	Prices for goods and gratuities
	Lamson and Hubbard	Lamson and Hubbard, Boston	ND	
	Hudson's Bay Co.	London	ND	
Wrigley	Northern Trading Co.	Winnipeg Fur Auctions	30	'Strong talk rather than price'
	Hudson's Bay Co.	London	70	
Simpson	Northern Trading Co.	Winnipeg Fur Auctions	ND	None. Colluded on prices
	Lamson and Hubbard	Lamson and Hubbard, Boston	ND	
	Hudson's Bay Co.	London	ND	
Liard	Lamson and Hubbard	Lamson and Hubbard, Boston	ND	None. Colluded on prices
	Hudson's Bay Co.	London	ND	
Nelson	Hudson's Bay Co.	London	ND	Indian loyalty
Providence	Northern Trading Co.	Winnipeg Fur Auctions	ND	Liberal gratuity system
	Lamson and Hubbard	Lamson and Hubbard, Boston	ND	
	Hudson's Bay Co.	London	60	
Ft Rae	Pinsky and Necrassoff	Edmonton	2	Aggressive fur pricing
	Northern Trading Co.	Winnipeg Fur Auctions	10	
	Lamson and Hubbard	Lamson and Hubbard, Boston	11	
	Hudson's Bay Co.	London	77	

Resolution	McQueen	?	4	Competitive fur and merchandise prices, tripping and liberal credit
	Alex Loutit	?	5	
	Lirette	Transient cash buyer	8	
	McDonald	Edmonton	10	
	Pinsky and Necrassoff	Lamson and Hubbard, Boston	14	
	Lamson and Hubbard	Winnipeg Fur Auctions	13	
	Northern Trading Co.	London	17	
	Hudson's Bay Co.	Edmonton	29	
Ft Smith	John Morie	Edmonton	ND	Competitive fur and merchandise prices
	L. Connibear	?	ND	
	Northern Trading Co.	Winnipeg Fur Auctions	ND	
	Hudson's Bay Co.	London	ND	
Fitzgerald	J.H. Russel	?	2	Competitive fur and merchandise prices
	Northern Trading Co.	Winnipeg Fur Auctions	4	
	Lamson and Hubbard	Lamson and Hubbard, Boston	9	
	Pinsky and Necrassoff	Edmonton	14	
	Hudson's Bay Co.	London	71	
Ft Chipewyan	23 small independents	Mostly Edmonton	ND	Competitive fur and merchandise prices, tripping and 'bootlegging'
	Hamden and Alley		ND	
	T. Woodman		ND	
	Colin Fraser	Edmonton	ND	
	Lamson and Hubbard	Lamson and Hubbard, Boston	ND	
	Hudson's Bay Co.	London	ND	
McKay	Nd	London	ND	'Bootlegging' and buying of contraband furs
Ft McMurray	Hudson's Bay Co.	London	ND	Competitive fur prices
	Many cash buyers	Edmonton	ND	
	Hudson's Bay Co.	London	ND	

ND = no data
SOURCE: HBCA PAM A 74/52

TABLE 12
Hudson's Bay Company fur trade, 1922: Athabasca District

Post	Competitors	External links	Share of furs (per cent)	Nature of competition	Profit/Loss	Gross margin goods
Little Red River	Lamson and Hubbard	Boston and Winnipeg	ND	Competitive fur and merchandise prices 'boot-legging'	(4,354.47)	
	Northern Trading Co.	Winnipeg	ND			
	Hudson's Bay Company	London	50			
	Revillon Frères	Paris/New York	ND			
Wabasca	10 opposing stores	Mostly Edmonton	ND	'unscrupulous bootlegger'	1,638.93	55
	Hudson's Bay Company	London	50			
Athabasca Post	ND	ND	ND		(6,705.61)	
	Hudson's Bay Company	London	ND			
Peace River	Many small stores	Edmonton, New York	40	Mostly cash buying of secondary trade	(6,898.35)	19
	Hudson's Bay Company	London	60			
Keg River	Keg R. Co. [Lamson's]	?	ND	Competitive fur and merchandise prices	(1,314.97)	60
	Hudson's Bay Company	London	ND			
	McLean of Caraçjou					
Upper Hay River	Lamson and Hubbard	Boston and Winnipeg	10	Competitive fur and merchandise prices		
	Northern Trading Co.	Winnipeg	ND			
	Revillon Frères	Paris/New York	10			
	Hudson's Bay Company	London	ND	Special prices for white trappers	7,883.45	71

Ft Vermilion	Lamson and Hubbard	Boston and Winnipeg	Competitive fur prices	14		
	Revillon Frères	Paris/New York	50 per cent higher than Edmonton	14		
	Sheridan Lawrence	Edmonton		21		
	Hudson's Bay Company	London	Considerable cash buying	50	(9,457.41)	54
Grouard	Transient cash buyers	Mostly Edmonton	Cash buying and 'moonshiners'	ND		
	Hudson's Bay Company	London		60	(164.65)	22
Ft St John	Many local merchants	Mostly Edmonton	Competitive fur and merchandise prices	ND		
	Hudson's Bay Company	London	Cash buying	60	781.77	34
Hudson's Hope	Hudson's Bay Company	London	Competitive fur and merchandise prices	25	4,884.20	33
	Small traders for Winnipeg fur auction	Winnipeg	Cash buying	75		
Whitefish Lake	ND	ND	ND	ND		ND
	Hudson's Bay Company	London		ND		
Sturgeon Lake	Revillon Frères	Paris/New York	Credit trading		(4,247.16)	41
	Small free traders [2]			70		
	Hudson's Bay Company	London	withdrew all credit	30	(796.00)	
District total or average					(18,750.27)	30

ND = no data
( ) = loss
SOURCE: HBCA PAM A 74/52

actions by whites served as a model for the Indians, who began to do likewise. Indian agents and game wardens encouraged Indians in this direction.[6]

Table 12 shows that throughout nearly the whole of the old Athabasca District (which included British Columbia eastward of the Rocky Mountains) Hudson's Bay Company traders faced conditions similar to those at Fort McMurray. The company's share of the local returns ranged from a high of 60 per cent to a low of 30 per cent. Gross profit margins on goods varied from 19 to 71 per cent while eight of the twelve posts registered a net loss on operations. The district manager's report for 1923-4 noted: 'practically every Post is accessible to transient cash buyers from Edmonton, apart from the many established firms and dealers located at the different posts.'[7] The district manager tried to keep fur-buying under reasonable control by gauging prices according to the Edmonton market and keeping post managers 'constantly in touch to the degree mail permitted.'[8] Because of the way older post managers responded to competitive circumstances he was not successful. For example, Fred Clarke, who was in charge of Keg River, was a 'zealous trader,' who had 'difficulty keeping to the tariff' in the face of stiff opposition by Revillon Frères, the Keg River Trading company (financed by Lamson and Hubbard), and two local operators by the name of McLean and Carcajou.[9]

Clarke and similar 'zealous traders' had to contend with local trappers who took advantage of the market information services provided by auctions houses, mail-order firms, and those who kept in touch with markets by telegraph. Well armed with information, they were in a good position to pit local traders and buyers against each other. The annual report for 1923-4 showed that at Peace River post there were four permanent buyers connected with the American houses and 'practically every skin that is brought into town is put up for competition.' Besides these residents, the 'competition' included outsiders, because 'when trappers arrive with their furs they immediately wire Edmonton buyers who take the first train up to be in on any competitive sale, consequently the trappers invariably realize more than their furs are worth.'[10]

In the past the officers could appeal to natives' loyalty and play on the fact the company was practically the only supplier of goods in an effort to secure their business. In a frontier district like Athabasca this approach no longer worked. Settlements had developed around most of the major posts, and merchants competed vigorously for the retail business of Indians, white trappers, and others. For instance, 700 residents lived adjacent to the Peace River post. There were twelve stores and a Revillon Frères wholesale outlet. The district manager complained that these stores had 'nil overhead, no fixed prices or set profits.' Instead, 'orders are sent into town and peddled around to the different stores, and it is known that most of this business is done on a 5% basis.'[11] Even in the much smaller community of Grouard, which had only two stores, merchants undersold the company on many lines.[12] The Hudson's Bay Company's gross profit margin was just under 30 per cent.[13] To a significant extent this low margin resulted from the increasing tendency for white and Indian clients to buy more of their dry goods from new competitors and their groceries from the Hudson's Bay Company. Groceries were the least profitable aspect of retail sales, averaging only 13.9 per cent over the cost landed price at Peace River in 1923.[14]

Some of the company's Athabasca officers faced another problem – 'bootleggers.' These opponents generally brewed their contraband in the Indians' camps. They were active around Grouard and Little Red River. At the latter location the 'unscrupulous' Revillon manager reportedly sold unlimited quantities of 'extracts' – presumably because they contained large amounts of alcohol.[15] There was little the company men could do about this activity but press for more rigorous law enforcement.

Compared with Athabasca the Saskatchewan district seemed quiet, judging from the written reports. Revillion Frères was the principal opponent and it was most active along the railway lines, where it sent its cash buyers. Some smaller operators were also present, particularly in the vicinities of Prince Albert and The Pas.[16] Cash transactions accounted for a small portion of the merchandise turnover (fig. 39). The gross profit margins of the majority of the posts in the district were more favourable than most of those in the Athabasca region. The results of fur buying, however, were only marginally better. More than half of the posts registered losses (table 13), and the district as a whole showed only a slim profit of $6,464.31.

The Lake Superior and Lake Huron districts were similar to the Athabasca-Mackenzie District in terms of the intensity of competition. Gross profit margins on goods were slim, being below 50 per cent at sixteen of the twenty-six posts (tables 14 and 15). Worse, twenty of them suffered net losses. The company's officers faced all the same problems here that their colleagues in Athabasca did. These tables and

TABLE 13
Hudson's Bay Company fur trade, 1922: Saskatchewan District

Post	Merchandise Sales: Cash trade	Credit trade	Barter trade	Total sales	Cash share (per cent)	Furs: profit/loss
Buffalo River	866.70	12,009.25	0.00	12,875.95	7	(4,182.70)
Cedar Lake	1,041.80	13,369.90	15.00	14,426.70	8	(2,319.19)
Cold Lake	4,884.41	37,090.81	89.20	42,064.42	13	(2,843.09)
Cumberland House	1,655.39	19,032.89	0.00	20,688.28	9	(1,981.48)
District Office	689.54	10,652.58	0.00	11,342.12	6	12,850.32
Ft à la Corne	2,513.70	9,477.77	0.00	11,991.47	27	(282.50)
Green Lake	2,807.55	31,057.66	0.00	33,865.21	9	1,848.98
Ile à la Crosse	1,460.95	9,499.17	0.00	10,960.12	15	(1,760.94)
L.L. Ronge	3,879.13	29,510.66	0.00	33,389.79	13	2,787.71
Lac Brochet	1,636.10	50,712.40	1,413.00	53,761.50	3	(543.23)
Montreal Lake	1,551.78	12,352.44	0.00	13,904.22	13	1,746.60
Onion Lake	6,415.92	11,335.19	72.30	17,823.41	56	2,955.07
Pas Mountain	2,901.25	13,321.78	0.00	16,223.03	22	2,945.90
Pelican Narrows	1,954.95	15,198.32	44.50	17,197.77	13	(9,191.01)
Pine River	111.35	17,441.76	0.00	17,553.11	1	(300.93)
Portage la Loche	846.65	20,545.62	0.00	21,392.27	4	2,157.01
Pukkatawagan	563.15	17,441.76	0.00	18,004.91	3	(2,561.94)
Stanley	1,445.35	14,878.47	0.00	16,323.82	10	5,160.54
The Pas	17,460.18	76,138.61	334.85	93,933.64	23	(25.81)
Total or average	54,685.85	421,067.04	1,968.85	477,721.74	13	12,961.20

( ) = loss
SOURCE: HBCA PAM A 74/52

the accounts on which they are based suggest that competition was now centred along the Canadian National Railway (formerly the National Transcontinental Railway).[17] Bootleggers were particularly vexatious here. The train conductors were the worst of them, according to the company's traders. Conductors ran their illicit operations from aboard the train and from selected stations along the route. The company's officers claimed that one of the reasons that Indians wanted cash for their credit balances was to buy 'moonshine.'[18] Traffic in contraband furs, mostly beaver and otter, was another problem along the railway. Apparently this practice was most widespread along the Canadian Pacific line, particularly near Lake Nipigon and Montizambert.

TABLE 14
Hudson's Bay Company fur trade, 1922–3: Lake Superior District

Post	Profit/Loss 1922	Value of fur returns, 1923[a]	Profit/Loss 1923	Gross profit margin on goods (per cent)
Bucke	1,077.95	33,869.70	(4,386.65)	49
Cat Lake	18,664.22	32,377.10	(2,984.05)	54
Dinorwic	1,936.15	33,793.85	1,593.12	51
Fort Hope	19,983.16	56,784.55	(278.87)	52
Fort William	ND	4,401.72	ND	ND
Graham	(4,008.53)	26,936.23	(7,974.11)	20
Grassy Narrows	3,582.24	18,185.77	851.64	52[b]
Hudson	4,053.67	26,869.09	(1,510.03)	25[b]
Lac Seul	9,341.85	34,730.13	(290.00)	79
Long Lake	10,824.64	45,114.15	5,886.92	42
Minaki	3,883.88	22,250.29	6,403.27	50
Missanabie	(431.03)	38,201.08	(3,610.10)	30[c]
Montizambert	7,690.60	24,837.53	(5,935.67)	36
Nipigon	5,160.03	34,434.57	(8,888.58)	39
Nipigon House	1,658.28	14,117.67	(765.81)	56
Osnaburgh	22,525.00	53,643.11	7,683.32	83
Pine Ridge	9,401.11	41,529.29	(2,356.63)	79
Total or average	115,343.22	542,075.83	(16,562.23)	50

a Valued at current standard
b Strong competition from Eaton's
c Mostly grocery sales
( ) = Loss
ND = No data
SOURCE: HBCA PAM A 74/52

Catalogue retailing was another important development that cut into the Hudson's Bay Company's profits in the region. By 1922 many line post managers complained that the T. Eaton Company was taking away the most lucrative aspects of the dry-goods trade. Eaton's began selling by mail in 1884, and by the turn of the century tons of their catalogues were distributed across the country.[19] White customers were the first to take advantage of this new opportunity, but Indians soon caught on. It was the development of this business that encouraged Eaton's and its rival, the Robert Simpson Company, to enter into a fur-marketing arrangement with Shubert of Chicago. Following the lead of Montgomery Ward and Sears and Roebuck in the United States,

TABLE 15
Hudson's Bay Company fur trade, 1922–3: Huron District

Post	Merchandise sales				Gross profit margin on goods (per cent)	
	Cash sales		Credit sales			
	1922	1923	1922	1923	1922	1923
Martens Falls	739.95	300.19	16,882.87	12,001.25	33	114
Senneterre	3,157.08	5,374.17	7,962.08	9,883.29	50	51
Mattice	16,819.56	11,560.87	14,918.05	22,810.70	47	45
Biscotasing	9,547.43	7,246.10	9,052.67	13,039.53	45	42
La Sarre	671.34	10,962.20	6,800.80	70,189.98	56	41
Grand Lake	1,378.63	834.27	13,572.23	15,971.36	36	40
Temagami	12,008.74	16,056.34	11,659.49	13,110.48	28	33
Barriere	301.94	866.22	28,730.55	20,683.41	35	24
Gogama	3,702.90	4,039.92	22,568.16	19,635.50	29	21
English River	566.40	1,191.90	10,786.42	11,739.31	40	13
Total or average	48,893.97	58,432.18	142,933.32	209,064.81	40	42

SOURCE: HBCA PAM A 74/52

these two Canadian retailers used Shubert's services to dispose of their fur collections.[20] This development most strongly affected the fur trade in frontier districts and in the marginal trading areas where farmers trapped on a part-time basis.

In 1931, nearly a decade after Hudson's Bay Company traders began to complain about competition from Eaton's, the district managers suggested that the company should advertise for furs at its retail stores in competition with the Toronto-based firm and hand over the returns they collected to the fur-purchasing agencies. H.P. Warne, who managed the fur-purchasing agencies, replied that the company already had considered and rejected such an idea because, unlike Eaton's, the Hudson's Bay Company retail stores no longer issued catalogues.[21] Ralph Parsons, the company's fur trade commissioner, offered the opinion: 'there was no reason why our posts should not meet the competition of Eaton's mail order house, provided that they had the right kind of merchandise. The class of dry and fancy goods carried at the majority of posts was not suitable for the present day trade and district managers should see to it that old stocks were cleared up as quickly as possible and new fancy goods taken in small quantities giving a large assortment.'[22]

In 1922 the Hudson's Bay Company traders confronted another short-term, but very frustrating, merchandising problem. Many of their small opponents were selling goods they had obtained at bankruptcy sales which were commonplace in the aftermath of the market crash of 1920. Presumably Hudson's Bay Company traders faced this difficulty elsewhere in the north in 1922, but the men in Lake Superior and Lake Huron country paid the most attention to it.[23]

The competition in the James Bay District differed from elsewhere in Ontario. Here Revillon Frères vigorously challenged the Hudson's Bay Company from 1901 until the late 1920s; small operators were not significant. Generally company officials regarded the French-owned concern as one of the more 'sane competitors.' This meant, in effect, that Revillon Frères waged the struggle along more traditional lines. Thus, cash fur buying did not become an important aspect of the business. On the other hand, because of the strength of Revillon Frères' opposition, the results of trading operations were bleak. Only two of the thirteen posts registered a significant profit (table 16). These two, Great Whale River and Fort George, were arctic fox posts. In good years these posts were very lucrative. Elsewhere, the competitors struggled to control only slim returns.

In many respects Keewatin was a transitional district where both 'traditional' and 'frontier' trading took place. Most of the competitors were active along the old transportation axis (Lake Winnipeg / Hayes River). But, they were also moving northward along the Hudson's Bay Railway line which was under construction. Opponents were particularly active at Norway House, Oxford House, God's Lake, and Nelson House. Also, they resorted to tripping on a wide scale. Most of the small operators had direct financial links with Winnipeg or connected indirectly with that city via Selkirk.[24] The district ranked second in terms of gross profit margins on merchandise, averaging just under 70 per cent, and eight of the twelve posts turned significant profits (table 17).

In 1922 the most remote area of the Hudson's Bay Company was that of the Nelson River District. Here the company's opposition was largely limited to Revillon Frères at Wenusk and Lamson and Hubbard on the west coast of Hudson Bay. Also, there were some small operators at Trout Lake.[25] Reflecting its isolated position, this district had the highest average gross profit margin (six of the nine posts exceeded 100

TABLE 16
Hudson's Bay Company fur trade, 1922–3: James Bay District

Post	Profit/Loss 1922 ($)	Profit/Loss 1923 ($)	Gross profit margin on goods (per cent)
Moose Factory	10,404.00	(5,011.00)	53.80
New Post	575.00	(2,097.00)	36.60
Albany River	(17,167.00)	(15,803.00)	47.00
Attawapiskat	6,701.00	(5,737.00)	72.00
Rupert House	8,839.00	(203.00)	95.00
Mistassini	11,793.00	(3,516.00)	45.00
Woswonaby	19,655.00	(1,782.00)	39.00
Neoskweskau	12,254.00	(169.00)	29.00
Nemaska	3,857.00	(1,135.00)	66.00
Eastmain	11,035.00	(1,166.00)	46.50
Fort George	17,930.00	6,066.00	58.00
Great Whale River	46,141.00	56,546.00	79.16
Charlton Depot	4,172.00	260.00	
S.S. Innew	135,611.00	62,872.00	
Total or average	271,800.00	89,125.00	55.59

( ) = Loss
SOURCE: HBCA PAM A 74/52

per cent), the second-lowest portion of its merchandise sales consisting of cash purchases, and most of its posts showed substantial gains on their fur sales (fig. 39 and table 18).

As we saw earlier, by the eve of the First World War senior Hudson's Bay Company officials had decided that the expanding transportation networks, most notably the railways, were pushing back the frontiers of the traditional fur trade areas by opening up new territories to modern competitors. They believed that the company could be carrying on in the older more profitable ways only in the Arctic. Developments during the war, particularly the extreme inflation of fur prices which set off a stampede of buyers into the north, served to confirm the wisdom of the directors' 1913 conclusions. Also, arctic fox prices were still very strong (fig. 41). Accordingly, the directors reactivated the plan they previously had shelved. With much publicity the company set about building a line of posts in the central and western Arctic for the first time.

TABLE 17

Hudson's Bay Company fur trade, 1920–2: Keewatin District

Post	1920 ($)	1921 ($)	1922 ($)	Total ($)	Average gross profit margin on goods (per cent)
Norway House					77
Cash	6,286.31	4,384.97	3,532.57	14,203.85	
Credit	33,592.75	37,495.87	33,703.71	104,792.33	
Barter	3,550.90	2,702.20	1,697.65	7,950.75	
Total	43,429.96	44,583.04	38,933.93	126,946.93	
Nelson House					76
Cash	2,133.48	633.92	1,070.34	3,837.74	
Credit	22,815.51	25,079.22	26,145.84	74,040.57	
Barter	10,093.10	922.25	1,722.45	12,737.80	
Total	35,042.09	26,635.39	28,938.63	90,616.11	
Split Lake					77
Cash	1,912.25	2,441.70	1,151.80	5,505.75	
Credit	20,864.48	23,213.62	21,457.45	65,535.55	
Barter	5,339.40	9,226.60	7,513.95	22,079.95	
Total	28,116.13	34,881.92	30,123.20	93,121.25	
Oxford House					86
Cash	2,545.05	1,756.95	1,052.31	5,354.31	
Credit	25,678.54	23,286.38	18,861.13	67,826.05	
Barter	8,379.65	10,285.00	2,547.25	21,211.90	
Total	36,603.24	35,328.33	22,460.69	94,392.26	
God's Lake					64
Cash	416.05	209.75	300.05	925.85	
Credit	12,655.07	14,575.75	15,854.64	43,085.46	
Barter	12,990.75	9,424.20	4,418.85	26,833.80	
Total	26,061.87	24,209.70	20,573.54	70,845.11	
Island Lake					81
Cash	1,688.85	1,060.72	852.72	3,602.29	
Credit	31,990.42	41,014.85	24,710.49	97,715.76	
Barter	2,846.90	1,047.12	637.90	4,531.92	
Total	36,526.17	43,122.69	26,201.11	105,849.97	
Berens Rivers					46
Cash	5,759.41	11,149.41	1,933.50	105,849.97	
Credit	2,812.85	13,887.18	2,299.00	105,849.97	
Barter	2,455.90	12,114.34	344.30	211,699.94	
Total	308,788.48	927,807.54	102,278.80	423,399.88	

TABLE 17 – continued

Post	1920 ($)	1921 ($)	1922 ($)	Total ($)	Average gross profit margin on goods (per cent)
Little Grand Rapids					105
Cash	2,825.90	1,555.15	1,636.50	6,017.55	
Credit	17,047.19	18,969.19	17,977.73	53,994.11	
Barter	5,114.60	7,941.50	4,142.25	17,198.35	
Total	24,987.69	28,465.84	23,756.48	77,210.01	
Fort Alexander					43
Cash	4,119.15	2,459.15	2,404.74	8,983.04	
Credit	5,129.61	11,318.81	6,942.44	23,390.86	
Barter	426.17	586.88	195.50	1,208.55	
Total	9,674.93	14,364.84	9,542.68	33,582.45	
Setting Lake					11
Cash	–	–	2,707.88	2,707.88	
Credit	–	–	896.00	896.00	
Barter	–	–	154.15	154.15	
Total	–	–	3,758.03	3,758.03	

NOTE: The report indicated that Fort Alexander, Berrens River, and Setting Lake had low profit margins because of the closeness of 'civilization.'
SOURCE: HBCA PAM A 74/52

Company managers also considered moving back into the Yukon. On 16 September 1920 the commissioner's office sent a detailed report to the governor and committee outlining the trading prospects in this frontier area. The report ruled out expansion for several reasons. Fur returns were limited and would barely pay freighting costs. Aggravating the situation, the closed season on beaver would not be lifted until 1923, and Yukon Commissioner George P. Mackenzie announced that the government planned to impose a closed season on marten.[26] Merchandising prospects were also bleak. The old Northern Commercial Company, an American concern, controlled retailing in the northern half of the Yukon. Regarding this firm, the Hudson's Bay Company commissioner's office reported: 'their policy has been to purchase or freeze out opposing firms, and fortune has favoured them. In Dawson, 9 out of every 10 stores are closed.'[27] It was not wise to tackle such a formidable opponent for doubtful returns, given the economic climate at the time.

TABLE 18
Hudson's Bay Company fur trade, 1922–3: Nelson River District

Post	Profit/Loss 1922 ($)	Profit/Loss 1923 ($)	Average ($)	Gross profit margin on goods (per cent)		
				1922	1923	Ave
York Factory	44,425.00	32,871.00	38,648.00	92	87	89
Baker Lake	29,854.00	92,781.00	61,317.50	215	186	151
Trout Lake	25,257.00	13,924.00	19,590.50	120	101	111
Churchill	8,960.00	10,414.00	9,687.00	138	129	133
Severn	8,105.00	7,883.00	7,994.00	152	170	161
Chesterfield	4,415.00	7,433.00	5,924.00	148	237	192
Eskimo Point	3,856.00	52,334.00	28,095.00	189	123	156
Repulse Bay	(3,039.00)	12,536.00	4,748.50	40	35	38
District Office	(3,504.00)	791.00	(1,356.50)			
Wenusk	(4,068.00)	(4,400.00)	(4,234.00)	104	80	92
Net gain	114,261.00	226,567.00	170,414.00			
MSYork Factory	(1,709.00)	1,383.00	(163.00)			
MS Chesterfield	(25,728.00)	(1,912.00)	(13,820.00)			

( ) = Loss
SOURCE: HBCA PAM A 74/52

HBC : competition + mergers

Although trading prospects in the subarctic beyond the Yukon were no longer as rosy as they had been in the past, Hudson's Bay Company officials had no intention of abandoning the area to the opposition. Rather, they decided to try to eliminate their larger opponents by fierce head-to-head competition and by take-over challenges. The market collapse following the First World War and during the depression of the 1930s provided important opportunities to make these moves. In this respect developments in the fur trade paralleled trends in the larger economy. Economic historians have noted that the merger movement of the late 1920s was one of the most intensive in modern Canadian economic history.[28]

During its first two years of operations, Lamson and Hubbard Canadian Ltd made enormous profits. The company's traders were very cocky. On a trip to the Peace River and Edmonton areas in the autumn of 1919, Sir Augustus Nanton, chairman of the Hudson's Bay Company's Canadian Advisory Committee, had an extended conversation with an official of Lamson and Hubbard in which this opponent bragged about his firm's successes. In a letter he wrote to the company's commissioner about their talk, Nanton reported: 'his firm had some 18

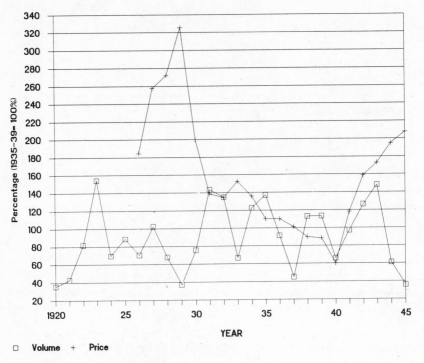

Figure 41
Canadian arctic fox production, 1920–45

small stores in the Mackenzie River District, which were stocked with goods ranging from $30,000 to $50,000 at each store and that he had authority, which he was going to carry out shortly, to open an additional 8 or ten trading posts.' Nanton continued:

He claimed he was doing well and intimated that although they tried to pay for as many furs as possible on goods, they always had a certain amount of cash at their posts, and as they bought furs according to value they gave their representatives discretionary powers to pay cash, or part cash and part goods. He did not know who I was and although he did not in any way run down the Hudson's Bay Company, he let me gather from his remarks that their policy was such that if they came in competition with the Hudson's Bay Company, nine times out of ten they got the furs if they wanted them.[29]

Lamson and Hubbard's aggressive approach led the company to

expand from seven posts in 1918 to thirty-five posts in 1919. The assets of the firm rose from $200,000 to an estimated $2 million during the same period. The problem was that the company's directors plowed all the profits into expansion and they did not build any liquid reserves. Furthermore, they planned for the trading year of 1920 on the assumption that the abnormally high fur prices would continue. As a result, when the market broke, Lamson and Hubbard was left in an extremely vulnerable position.[30]

Hudson's Bay Company officials wasted no time in taking advantage of the situation. Under the leadership of Fur Trade Commissioner Angus Brabant, who acted on the advice of his senior traders, the company mounted a systematic attack on the vulnerable Lamson and Hubbard organization.[31] As the officers had predicted, Lamson and Hubbard lacked the financial and manpower resources for a protracted struggle under 'normal' conditions. The company ceased operations in March of 1923. The following month the Hudson's Bay Company bought the assets from the assignees of the old company and incorporated a new firm in Winnipeg under the name of Lamson Ltd. By April 1924 the Hudson's Bay Company had obtained all the shares of Lamson Ltd.[32]

This success presented the Hudson's Bay Company with another opportunity – the take-over of the Alberta and Arctic Transportation Company, which was a subsidiary of Lamson and Hubbard. Incorporated in Edmonton in 1921, this concern fiercely competed with the Hudson's Bay Company for the transport business of the Athabasca-Mackenzie region. The company resulted from the merger between the British Columbia Express Transportation Company of Prince George and Ashcroft (known as the B-X Company) and the transport arm of Lamson and Hubbard.[33] The completion of the Grand Trunk Pacific Railway had put the B-X Company out of business. To deal with this development its president and main shareholder, Charles Millar, a lawyer from Toronto, joined forces with Lamson and Hubbard.[34] Lamson and Hubbard held 71 per cent of the shares of the Alberta and Arctic Transportation Company and the B-X Company had 24 per cent. There were seventeen other minor investors.[35] Following the merger, the B-X Company moved its craft (the most important of which was the stern-wheeler B-X), boat-building, and repair facilities from the Fraser River to the Peace River.[36] According to Colonel Cornwall, former B-X Company President Millar used his political connections to obtain government shipping contracts for the newly formed Alberta and Arctic Transportation Company, and Hudson's Bay Company records lend support to his assertion.[37]

In spite of its considerable success, the Alberta and Arctic Transportation Company fell victim to the financial difficulties of its parent. In 1924 the Hudson's Bay Company bought the firm. Between 1924 and 1942 the Hudson's Bay Company continued to operate the Alberta and Arctic Transportation Company as a wholly owned subsidiary under its original charter. The company did so for publicity reasons. In 1924 senior officials reported that the Hudson's Bay Company had lost a good deal of the transportation business because it gave priority to the needs of its own fur trade department, and it paid only scant attention to those who used its shipping services.[38] By continuing to operate the Alberta and Arctic Transportation Company as a subsidiary, officials hoped they could get around this problem. The difficulty was, however, that one of the main purposes of the take-over was to eliminate the competition for river traffic that had served to open the territory to opposition fur traders by forcing down freight rates.

Despite years of experience and considerable resources, Revillon Frères fell on hard times beginning in the 1920s. Excluding gains from wholesale operations, the firm lost roughly $335,000 between 1921 and 1926.[39] The future looked bleak. In nearly all instances post operating expenses exceeded the profit margins earned on merchandise sales. Additional reductions in operating costs were not possible.[40] Faced with these difficulties, the company began to retreat from the north. In the spring of 1925 the Revillons sold their operations in Labrador to the Hudson's Bay Company, and in the spring of 1926 negotiations began for the sale of controlling interest in the remaining fur trade business. According to the terms of agreement the Hudson's Bay Company secured 51 per cent of the stock of Revillon Frères. Direction of the French company was left in the hands of the current managers, although the Hudson's Bay Company reserved the right to place a majority on the board of directors. Revillon Frères and Hudson's Bay Company management were supposed to exchange information freely.[41]

This take-over served the Hudson's Bay Company's interests in several important ways. The directors did not want to eliminate what they regarded as a 'sane and reasonable competitor.' Also, they feared that the Indians and the Canadian government would react adversely to the loss of competition in the north.[42] It was partly for this reason that the Hudson's Bay Company planned to operate Revillon Frères as a separate entity – preferably without the merger's becoming public knowledge. By co-ordinating the actions of the two companies, the senior managers hoped that they would be able to regulate debt; curtail the trade in unprime fur; set fur prices in relation to prevailing world prices rather than local circumstances; reduce labour costs by eliminating competition for employees; reduce outposts and tripping; discourage third-party competition; and eliminate duplicate transportation systems.[43]

From the outset there were problems. Rumours of the take-over were widely reported in industry publications, and they circulated among the native people. Many Revillon Frères and Hudson's Bay Company post managers refused to co-operate; contrary to their instructions, many competed with one another as before. Only in the area of transportation did the new arrangement work well.

The deteriorating business climate worked against Revillon Frères, however, and the firm suffered heavy losses. In 1934 the Revillon Frères had to liquidate their investments to pay off the company's current indebtedness. The Hudson's Bay Company made a buy-out offer which the Frenchmen refused. But, the following year they sold eleven posts to the Hudson's Bay Company – three in the James Bay District and eight in the Athabasca-Mackenzie area. Finally, in 1936 the Revillons sold their remaining shares of Revillon Frères to the company.[44] *1929 crash*

The boom of the 1920s ended abruptly with the stock market crash in 1929. As was the case in most industries, the collapse of prices had major repercussions on the fur trade. Of particular relevance here, the panic offered the Hudson's Bay Company the opportunity to regain lost ground in the fur-marketing aspect of the business. The company began by seeking to wrest control of one of the Winnipeg Fur Auction Sales Company's major suppliers of fur.

When A. and W. Nesbitt, Ltd, went bankrupt immediately after the First World War, it left the Edmonton-based Northern Trading Company in a difficult position. The latter company owed considerable debts to Nesbitt which it could not pay. Given these circumstances, Nesbitt's liquidator forced the Northern Trading Company into receivership in 1925. Since the Northern Trading Company disposed of an average of $180,000 worth of fine furs at its sales every year, this action represented a threat to the Winnipeg Fur Auction Sales Company.[45] The Winnipeg dealers were anxious that the company not fall into the hands of the Hudson's Bay Company or those of rival Montreal

interests.[46] They had good reason for concern. On 23 December 1924
the deputy chairman of the Canadian Advisory Committee of the
Hudson's Bay Company (the creation of this committee is discussed
below) in Winnipeg wrote to the governor and committee, informing
them that 'Mr Brabant (commissioner) states that a number of Winnipeg Jewish traders connected with the Winnipeg Fur Auction Company are now endeavouring to acquire the assets of the Northern
Trading Company. It is to prevent the invasion of the territory by these
people that the Commissioner considers the Hudson's Bay Company
should acquire the assets of the Northern Trading Company and maintain a separate subsidiary trading Company in the territory.'[47] Besides
wanting to keep the Winnipeg Jews out of the Athabasca-Mackenzie
territory, Brabant wanted to make a bid for the company because he
wanted to combine the transport service of this company with that of
the recently acquired Alberta and Arctic Transportation Company.[48]

Following the advice of commissioner Brabant, in 1925 the Hudson's
Bay Company made a $140,000 bid in the Supreme Court of Alberta
for the assets of the Northern Trading Company. At the last possible
moment the company's founder, Colonel J.K. Cornwall, made a
$150,000 counter-offer. Cornwall had obtained the backing of a number
of important Jewish fur dealers from Winnipeg. The most important
of these were Max and Moses Finkelstein, who held interests in the
Winnipeg Fur Auction Sales Ltd and owned the North-West Hide and
Fur Company of Winnipeg.[49] The court accepted Cornwall's offer, to
the great irritation of Hudson's Bay Company officials, who believed
the judge acted unfairly. After 1925 the Edmonton-based Northern
Trading Company operated under the name Northern Traders Ltd and
maintained its head office at Fort Smith.[50] Unfortunately for Cornwall's
new Winnipeg partners, Northern Traders continued to lead a tenuous
existence. This situation led Max Finklestein to approach the Hudson's
Bay Company for a loan of $200,000 in 1929. Finkelstein and the board
reached an agreement according to which Northern Traders agreed to
put up 51 per cent of its shares as collateral, and it guaranteed to ship
$1 million worth of furs each year to the Hudson's Bay Company's
auctions in London. Furthermore, the Hudson's Bay Company was
given the option of acquiring a 49 per cent interest in the Winnipeg
Fur Auction Sales Ltd.[51] Finally, the directors of Northern Traders
guaranteed to maintain the net assets of the company at $438,000.

The depression crippled Northern Traders even further. In 1930
Max Finkelstein had to approach the Hudson's Bay Company for an

additional loan of $125,000. The governor and committee refused this request because Northern Traders already owed $73,000 to the Hudson's Bay Company for transportation services. Furthermore, it owed about $230,000 to other creditors, including the Bank of Montreal, and the net assets of the troubled organization had fallen below the guaranteed limit.[52] On 10 June 1930 the Hudson's Bay Company served notice to the shareholders of Northern Traders that they had to make a payment of $83,663.78 to the latter company to bring the assets up to the agreed limit.[53]

For the next nine years the principal creditors of Northern Traders managed the affairs of the troubled company. After suffering an additional net loss of $69,150 in 1931, they tried to persuade the Hudson's Bay Company (the largest creditor) to acquire the remaining assets. After carefully considering the matter, the Canadian Committee decided that the company had little to gain from the proposed take-over. Having failed either to find a suitor or to turn Northern Traders' fortunes around, the creditors decided to liquidate the firm. At this time the Hudson's Bay Company agreed to purchase the remaining inventory at forty cents on the dollar to prevent the disposal of the stock in the Mackenzie River area at cut-rate prices. However, the company refused to buy the trading posts, considering that most of them were in poor repair and they were located at places where the English firm already had establishments. It was not until 1946 that these properties were sold and Northern Traders' affairs concluded.[54]

Although Northern Traders remained on the scene much longer than Brabant would have liked, the take-over battle of 1925 did accomplish one of his original objectives. The beleaguered firm had to give up the transportation business. Accordingly, on 6 November 1926 Northern Traders contracted to have the Alberta and Arctic Transportation Company handle its shipping requirements between Waterways, Alberta, and its posts in Alberta and the Northwest Territories. Also, it assigned its shipping contracts to the Hudson's Bay Company subsidiary.[55] In this way the company did strengthen its position on the waterways in this important district.

Generally the company's take-over strategy achieved very little because small operators took to the field in growing numbers. Unfortunately, few records of these opponents have come to light to date, so glimpses of the industry from their perspectives are rare at present. One of the few, and very interesting accounts is that of Peter Baker.

Baker was born in 1887 in what is now Lebanon. According to his autobiography he was a Christian who left the Middle East in 1907 to avoid being conscripted into the Turkish army to fight rebels in Yemen.[56] After a brief stay in the United States he immigrated to Canada. In 1921, like so many others, he set out from Edmonton in the hope of profiting from the 'oil boom' under way in the Mackenzie Valley. He headed for Fort Smith to establish a small 'store' in a tent. His partner, John Morie, made all the arrangements and obtained their goods in Edmonton, mostly on credit.

Initially, Baker and Morie were not primarily interested in trading furs. Rather, they intended to sell merchandise to prospectors and to take part in the business that would follow the signing of Treaty 11 that year. Regarding that event, Baker wrote: 'John suggested I go to Fort Resolution and take some oranges, chocolate bars and orange drink mixture and the five gallon bottle with its tap to serve orange drinks ... We would introduce something that hadn't been done before.'[57] Although an outbreak of fever among the local dog population prevented the Indians from visiting Baker, the venture was still a success. He sold his drink and candy to the town's residents and some nearby Indians for a tidy profit of $800 before returning to his base at Fort Smith. Thereafter the Indians referred to him as 'Jiac Oza,' or the 'orange man.'

The local Hudson's Bay Company men frowned on Baker's activities. According to Baker, they set out to discredit him before he got established by telling the Indians that he was a Jew. Baker claimed he 'had never heard anybody mention such a word as "Jew." ' He added: 'In those days, when anybody was called a "Jew," it meant outcast and despised, because a "Jew" was a "Christkiller." I was called that most often.'[58]

Baker described the tactics of his Hudson's Bay Company opponent as follows: 'When I got supplies in, the Hudson's Bay took notice ... I was told that Willy Lyall [manager at Fort Fitzgerald] told District Inspector Harry Godsall [Phillip H. Godsell], "If you give me the Fort Smith post, I'll fix that Jew for you and make sure he gets no fur!" '[59] The company did post Lyall to Fort Smith and, according to Baker, he set about carrying out his threat: 'he told people all about the "Jew" and made up a name for my place, the "Jew's Store." The people, Indian, Métis and whites came and told me that he was spreading false propaganda about me.'[60]

Apparently Baker bore up well against the war of gossip the local company men were waging against him. He boasted that he even turned it to his advantage. For example, while visiting a Chipewyan chief at Fort Norman one Easter weekend, Baker was asked: 'Why did your people kill Jesus Christ?' By his account he replied: 'Look, tomorrow is Easter Sunday. You are happy to have confession and attend Mass and your soul is saved. If Jesus had not been killed you would go to Hell!' The chief reportedly replied: 'Equee!' meaning 'Correct,' and gave a big laugh. Thereafter he was a steady client. Baker claimed that even though Lyall and his followers tried hard to ostracize him, he had a great number of friends.[61]

However, the 'Arctic Arab' as he was also known soon discovered that Lyall had other ways of harassing him. He kept a close eye on Baker's store. When Indians came to trade, Lyall often sent a man over to lure them away. Sometimes he came in himself. On at least one occasion Lyall stole wood from Baker. There was little Baker could do about it, however, because the local police inspector, Fred Fletcher, was a close friend of Lyall. A short while later Fletcher arrested him on what Baker claimed was a trumped-up charge of knowingly receiving stolen property. At issue was a small amount of tobacco he had purchased from a Hudson's Bay Company outpost manager of Indian descent named Alex Daniel. Baker was held in custody for three weeks until he arranged bail. Eventually he received a six-month suspended sentence from a local judge following a trial without a jury. Baker believed he had no choice but to accept the sentence. Reflecting on this episode, Baker wrote:

'I had to let it go at that, what could really be called a kangaroo court.

Before the Judge started the hearing he went around to study the attitudes of all the prominent people. Father Manseau and Dr. MacDonald recommended dismissal of the case, while Mr. Card also did what he could to help. There was hardly anyone who didn't have a good word for me, except Willy Lyall. He said I should be given two years in the penitentiary and deported from the Northwest Territories ...

Corporal Walters told me, 'As a self defence man you did as well as anyone could possibly have done. Of course, if you had a good lawyer it would have been a different story with no conviction but, anyway, you are free now and it's all over with.'[62]

These episodes are interesting for several reasons. The most challenging newcomers to the industry were the smaller traders, whom company men referred to as Jews and Assyrians. These merchants were included in the ranks of immigrants from eastern and southern Europe who came to Canada at the turn of the century. Baker, who admittedly may have had an axe to grind, suggests that the company's officers' disliked these intruders, an aversion that may have had racial overtones. Although the company's records do not provide the information needed to confirm or refute Baker's story, they do make it clear that the officers did not refer to competitors associated with Revillon Frères and Lamson and Hubbard in derogatory ways. Of greater importance here, Baker's narrative tells us that competition was not waged simply along economic lines (e.g., in terms of price, merchandise selection, credit, and gratuities), in contrast to the impression the Hudson's Bay Company's records create. Local social connections and political pressure were part of the traders' arsenals.

So, Baker learned the hard way that the Hudson's Bay Company was still the dominant force in the territory and that the local company officers had a variety of ways to discourage competition. Senior officials had no knowledge of many of them. Yet, in spite of the local officers' flexing of their muscle, Baker and others like him thrived. This posed a growing problem for the company. Past experience had demonstrated that it did not make good business sense to buy out these small opponents when efforts to drive them out failed. Usually these 'free-traders' were willing to sell only when they were in serious financial difficulty. This meant that buy-outs often gave them urgently needed cash. In any event, given that liberal credit generally was readily available (except during the depths of the depression) these men were able to re-establish themselves in new locations with great ease.

It was for these various reasons that the take-over strategy failed. In fact, it was probably counter-productive. As company traders often pointed out, it made better sense to collude with large operators like Revillon Frères to fix prices, share local markets, and make it more difficult for small independents to earn enough to establish themselves. Being unable to eliminate its opponents, the Hudson's Bay Company continued to decline. Figure 42 shows the extent of the company's slide between 1926 and 1932 by indicating the share of company's returns collected by trading posts (districts) and fur-purchasing agencies. The latter handled most of the ranched furs and 'secondary collections.' During the Second World War the Hudson's Bay Company slipped further behind in spite of moving its operations to New York in an effort to avoid the problems of the First World War. In 1945 its

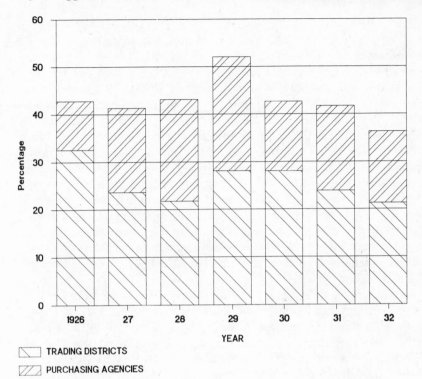

Figure 42
Hudson's Bay Company share of Canadian fur production, 1926–32

various selling organizations collectively handled 35 per cent fewer furs from around the world than they had in 1938.[63] The decline in the company's share of the marketing of North American furs was not as extreme, but it was substantial none the less, decreasing from 19 to 15 per cent.[64]

In Canada alone the Hudson's Bay Company's record was much worse. Furs consigned to the company's Montreal Sales Department for private treaty disposal or to Lampson, Fraser and Huth declined steadily, and by 1945 they accounted for only 2.5 per cent of total Canadian production. This poor performance was largely the result of the company's failure to secure a significant share of the ranched fur business which was increasingly handled by breeders' associations.[65] The track record of the company's Fur Trade Department was just as dismal. In 1943–4 it obtained only 23 per cent of total Canadian fur output – a decline of 13 per cent from the early 1930s.[66]

Immediately after the war the Hudson's Bay Company directed two of its most experienced fur graders and sellers, Norman Beynes, who had worked in the London warehouse, and Charlie Wilson of Winnipeg, to take stock of the fur trade for the Hudson's Bay Company and to assess its position in the industry.[67] These two men noted that in Canada (table 19) the company operated 116 posts and faced twice that number of resident traders. In addition, there were an unknown number of travelling buyers. Not counting Quebec, there were almost 1,500 fur dealers, who dealt with trappers, traders, auction companies, and manufacturers. Most of the resident traders in Quebec sold their furs to large Montreal dealers or to travelling buyers. Only a few of them consigned their collections directly to the Canadian Fur Auction Company in Montreal. This company had remained the country's largest auctioneer. Most of the furs it handled were destined for the United States.

In Ontario the Hudson's Bay Company still regarded the country north of the Canadian National Railway main line as a remote area, even though it faced at least thirty resident traders there. These rivals sold their furs primarily at points along the railway (the town of Cochrane was the leader) to Montreal dealers, or they consigned them to the Canadian Fur Auction Company.

In Manitoba the opposition concentrated its activities along the Hudson Bay Railway. The Pas, for example, was a thriving regional fur market. Most of these opponents' furs went to the two Winnipeg auction houses which collectively handled about two-thirds of the volume of their Montreal competitor. A sizeable portion of the Winnipeg fur auction business came from Saskatchewan, Alberta, the Northwest Territories, and northwestern Ontario. This situation arose partly because Winnipeg dealers and auction houses were very active in all these areas.

In Saskatchewan the government was heavily involved in fur marketing, handling the bulk of muskrat and beaver collections. According to the Hudson's Bay Company, 'all provincial government employees in the north are agents for the Government Marketing Service in the fur season, and solicit consignments from all trappers and traders contacted in the course of their duties.'[68] In both Saskatchewan and Alberta a substantial number of the fur dealers still were country storekeepers – over 80 per cent in Alberta. They sold their furs roughly

TABLE 19
Overview of the fur trade, 1947

Province	Total HBC posts[a]	Line posts	HBC posts without opposition[a]	Resident traders[b]	Transient buyers	Dealers	Major auctions	Average value 1942–7	Break-even point
Quebec	28	4	6	35	25	ND	Canadian Fur Auctions	7,705,883	5,000,000
Ontario	12		10	30	ND	406	None		
Manitoba	23	6	ND	80	ND	300	Soudack Fur Auctions	2,705,200	2,000,000
							Dominion Fur Auctions	2,328,900	1,750,000
Saskatchewan	16		ND	19	ND	247			
Alberta	20	4	ND	40	ND	365	Edmonton Fur Auctions[c]	1,728,950	ND
British Columbia	17	4	ND	28	ND	136	W. Canada Raw Fur Auctions[d]		
							Little Brothers[e]	1,324,421	ND

a North of the Canadian National Railway in Ontario and 52n parallel in Alberta
b North of the Canadian National Railway and includes resident and transient traders
c Established in 1935
d Established in 1941
e Taken over by Seattle Fur Exchange in 1945
ND = No data
SOURCE: Beynes and Wilson, 'Canadian Fur Marketing Research,' HBCA PAM, GD 104/Box 13 FT

every ten days during the trapping season to larger collectors who visited them by truck. By this time native people played only a minor role in the fur trade of the prairie area.

By the end of the Second World War the fur auction business had expanded in Alberta and British Columbia. There was one major house in Edmonton and two in Vancouver. However, the hinterlands of these two cities were small when compared with those of Montreal and Winnipeg, being largely limited to their respective provinces.

When reflecting on their survey, Beynes and Wilson wrote: 'Our study has proved to our satisfaction that the company, in its past policies, paid insufficient regard to the evolutions taking place in the Canadian raw fur business. Failure to adjust our methods to meet what was happening in the trade has not only built up our competitors, but also has had a detrimental effect on the Canadian Fur Trade Department.'[69]

7

Attempts to revitalize
the Hudson's Bay Company's
Fur Trade Department,
1920–1945

When is a business not a business? When it is a fur trade.
(Thomas Bell, Rupert's House)

Part of the reason that the Hudson's Bay Company continued to lose
ground after the First World War in spite of eliminating its larger
opponents related to problems within the organization's Fur Trade
Department. In the 1920s the Canadian and London committees were
mostly concerned with the retail stores division, where they made
heavy investments but suffered substantial losses.[1] Meanwhile, the fur
trade department was largely left on its own. When the directors, most
notably the Canadian Committee, finally turned their attention to this
department, their efforts to regain a comparative advantage in the
industry were dogged by inconsistencies in approach and by conflicts
with senior fur trade officers and key members of the London board.
The basic problem was that Canadian Committee members believed
they could resolve the department's problems by applying modern
business procedures, but senior officers and some members of the
board thought the reintroduction of 'glorious' old traditions was the
answer. While they attempted to resolve these conflicting opinions,
the trade continued to slip away, and the once-proud officers had
become an increasingly demoralized force.

There is an enduring popular belief that the company's Fur Trade
Department was a highly disciplined and effective, if rather conservative, organization. On the contrary, company records reveal that this
was not the case. The department was disorganized for most of the

first half of this century. When Chipman left the commissioner's office in 1910, the company reversed its previous course and began to decentralize authority within the department. The potential advantage of taking this approach was that it gave district and post managers flexibility to deal with the increasingly competitive and varied fur trade. But, for this to be a successful business strategy the company needed high-calibre, well-trained managers; a commissioner who provided effective leadership; and someone, or a management group, who kept a watchful eye on total operations and a firm hand at the helm. For a variety of reasons almost none of these conditions was met between 1910 and 1940.

By 1911 the London board had concluded that the company's business had become too complex for it to conduct Canadian operations without having regular access to first-hand business information and local professional advice. Accordingly it established the Canadian Committee Advisory Board composed of leading Canadian (mostly western) businessmen. Sir Augustus Nanton, a leading Winnipeg businessman, served as its first chairman.[2] At first this body served in a strictly advisory capacity. However, as time passed, the committee was given more responsibility. In 1923 the board renamed it the Canadian Committee in recognition of this development. Seven years later the board empowered the committee to make all the senior administrative appointments for Canadian operations.[3]

In the beginning the Canadian Committee was preoccupied with problems in the stores division and its members had little familiarity with the fur industry. Consequently, they showed little interest in the Fur Trade Department before the late 1920s. Making matters worse, during the First World War members of the London board devoted most of their attention to the highly lucrative wartime supply-contracting business just at the time competitors took to the field in the Canadian north in unprecedented numbers. As we have seen, although the board refused to take an active part in the management of the division during the First World War, it also was unwilling to give Commissioner Bacon a free hand to conduct affairs as he thought best. His resignation in disgust in 1918 demoralized the officers and men. Compounding the department's problems even more, substantial numbers of the company's most experienced post managers enlisted in the armed services during the war. Others deserted to the opposition until the company introduced a bonus scheme in 1919.[4] As we have seen, to make up the shortages district managers recruited considerable numbers of native men.[5] Without being specific, company officials complained that native post managers were unable to cope with the changes that were taking place. This is understandable, given their low level of training and the social setting they had to operate within. The native post managers were under considerable pressure to extend credit to relatives regardless of business considerations, and they had to dispense relief generously. For these various reasons most native managers were unsatisfactory. On the positive side, however, their kinsmen tended to be loyal customers, a fact that apparently was not appreciated by the Canadian Committee.

As early as the mid-1920s the Fur Trade Department had deteriorated to the point that a major renewal program was desperately needed. In preparation for this the Canadian Committee initiated a series of detailed analyses of all aspects of departmental operations.[6] This research began in 1929 and continued throughout the 1930s. The committee's first major action came in 1930. Exercising its new authority to make appointments, it replaced the current fur trade commissioner, Charles French, with Ralph Parsons.[7] The committee thought French was incompetent. His replacement was a very promising Newfoundlander who had joined the company as an apprentice clerk in 1900 at the age of nineteen. After serving four years in that capacity in the Labrador District, Parsons had been sent to Rigolet Post as a clerk. In 1906 he became manager of Wolstenholme Post and in 1917 he was appointed inspector of the Labrador District. Two years later he was promoted to manager of the district. In 1920 the company merged the Labrador and St Lawrence districts and Parson took charge of the combined district, serving in that capacity until 1931, when he assumed his new duties.[8] In other words, Parsons had established an excellent record in the company's Fur Trade Department by the time Canadian Committee chose him to direct it. By selecting such a man, the company officials were reverting to a much older hiring tradition which they had broken with when they appointed Wrigley and Chipman, neither of whom had had any previous company experience.

Besides recommending the replacement of the current commissioner, the Canadian Committee proposed that new terms of reference be drawn up for future commissioners to tighten the committee's reins on them. In particular, they wanted the commissioner to follow broad management guidelines which the committee would draft. They added: 'We also desire that at the same time the Commissioner shall be informed that, in all matters involving broad policies, expenditure of moneys other than in normal course of business, and senior appointments in the Department, he must consult with the Canadian Committee and obtain their approval before any commitment of any kind is made.'[9]

When Parsons assumed his new duties in 1931, the board promoted P.A. Chester to general manager of Canadian operations and they made him a member of Canadian Committee to streamline the administrative structure. He became Parsons's immediate superior. Chester had grown up in a working-class family in Derbyshire, England. He joined the company as an assistant accountant in the London office in 1923. In 1924 the board transferred him to Canada to review the accounting system being used in Winnipeg. In 1925 he became the chief accountant there, serving in that capacity until he took up his duties as general manager.[10]

Finding suitable senior managers was not the only problem the company faced in the 1920s. The whole command structure of the Fur Trade Department was in disarray. There were several reasons. The program of decentralization after 1910 and the movement away from the traditional authoritarian labour / management system had gone too far. By the end of the First World War post and outpost managers often ignored policy directives issued by district headquarters or by the commissioner. This insubordination led the Canadian Committee to complain in 1930 that: 'the District Managers, to all intents and purposes have merchandised their units according to their own lights, run their own transport, supervised and controlled their own personnel, and in some cases run other subsidiary operations.'[11]

The physical appearance of many of the Hudson's Bay Company's posts reflected years of neglect and the growing disillusionment of the men who were responsible for their upkeep. One of the regions suffering most was the James Bay District. In 1920 inspecting officer Louis Romanet described the situation as follows: 'a sort of general discouragement, a fatalism, seems to have put a drag to better activity. James Bay looks like a little kingdom living in its past, and walking slowly towards its ruin. The officers in charge, facing a too visible decline of their post, seem to accept passively, and as an unavoidable fatality, the decay of the oldest District of the Company.'[12] Regarding the manager of the district, Romanet added 'he is rocking his pride in the chair of illusions.'[13]

Clearly something had to be done to address what the Canadian Committee termed: 'the vital factor, namely, the loosening of the reins of control from Winnipeg, which has resulted in lack of control, co-operation and efficiency.'[14] Parsons's solution to the problem involved 'bringing in' district headquarters offices to a few locations where he could control them more easily. Under his scheme he established the headquarters for British Columbia in Victoria; Athabasca-Mackenzie in Edmonton; Saskatchewan, Keewatin, Superior-Huron, Nelson River, and the Western Arctic in Winnipeg; and St Maurice and St Lawrence in Montreal. He planned to relocate the James Bay and Ungava offices in Winnipeg later.[15] Beginning in 1926 the commissioner held fur trade conferences in Winnipeg for district managers so they could exchange ideas. In some respects these were similar to the departmental council meetings of the pre-1870 era except that the assembled men did not pass rules and regulations. Starting with the 1933 meeting, managers who had special expertise in certain areas of operation gave papers at the request of the commissioner. The topics presented included controlling credit, operating line posts, and conducting trade with Indians.

Three years after becoming company governor in 1931 Sir Patrick Ashley Cooper visited Canada to inspect general operations. Following his visit, he prepared a comprehensive report that dealt with the key aspects of the Fur Trade Department and he included a series of recommendations for further changes. The governor, who was a strong supporter of Parsons, wrote approvingly of the commissioner's centralization effort:

since the brains and imagination for the Trading Posts have got to be supplied from Head Office, it follows that a very complete system of contact with the Posts and other outlying units is essential. Such a system will be facilitated to a material extent by what has been done already in centralizing the head Office of a number of districts in Winnipeg. This has meant a physical proximity between District Managers and between them and the headquarters staff which must in itself have been helpful.[16]

However, the governor believed that additional managerial and organizational changes were urgently needed before the plan could work. When discussing the company's administration, he drew an analogy between the fur trade and the army – both needed a first-rate headquarters staff and regimental officers and men. He believed both were lacking in 1934, and he offered the opinion that: 'at present our chief problem is to provide: (1) a central administration or general staff,

(2) a commercially-minded F.P.A [fur-purchasing agency] organization, (3) a hard working, economical Post personnel, and (4) a number of scientifically or commercially trained men for various specialized departments.'[17] The governor thought these problems could not be overcome until the company developed a system for the selection, training, and promotion of men competent to fill higher positions in the organization.

For these men to be effective, improvements had to be made in the command structure beyond those initiated by Parsons. Governor Cooper thought that a 'family tree' (organizational chart) was needed to show the ultimate kind of organization the company hoped to achieve, to help define lines of administrative authority, and to clearly establish the relationships that were to be developed between internal departments.[18]

The London board considered the governor's report before sending it to the Canadian Committee with the instruction that members were to study it carefully. Also, the board provided an extra copy which it asked the committee to pass along to Commissioner Parsons. These instructions and the report provoked a hostile reaction from the committee. On 13 December 1934 Canadian Committee Chairman George Allan (one of the committee's founding members, who had assumed the chairmanship in 1925 and board member since 1925) wrote a carefully worded private and confidential reply to the board.[19] After observing politely that the committee had studied and considered the observations of the governor with the greatest interest, Allan went on to rebuke the board for going over the committee's head. He stressed: 'we know you agree with us that one of our most important responsibilities with our administration of all departments of the company's business and of its subsidiary Companies in Canada, has been the establishment of administrative control, and the proper assignment of duties and responsibilities down the line of our organization, and that it is fundamentally important there should be no deviation from our chain of constituted authority.'[20] Regarding the chain of command, the committee noted that it always dealt with General Manager Chester, who in turn communicated with the fur trade commissioner, the heads of other departments, and managers of subsidiary companies. In other words, the governor, who had stressed the need to develop clear lines of authority, was, in the committee's opinion, acting in a contrary fashion.

Having made its procedural point, the committee got down to the

Northern Traders' (formerly Northern Trading Company) post at Fort
Providence, NWT, ca 1928

A Canadian Automobile Association test vehicle at Moose Factory, 1931

'Oh, what are those cute little animals? Why up here we call 'em muskrats, but when they reach the city they're Hudson Bay Seals.' Cartoon commentary on growing practice of dyeing and treating cheap furs to resemble more expensive varieties

Fashion sketch of an ermine cape

THE
LATEST
FROM
PARIS

Model by
Fourrures Max :
Ottoman
Silk, trimmed
Hudson Seal

*Drawn exclusively or
"The British Fur Trade"*

A silk coat trimmed with 'Hudson Bay seal' (muskrat)

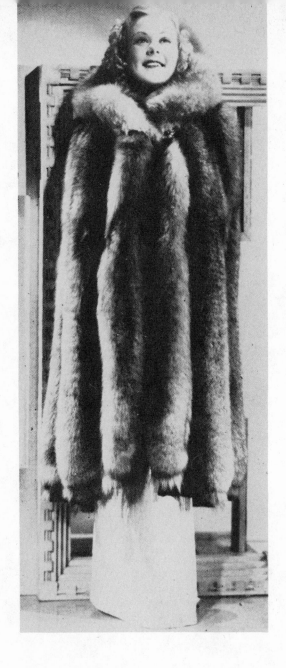

Sonja Henie of Twentieth Century Fox modelling a luxurious blue fox cape; in the 1930s the fur industry used Hollywood movie stars to promote fashions, and fur capes regained popularity in 1934.

The twin silver fox scarf shown here was strongly promoted in women's fashion magazines throughout the United States in the spring of 1938.

This twin-engined Beechcraft was the first airplane purchased by the Hudson's Bay Company, 1939. From the left: Harold Winny (pilot), Patrick Ashley Cooper (governor), Duncan McLaren (mechanic), Paul Davaud (transportation manager), P.A. Chester (general manager), and R.H. Chesshire (manager, Fur Trade Department), June 1939

Hauling supplies from Moose Factory to Rupert House, 1934

Treaty 9 payment at Lansdowne House, Ontario, 1942

Charles N. Stephen of the Hudson's Bay Company with radio equipment at
Lansdowne House, Ontario, 1941–2

Trapper Isaiah Clark giving his order to the Hudson's Bay Company Chief Clerk Joe Keeper at Norway House, 1943. Keeper, one of many Hudson's Bay Company employees of Indian-European descent, was born at Walker Lake in northern Manitoba in 1888 and attended the Brandon residential school. In 1911 he set the Canadian record for running ten miles, which was not broken for twenty-five years. In 1912 he represented Canada at the Stockholm Olympics placing fourth in a field of seventy-five men in the 10,000 metre race. He served with the Royal Winnipeg Rifles, 107th Battalion, and was decorated for bravery at Cambrai in 1917. Between 1930 and 1937 Keeper worked part time at Norway House, becoming a permanent employee in 1938. He served variously as a camp trader, carpenter, and assistant at Island Lake, God's Lake, Sandy Lake, Little Grand Rapids, and Norway House. He died in 1971.

Hudson's Bay Company Norway House Manager Allan Fraser appraising furs brought in by trapper Isaiah Clark in 1943

Inside the Hudson's Bay Company store at Lac La Ronge, autumn 1946

business of considering the recommendations that the governor had made. By 8 February 1935 the committee had prepared a series of notes for Chester to deliver in person that spring. By this time the committee members had lost faith in Parsons because they had discovered that he had a 'tremendous resistance to delegation of any kind.'[21] As long as the commissioner behaved in this way, it made little sense to develop a good headquarters staff.

In this particular instance the Canadian Committee members did not openly question the governor's support of Parsons's program of 'bringing in' the district headquarters, but they held serious reservations about the move none the less. A year earlier they had told the board that they feared Parsons would become too involved in routine administrative details and they believed managers would lose touch with their territories. The subsequent course of events convinced them that their worries had been well founded. On the eve of the Second World War the Canadian Committee sent the Board a memo regarding the reorganization of the western districts (Athabasca, British Columbia, Western Arctic, and Edmonton) which was under way.[22] In this memo they complained that posts usually received only one inspection per year. Even worse, all too often it was done at the most comfortable travelling time for the district manager, the summer, which was the slack operating season. As an added problem, the committee noted that district managers spent about half the year or less inspecting, and they did not know what the managers did with the balance of their time, except, perhaps, engage in endless correspondence and the compilation of innumerable accounting returns. In short, the Canadian Committee complained that the inspections were only audits, not practical operating surveys.[23]

The committee continued to attack Parsons's organizational structure in subsequent correspondence with the board. In 1942 it caustically observed: 'the Department built up a great paper administration. Post managers were compelled to keep elaborate accounts, prepare complicated monthly statements, and write reports and numerous letters. District managers stayed in their offices when they should have been out in the field and tried to administer their district by correspondence. When they did get out, the main objective of their inspections was the preparation of long routine reports for head office which, in the main, were valueless.'[24] The committee went on to say that the heavy demand for paperwork by the commissioner's office turned district managers into accountants and post managers into bookkeepers, setting in motion a downward spiral in operating standards as well as morale.[25] It was the committee's view that 'the trade is entirely in the hands of Post Managers, and five minutes' discussion with a Post Manager at his Post is worth a ton of letters and accounting returns.'[26]

One of the primary reasons for this sustained attack on Parsons was that Canadian Committee members were convinced that the fur trade could be conducted by applying the same 'scientific management' principles they currently were using in the stores division. According to this outlook, every business function was supposed to be divided into its component parts, so that rationally controlled tests could be applied to each of them to determine the most efficient way to carry them out. To develop a properly rationalized, streamlined, and efficient administrative system experts had to be effectively utilized.[27] For this reason Parsons's business philosophy was not acceptable.

The London board members, on the other hand, held a very different view of the matter. They believed that the fur industry was unique and that it required a different managerial approach from other businesses. This clash of outlooks meant that there was a strong difference of opinion between the two groups about how the department should be managed and what kind of men were needed for the job. The Canadian Committee held the view that the commissioner should devote his attention to basic policy matters and leave the day-to-day conduct of the business to highly trained specialists. In contrast, the board, particularly Governor Cooper, favoured having a generalist like Parsons in charge. As early as 5 May 1933 Chester discussed with the London Board the issue of appointing experts to direct subdepartments in the commissioner's office. The new positions proposed included those of assistant fur trade commissioner, controller (there had been a chief accountant since 1925), merchandise manager, transport manager (with an engineering assistant), and supervisor of the raw-fur department (with an assistant who was expected to be experienced in developing country markets and trade).[28] The board acceded to this suggestion, and by 1 May 1938 all these units had been created and an organizational chart (fig. 43) had been drawn up to show how they were interrelated.

The stage was now set for the committee to push Parsons aside.[29] Because he would not delegate authority to his 'experts,' the Canadian Committee began to work around him. When Robert H. Chesshire, a protégé of Chester, was given the job of reorganizing the Mackenzie valley transportation system in 1937, the committee struggled to keep

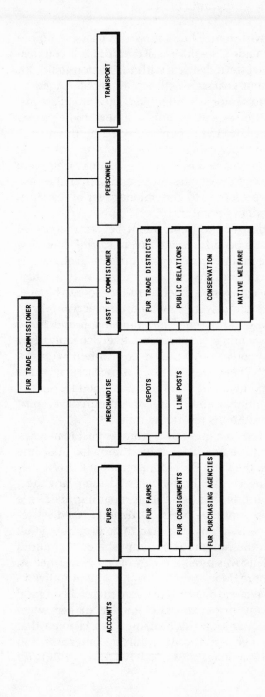

Figure 43
Hudson's Bay Company, Fur Trade Department organization, 1938

Parsons from 'interfering' with him. They found this task even more difficult in 1938 when they made Chesshire assistant fur trade commissioner and manager of the western districts with the responsibility for reorganizing them. The same year a 'strictly confidential' Canadian Committee series of notes on senior personnel indicated that Parsons: 'is not a good administrator or executive, and will have to be retired sooner or later.'[30] Two years later the committee acted on this assessment and forced Parsons to retire. Chester took direct control of the department and Chesshire served as his assistant.[31] In 1942 Chesshire became the general manager of the department, serving in that capacity until 1945 when he was promoted to general manager of the Hudson's Bay Company's Canadian operations.[32]

Even before reorganization of the department began, the critical personnel problems had to be addressed. In 1925 the company launched another major recruitment drive in northern Scotland. At first the company's agents concentrated most of their activity in Aberdeenshire. According to the company's chief recruiter, George Binney, most of the men who were hired were low-paid farm servants who had left school at the age of fourteen. The company found these men attractive because they could be engaged relatively cheaply, they accepted slow rates of promotion, and they were content with the lonely life of the service.[33] There were serious drawbacks to these recruits, however. Binney pointed out that these Scotsmen lacked the 'quick intellect and the potential ability and the progressive spirit required to meet today's conditions in the fur trade.'[34]

Indeed, the company expected a great deal from its post managers. Parsons noted: 'Besides requiring to have a good knowledge of furs and general merchandising, the ideal Post Manager must know something of accounts, extending credit, the natives and their language, carpentry, engineering, painting, boat or canoe repairing, medicine and first aid, and, at certain southern posts, gardening. Needless-to-say, it is almost impossible to train any one man to be proficient in all these, but the list indicates the numerous accomplishments required of a man at a Fur Post.'[35] This was a tall enough order. Nevertheless, the company demanded more. Managers had to be willing to live in relative isolation, and they were expected to impose their will on local natives. Repeatedly company inspectors said good managers were those whose 'word was law' among the Indians. They claimed that natives liked and respected men of authority. While the latter assertion is doubtful, obviously native managers would have found it difficult to rule over their client relatives given that their traditional society was egalitarian in nature.

Considering these requirements and the limitations of the Scottish farm hands, beginning in the spring of 1927, Binney cast his net more widely, and he sought apprentices from all areas of England and Scotland. He was particularly interested in English and Scottish elementary and secondary school boys. By 1929 55 per cent of all new apprentices came from various areas of Scotland and 45 per cent from England. In 1930 the figure had been 60 per cent and 40 per cent, respectively.[36]   *immigration restrictions*

The depression disrupted the company's recruitment program. As the unemployment rate soared, the Canadian government passed immigration restrictions. This action caused concern to board members, given their traditional preference for Scottish men over Canadians. Furthermore, they wanted to have the same freedom as they'd had in the past to transfer men from London headquarters to Canada whenever it served their interests to do so. For these reasons, the board intended to petition the Canadian government to have the company exempted from the immigration regulations. The Canadian Committee disapproved. Its members believed that it was politically unwise to do so, given the economic circumstances. To make their point Chester informed the board in 1933 that an advertisement the company had recently placed in Winnipeg newspapers announcing twenty vacancies for fur trade apprentices had generated 823 applications.[37] He added that in view of these circumstances the Canadian Committee believed strongly that any attempt to recruit men in the United Kingdom would adversely affect the company's image in Canada.[38] Apart from this consideration the committee contended that Canadians could make satisfactory recruits.

On 5 May 1933 the board unanimously concurred with the committee and agreed not to recruit in the United Kingdom for the time being.[39] But, board members stated that as soon as prosperity returned, they expected that Canadian apprentices would leave the company's service for higher-paying jobs in the cities. In view of this probability they ruled: 'whilst agreeing with the Canadian Committee's recommendation, [we] decided that we should proceed with steps already initiated ... to secure the right to send Apprentices from the United Kingdom to Canada and to interchange members of the existing staff, so that, when conditions improved in Canada, the Company could resume its former policy of appointing Apprentices from the highlands of Scotland.'[40] For this reason the governor closed the discussion by stressing the need, in the meantime, to avoid appointing too large a portion of Canadians to the staff. As the staff rejuvenation program went forward, nearly all native managers were 'weeded out.'

Training the new recruits was another serious staff problem the company struggled with, largely unsuccessfully, between 1926 and the Second World War. Considering that senior officials regarded many of the post managers of the immediate post – First World War era as being incompetent, assigning new recruits to them for training made no sense. In 1926 the company tried to get around this difficulty by having Fur Trade Commissioner French identify those posts that had managers who were capable of doing the job and had suitable accommodation for one or two trainees. Twenty-one posts were chosen as training stations for apprentices who had been specially selected from among the new recruits.[41] The company promised managers a bonus of $100 for each apprentice they successfully trained. The instruction they offered was supposed to include merchandising, salesmanship and barter, store and post management, accounting, languages, treatment of natives, and fur grading.[42] The commissioner warned managers that apprenticing clerks were not to be regarded merely as regular staff for the work at the post. Rather they were to be treated as supernumerary personnel primarily for training.[43] This was a departure from previous practices. By giving this instruction, Commissioner French hoped that the selected managers would train men much more quickly than had been done in the past.

The 1926 initiative failed for the most part. On 12 May 1928, while he was still manager of the Athabasca-Mackenzie District, Parsons noted that the demands of the business meant that apprentices often had to be transferred from post to post before their training was completed. The training bonus system was unworkable under these circumstances. Even more serious, many of the apprentices that recruiters selected for special training turned out to be not as good on the job as those who were passed over. For this reason Parsons concluded men should not be chosen for special instruction until they had proved themselves under actual working conditions.[44]

In the summer of 1927 the company tried a new approach. While its ship, the *Bayrupert*, sailed from Ardrossan to Montreal, Binney drew up a syllabus and conducted a daily training program for the raw apprentices. Once the trainees had finished their course of instruction, he expected them to write a 1,000-word essay discussing the qualities they had to develop to become a successful fur trader. The best essayist received a prize.[45] The board members were impressed with Binney's efforts, and they thought that his program would be of 'extraordinary value to the apprentices.'[46] However, it was too short to be effective.

In January of 1937 the fur trade commissioner's office devised yet another training scheme in the hopes of dealing with persistent staff problems. The new scheme handled twelve trainees at a time over a three-month period in Winnipeg. Instruction time was allocated as follows: 45 per cent for fur pricing and grading, 26 per cent for merchandising, 13 per cent for accounting, 10 per cent for native welfare and history, and 6 per cent for questionnaires and exams. Douglas McKay taught the history component. He had just published the popular, and to this day still widely cited book, *The Honourable Company*.[47] Company officials intended that McKay's history lessons would forcibly portray the great traditions of the company and imbue a sense of institutional loyalty.[48]   *marriages*

Keeping good men in the service was increasingly difficult. Senior officials knew that they had to do everything they could to make it easy for post managers to marry. This meant providing adequate salaries and suitable housing for married couples. Whenever possible, an effort also had to be made to ensure that managers with older children received postings where education was available.[49] Chester underscored the importance of having married managers when he wrote: 'the presence and influence of a manager's wife, if she is the right type, is a powerful factor in helping them through the early years while they are accommodating themselves to the new, strange and lonely life.'[50] He added that a good domestic life improved the diet and health of the managers.

But although the company was eager to have its post managers take wives, it no longer wanted them to marry native women. Accordingly, in 1940 the Canadian Committee passed a resolution prohibiting such marriages, but they 'decided it was not advisable to announce this policy or include it in our written personnel policies.' Instead, when necessary men were to be warned that they would be fired if they entered into such marriages.[51] In effect, this move resurrected a long-abandoned eighteenth-century company policy.

Besides improving the lot of the post managers, some senior officials believed that it was time to put 'snap' back into the organization by reviving other defunct traditions. Movement in this direction began in 1927 when the board reintroduced the titles of chief factor and chief trader. The following March the company recommenced issuing commissions to chief factors.[52] New rules and regulations were drafted. These codes specified that officers were to maintain discipline but also treat their men with respect and as potential future officers. Uniforms were brought back, and in 1929 managers were cautioned that 'caps, badges, etc. should never be ridiculed, but looked on as one of the very best encouraging features of our whole organization.'[53]

In 1936 Mr M.A. Lubbock, who was in charge of merchandising in the Winnipeg depot, accompanied Commissioner Parsons on an inspection tour of the Mackenzie District. This trip led Lubbock to conclude that the company had to recreate a real pride in the company, 'not merely a sentimental appreciation of its greatness' and an active desire among the officers to maintain its traditions, customs, and outward show. To accomplish this, he thought, 'Flags and signs should be new, flag poles painted white; post grounds should be kept in perfect order; Company customs should be vigorously maintained; post managers and apprentices should wear their caps, and there should be a greater discipline as between ranks. No one expects a man to be too well dressed, but he should certainly be more neatly turned out when the District Manager or Fur Trade Commissioner is inspecting his post than at other times.'[54]

To give good men a reasonable prospect for advancement the company tried to place new recruits at posts where they could obtain the greatest all-round experience in the shortest time feasible. When possible, those who showed the greatest potential were moved at least every two years. Similarly, post managers were to be moved regularly to broaden their experience.[55] Henceforth, men were supposed to be evaluated for promotion on a regular basis. In the 1930s the commissioner's office began drafting a complex series of personnel rating sheets which included forty-two different criteria grouped into the following six categories: personality, physique, mental equipment, technical ability, knowledge, and dealings with natives. The commissioner intended to use a five-point rating scale for each item. I have reproduced the last section of the evaluation form in table 20.

In devising this evaluation procedure the commissioner's office staff believed they were applying current 'scientific management' techniques. The London board sent copies of the rating sheets and various memos regarding personnel management proposals to Mr G.H. Miles of the National Institute of Industrial Psychology in London and asked him for comments. Previously the board had retained the services of

TABLE 20
Hudson's Bay Company's proposed post manager evaluation form
(portion dealing with management of native customers)

ATTITUDE

Contemptuous	Indifferent	Average	Good	Excellent

HANDLING

Doesn't	Crude	Average	Good	Excellent

NATIVE CRITICISM

Very adverse	Some	None	Respected	Highly respected

LANGUAGE (native)

None	Little	Medium	Good	Excellent

SOURCE: HBCA PAM SD A 102 Box 86

Miles's organization to help them deal with problems in the London warehouse which had arisen because of staff-cutting measures implemented during the early years of the depression. Miles did not think much of the tentative scheme. He believed that it relied too much on textbook information and did not give enough consideration to the underlying principles or to the practical needs of the company.[56] Miles thought that it would make better sense to select a few key posts for an intensive job analysis which could serve as a basis for drawing up a more appropriate set of ratings scales, tests, and personnel records which would yield beneficial results to the company.

By the outbreak of the Second World War the company had made little headway in resolving its post-management personnel problems in spite of this series of initiatives. On 6 October 1938 the Canadian Committee members sent a memo to the London board stating that the most pressing problem in the Fur Trade Department remained post administration. They observed that most of the company's district managers were unsuitable and were not the type of men required for the job. Making matters worse, the company did not have men trained, or even partially trained, to help correct this state of affairs.[57]

transportation As in earlier years the Hudson's Bay Company continued to operate a sprawling transportation system (fig. 44). Beating the competition, keeping the equipment up to date, and taking full advantage of the expanded services offered by common carriers was a never-ending challenge. Two of the most important transportation developments that took place in the interwar years were the completion of railway lines to James Bay (in 1932) and to Churchill (in 1929) and the establishment of commercial air service beginning in the 1920s. As early as 1901 the company anticipated the building of the James Bay railway, and Chipman began making plans to take advantage of this eventuality. He was particularly interested in the prospect of eliminating Moose Factory as a port of entry and doing away with its costly shipbuilding and repair facility.[58] As soon as the line was finished the company began to dispatch outfits by rail from the south, redistributing them from the railhead by ship. The company dismantled the 'Moose Works' and the Moose Factory – Moosonee area became the 'end of steel,' as it is known today, rather than the major gateway it had been. The community of Moose Factory went into protracted economic decline as a result. Farther west the completion of the railway to Churchill cut through the heart of the northern Keewatin District which had been a remote district previously. Competitors moved forward with the railhead and the whole district was overrun by them by 1930.

The rapid development of bush plane service immediately after the First World War had an even more revolutionary impact because it opened the whole of the north to competitors. As soon as the First World War ended, retired military pilots approached the company and offered to provide their services. Although the board refused their initial overtures, none the less, members watched developments closely and they were eager to experiment with this new form of transportation. The earliest uses of airplanes that captivated the board's interest were the Canadian government's air photo survey of James Bay undertaken in the summer of 1920 and the Imperial Oil Company's purchase of aircraft that same year for use between Edmonton, Fort McMurray, and Fort Norman. It drew these developments to the attention of the Canadian Committee and asked if the company also could put airplanes to good use. The committee replied that it had already discussed the subject with Fur Trade Commissioner Brabant. The conservative-minded Brabant in turn said that he did not think that an air service

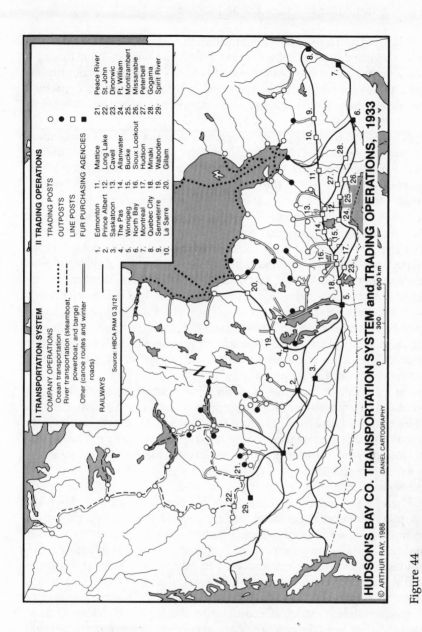

Figure 44

Hudson's Bay Company transportation system and trading operations, 1933

would be of much use to his department. But, given the board's interest in the matter, the committee again raised the subject with Brabant. Once more he said no.[59] At the time Brabant's attitude was not unreasonable. It was very costly to ship freight by air, and cargo capacities were extremely limited on most aircraft. Furthermore, winter flying was nearly impossible.[60]

In spite of these negative reactions in Canada, board members remained enthusiastic about the possibility. They continued to forward to the committee a series of articles on the progress of air service in northern Canada which they collected from newspapers and magazines. Of particular interest, the forestry service's use of airplanes for reconnaissance in northern Quebec and Ontario in the early 1920s demonstrated to them, and to the Canadian Advisory Committee, that airplanes could be very helpful to management by making rapid inspections possible. However, before permitting their employees to use commercial air service for company business, the directors had to settle the question of public liability. This issue had arisen as a result of workmen's compensation legislation passed in Quebec in 1928. In June of that year the company's legal advisers determined that use of air service did not put the company at greater risk. With this matter cleared up, the fur trade commissioner authorized employee air travel for company business after 26 July 1928.[61]

On 12 August 1929 the Hudson's Bay Company made the first recorded use of airplanes for shipping purposes when it sent 1,000 lbs of merchandise to Trout Lake and took out $55,000 worth of furs.[62] By this time bush planes were being used extensively in the north. By August of 1927 Western Canada Airways alone had already carried 1,000 passengers and 100 tons of freight and had flown over 100,000 miles since 1917.[63]

There were several reasons why the company moved slowly in adopting air service. Senior managers were fully aware that this new technological advance greatly accelerated the rate of movement of fur and merchandise inventories. Such a time saving minimized the risk of losses on falling fur markets, and it reduced the amount of capital tied up in stock at trading establishments. But, there were disadvantages. In 1934 these were fully discussed by W.E. Brown, manager of the Nelson River District, at a conference of company district managers held in Winnipeg. The commissioner asked him to present a paper that addressed the advantages and shortcomings of using commercial air service to replace canoes (many of which were now powered by gasoline engines) to supply the more remote posts.[64] In favour of bush planes, Brown noted that whenever there was little snowfall in winter, water levels were low the following summer, thus increasing the number of portages that had to be made. This made the work much more difficult, time consuming, and costly. Whenever natives has successful winter hunts, they did not want to engage in the strenuous transportation work during the following summer. Bush planes would eliminate these difficulties and accelerate capital turnover.

On the negative side, Brown noted that the use of air services would eliminate important summer employment opportunities for natives and increase their need for summer credit as a consequence. Furthermore, payments made to air service companies would be funnelled outside the local economy, thereby curtailing the purchasing power of native residents. After weighing these various issues Brown recommended that bush planes be employed only in northern Ontario, Manitoba, and Saskatchewan, where opponents already used them on a large scale. In the end company officials had to adopt these services more widely than Brown had recommended in order to compete with their rivals, who showed less concern than them about the resulting negative economic impact on the Indians.

When they made this decision, company officials also determined that because of the very high rate of depreciation on equipment they would not develop a company-owned air-freighting service. Also, the company lacked the technical expertise that was needed to operate such a facility. For these reasons it made better business sense to employ charter services.[65] On the other hand, for inspection purposes the purchase of a company aircraft seemed like a good idea. Such a plane could also be used for experimental purposes to test various possible transportation arrangements. Accordingly, in May of 1930 the search for an appropriate airplane began when the board wrote to the Ford Motor Company about its tri-motor aircraft which they had read about in an article in *National Geographic* in June 1930.[66] However, the company took no further action. It was not until 21 April 1937 that the Canadian Committee approved the expenditure of $50,000 to buy a plane. The board reconfirmed the decision on 10 May 1937.[67] In 1939 the company finally purchased a twin-engine Beechcraft and took delivery in Winnipeg at the end of March.[68]

Besides bush planes, the company used many 'winter roads' to link remote districts to railway lines or to ports of entry. Since the late nineteenth century company men had hauled cargo over these roads using horse-drawn sleighs. Immediately after the First World War, however, the Hudson's Bay Company began to experiment with 'motor sleighs' and tractors pulling large sleds. In this instance the company adopted a new technology very rapidly. It tested Bombardier's 'motor sleighs' almost as soon as they were invented. For instance, these forerunners of the snowmobile were employed on the inland route from Rupert House in the winter of 1922–3.[69] The initial trials were successful.

riverboats

By contrast, the company showed little initiative in the operation of its riverboat service in the Athabasca-Mackenzie area. Following its take-over of the Alberta and Arctic Transportation Company, the Hudson's Bay Company did little to upgrade the facility. Largely this was because the depression forced the company to delay making any major investments in equipment before Chesshire was given the job of reorganizing the system in 1937. By then most of the craft and shore facilities were outdated; extensive repairs and replacements were urgently needed. Accordingly, between 1937 and 1942 the company spent $500,000 for these purposes. In 1942 the Canadian Committee estimated that an equivalent expenditure was still needed to finish the modernization.[70]

communication system

In order to tighten management controls over the sprawling Fur Trade Department the Canadian Committee needed a good communications system. When reflecting on this problem in 1942 it observed: 'The Fur Trade Department is not a particularly large or complex operation but it has one outstanding feature, which distinguishes it from most businesses, in that it covers a territory almost as large as the United States, much of which lies in remote and isolated areas of northern Canada. This feature has been one root of the problems associated with every phase of the organization.'[71] The construction of telegraph lines in the late nineteenth and early twentieth centuries expedited communication only in the more southerly fringes of the company's fur trade domain. Elsewhere, information continued to move mostly by traditional methods until the end of the First World War. Many outposts remained out of communication with district headquarters during the closed water season. As we have seen, this meant that the managers of these isolated stations operated without direction or supervision for much of the year, and they had to buy furs without current market information. The highly volatile fur markets of the First World War period, especially the market collapse of 1920–1, made company directors acutely aware of the potential liability post isolation represented.

This concern made the prospect of using radio to break down the communications barriers very attractive to the Canadian Committee and to the board. Both were eager to experiment with the new equipment. In 1919 the deputy chairman of the Canadian Committee met in Montreal with the vice-president of the Marconi Wireless Telegraph Company of Canada. They discussed using wireless equipment to connect the mainline of the National Transcontinental Railway with James Bay, the Nelson River District, Norway House, The Pas, Fort McMurray, and to seven stations in the Mackenzie River District. Subsequently the Marconi company submitted a bid for the installation of the service. Once again it was the conservative Brabant who cast doubt on the proposal.[72]

None the less, the company moved forward. The first radio was installed at Norway House during the winter of 1921–2. Initially messages were broadcast using the *Free Press* station in Winnipeg. Much to the company's surprise and horror these announcements were picked up nearly 1,000 miles away in Windsor, Ontario.[73] To deal with the problem of maintaining the confidentiality of its broadcasts the company, in a manner similar to its competitors, transmitted fur prices in a special code. The earliest surviving one, that of 5 October 1922 is shown in table 21. They encoded other information using *Slater's Telegraphic Code Book* – one of the standards of the day.[74]

In these early days of radio the posts could not send messages. This meant that the Winnipeg headquarters had no way of immediately finding out whether or not their dispatches had been received. Eventually, of course, most of these initial problems were overcome, and by the outbreak of the Second World War some radio service was available even in the most remote districts. *merchandising*

According to the internal studies undertaken by senior officers and the Canadian Committee, one sphere of business where the Hudson's Bay Company remained surprisingly weak was that of merchandising. It had become non-competitive in this activity in most areas of the north by the 1920s, and it had not kept pace with native and white trapper's demands for new goods. Company officials blamed these problems partly on the conservative marketing attitudes of district and post managers. Most of these men were content to rely on the sales of the traditional quality items the company had built its reputation upon rather than take the initiative and introduce new products.[75] For example, in 1934 J. Bartleman, manager of the Athabasca-Mackenzie District, noted that for most of the nineteenth century the trade of his district consisted of few articles other than fowling pieces, powder and shot,

TABLE 21
Hudson's Bay Company telegraphic code for furs,
5 October 1922

Fur species		Code name
Bear:	black	Apples
	brown	Apricots
	white	Barley
Beaver		Carrots
Ermine		Corn
Fisher		Flax
Fox:	silver	Flour
	cross	Hay
	red	Hemp
	white	Oats
	blue	Onion
Lynx		Peaches
Marten		Pears
Mink		Plums
Musquash		Rice
Otter		Rye
Sable		Sugar
Skunk		Tea
Wolf:	timber	Tomatoes
	prairie	Turnips
Wolverine		Wheat

SOURCE: SD HBCA PAM A 102/Box 214

kettles, axes, nails, a few blankets, and a small assortment of woollen and linen piece goods. This situation began to change in the early 1880s when an independent trader named Elmore travelled down the Mackenzie River and began selling flour. The innovation irritated Chief Factor Gaudet, who then was in charge of Fort Simpson, and he believed it would lead to the decline of the local fur trade. According to Bartleman, other opponents were not as cautious as Gaudet and his fellow officers, and they quickly followed Elmore's lead. By the turn of the century flour had become a major trade item, and the company's slow response to this development gave their rivals a chance to establish themselves.

Bartleman's story simply highlighted an aspect of a more general trend. Sharply rising fur prices between the 1890s and 1920 heightened

the consumer demand of white and native trappers alike, while the ⌐
expansion of railway service during this era made it easier for traders
and travelling merchants to respond to this development. Flour was
only one of the exotic foods to become a staple. By 1910 canned foods
were commonplace among whites at the major trading posts served
by railways, steamboats, or ocean vessels, and they were beginning to
trickle in to the outposts where transportation was still a limiting
factor.[76] Although native people still wore some traditional clothing,
cotton and woollen garments had become the standard dress throughout the north by the eve of the First World War. Being lighter in weight,
these articles were relatively easy to ship to even the most remote
locations.[77] The old muzzle-loaders were still in widespread use, but
rifles were replacing them rapidly.[78] In northern Ontario by 1910 locally
manufactured birch-bark canoes were just beginning to be replaced by
imported freighter canoes. The outboard motor, ('the kicker') had not
yet made its appearance, but it became a standard accessory of hunters
and trappers shortly after the First World War.[79] So, it is clear that at
the turn of the century the pace of material culture change accelerated
rapidly in the north, and those traders who did not keep abreast of
developments were bound to lose customers to opponents who did.⌐

At the 1934 Fur Trade Department district managers' conference
Bartleman presented a paper in which he highlighted these other
retailing problems and suggested solutions. He argued that merchandise displays at line posts and 'Indian posts' were very backward. He
stated that in the past the company's posts were more like depots
where people got only what they asked for. To keep pace with new
developments, however, he stated that it was necessary to make them
places of interest where goods were properly displayed and prices
clearly marked.[80] Echoing some of the complaints and suggestions that
Inspectors Hardisty and Beeston had made over forty years earlier,
Bartleman stated that district and post managers did not keep up with
retail trends because they ordered most of their goods from catalogues
and company lists. He thought district managers needed to select their
goods first hand at the depots, where they could be apprised of retail
trends.

Besides often being unwilling to take the lead in introducing new
lines of merchandise, an added problem for the company in the Canadian Committee's view was that the post managers paid little regard
to the prices of their goods, since they were convinced that Indians
still were willing to pay premium prices for quality.[81] But, as small

merchants and 'free traders' overran the north in this century, and catalogue selling became more widespread following the introduction of mail service, Indian attitudes began to change, and the company lost business as a result.[82]

In order to regain its market share, the Canadian Committee believed that the company had to become competitive in its prices. Its attitude on this matter has to be understood in the context of the business they knew best – retailing. Following the collapse of markets in 1920, North American retailers were committed to discounting prices to maximize stock turnover while streamlining their purchasing operations. Under the leadership of the Canadian Committee the Hudson's Bay Company stores division followed suit.[83] Given their commitment to low-price selling in the retail division of the company, it is not surprising that the committee found fault with the Fur Trade Department's tradition of adding substantial mark-ups to the prime cost of merchandise to cover overhead and operating costs. In his 1934 paper Bartleman reiterated these concerns of the committee when he noted that stock-turn remained a problem, because managers did not make much of an effort to clear away stale items. He cited the example of men's suits, claiming that the company had not sold any in the north for some time because the stocks were old, out of style, made of the wrong materials, and crumpled from being folded up on the shelves for too long. However, Bartleman did note that the post managers were not entirely responsible for this difficulty; rather, the company's pricing policies were partly to blame, because it applied average mark-ups for whole inventories instead of using different ones for the various lines of merchandise. He recommended 75–100 per cent advances over cost-landed prices for fancy, dry, and hardware goods and 50 per cent for groceries. To clear dead stock, Bartleman proposed discounts of 10 per cent over cost. He wanted these 'bargains' placed up front in the stores on sales tables clearly marked with labels in English and in Cree syllabics where necessary.[84]

Merchandising problems were even more complex than the Canadian Committee or Bartleman indicated. Part of the difficulty related to the fact that there were, in fact, two different types of trade, which required separate approaches. This fact was made very clear in the presentations made by James Bay District Manager James W. Anderson and Saskatchewan District Manager R.A. Talbot. Anderson discussed the operation of line posts in frontier districts and contrasted it with traditional fur trading. He observed:

in many ways the methods adopted in catering to the native trade are directly at variance with the general business practice at line posts. White people coming to your store are treated as customers only and you use any and every available means to sell to them your merchandise. All you are concerned with is making a sale and securing the cash. With natives, however, the situation is entirely different, for while they are undoubtedly your customers you are also to some extent their boss, their guide, their friend and counsellor.[85]

Anderson observed that when acting in these latter capacities a good trader sometimes had to discourage Indians from making purchases.

Talbot made many of the same points that Anderson did, but he provided some additional insights. He noted that in the traditional trade socializing was a very important component of all transactions. For those men who were in charge of inland operations he stressed that it was important to remember: 'it is a very common practice for an Indian to come in to the post quite early in the day and when asked if he requires anything, he will simply answer in the negative. Some of our men in the past would be inclined to turn this man out, or have shut up the store, but after having lolled around the establishment for several hours, the native decides to make his wants known. This peculiarity has to be catered to by a successful trader.' Talbot continued: 'our establishments especially are looked upon as the local club or general meeting place for the natives, and we cannot afford to turn them away, and for that reason they must be made attractive as such and the idea fostered amongst the natives that they are the most important place in each settlement.'[86] Talbot emphasized that line posts were very different in this respect. White and native customers who visited these establishments conducted their affairs with dispatch.

To hold the trade of the more traditional Indian clients clearly it was not enough merely to be competitive in prices and up to date in terms of inventories. But, it also has to be pointed out that, even though Anderson and Talbot stressed the need to conduct line post and 'Indian post' affairs differently, these two men and the other managers were aware that line post trading was the way of the future, because 'free-traders' overran more of the country with each advance in transportation service. These troublesome intruders spread a 'source of dissatisfaction' among natives towards the company by creating sharp price differentials.[87]

The manner in which the company handled the distribution of its outfits also caused difficulties. The supply depots in Montreal, Winni-

TABLE 22
Fur Trade Department analysis of basic stock items, 1936

Category	Line posts	Mackenzie inland posts	Saskatche- wan posts	Western Arctic posts	Eastern Arctic posts
	Number of basic stock items in each category	Items similar to those required at line posts			

Category	Line posts	#	%	#	%	#	%	#	%
Yard goods	44	28	64	21	48	30	68	22	50
Smallwares	47	37	79	25	53	27	57	17	36
Drug sundries	57	29	51	18	32	12	21	10	18
Jewellery	17	16	94	15	88	15	88	15	88
Women's wear	29	16	55	29	100	15	52	12	41
Men's wear	56	48	86	42	75	47	84	37	66
Footwear	10	4	40	4	40	5	50	–	–
Hardware	122	114	93	85	70	92	75	79	65
Groceries	220	166	76	139	63	139	63	116	53
Total/average	602	458	76	378	63	382	64	308	51

SOURCE: 'Fur Trade Conference,' SD HBCA PAM A 102/Box 86

peg, and Edmonton were expected to make profits. Accordingly, they applied a surcharge of between 2.5 and 12 per cent to their prime costs when supplying the posts. In turn, post managers tried to fix their gross margins on merchandise at rates that enabled them to absorb all operating expenses and make a net gain. These series of advances meant that the company's trading tariffs wiped out all the potential competitive advantages the company should have derived from bulk purchasing. In other words, a problem Graham had identified in 1870 remained unresolved. For this reason Indian and white trappers obtained a disproportionate share of their groceries and staples from the Hudson's Bay Company, while they bought the newer lines of dry goods and hardware mostly from the company's rivals. This left the company with a relatively unprofitable retail trade.

In the late 1930s the committee and the commissioner's office made a concerted effort to address these difficulties systematically. They drew up basic stock plans for typical 'line post' and 'inland' operations. These are summarized in table 22.[88] Also, they consolidated purchasing activities, and the Fur Trade Department began to take advantage of the retail-buying offices of the company. The committee changed the operating policy for the depots by designating them as purely service units to be operated on a cost recovery basis rather than as units intended to make a profit.

In 1942 the Canadian Committee claimed that these various changes enabled the Hudson's Bay Company to provide a much better assortment of goods at competitive prices. Although the gross profit margins for items was lower, averaging only 33 per cent for remote posts between 1934 and 1941, this loss was more than offset by increased volume and an improvement in the ratio of dry goods and hardware sales to groceries.[89] For instance, in the western districts the company lowered the gross profit margin on merchandise by an average of 1 per cent between outfits 269 and 271, but the gross income from sales increased 36 per cent or $176,000.[90]

By the late 1930s it became clear to both the London board and the Canadian Committee that the Fur Trade Department was still in serious trouble in spite of their best efforts to turn it around. As we have seen, competitors were gaining an ever larger share of the business. The two groups fundamentally disagreed about who was responsible and how to solve this problem. The Canadian Committee wanted complete authority to conduct the affairs of the department. Among other concerns, it wanted to replace Parsons as head. The board, on the other hand, took the position that the fur trade was an international enterprise which was best managed from London. Furthermore, Governor Cooper remained a strong supporter of Parsons. In 1937 the board created a subcommittee of board and Canadian Committee members in an effort to resolve their differences.

On 7 December 1937 this group met. On this occasion the board representatives yielded on the two key issues by acknowledging that their policy 'had been wrong' and 'that there had been neither direction nor co-ordination in London.'[91] Representatives of the two groups unanimously agreed that an effort should be made to retain Parsons in the service in some capacity, while they recognized that in the end his dismissal might be necessary. Subsequently the Canadian Committee and the board ratified these decisions.

Despite this effort to come to an understanding, clashes between the two over basic issues continued unabated. They came to a head in 1942. On 18 February the board sent an eighteen-page memo to the Canadian Committee raising seventy-one different issues. In nearly every instance the board questioned previous conclusions and recommendations that the committee had made.[92] Not surprisingly, the Canadian Committee took exception to this letter. In March it mailed its annual report for the year ending 31 January 1942 and included within it a twenty-one-page (single-spaced) report that focused on the shortcomings of administration and policy that had affected every aspect of fur-trading operations since the turn of the century. It was, in effect, an extended attack on the London board.[93] The committee took the basic position that by the early 1930s 'the Department had entered upon the last stages of deterioration and, while the existing momentum was sufficient to keep it going for some time, the end, failing a complete transformation of policies and direction, was inevitable.'[94] In other words, the mess had been created before the Canadian Committee had assumed any significant responsibilities. When it did take a more active part, the depression and the war made it very difficult to make headway. Of course, the board rejected this view.

While we might be tempted to ascribe the bickering merely to efforts by the two groups to shirk responsibility for serious problems, or to see the wrangling merely in nationalistic terms, it appears that the root of the problem was one of competing philosophies of management. The London board still placed a high value on tradition, and it was more sympathetic to the old view that the fur trade was very different from most other lines of business. So, it took a generally conservative stance with regard to the introduction of new business practices (but not new technologies), and it continued to believe that its managers should be moulded in the course of service. The Canadian Committee, on the other hand, was more disposed to handle the affairs of the fur trade department as it did the retail stores by sacrificing company traditions for the latest business practices.[95] It was strongly committed to employing highly trained experts educated outside the fur trade to oversee the affairs of the department. Reflecting on their differences, the board pointed out to the committee: 'there is a possibility, in our long-established Company, that many problems are not in fact entirely so new as at first sight they may appear to those who have ignored past experience. In other words, experience is apt to be re-bought more than once and, while a new managerial generation may avoid the most glaring mistakes of its immediate predecessors, it may repeat some of the mistakes of the last generation but one.'[96]

8

The native people, the Hudson's Bay Company, and the state in the industrial fur trade, 1920–1945

It is true that the natives are our assets, that we must keep them alive for future profits even though we carry them at a loss till such time shall come. On occasions we have taken large profits out of the posts.
(George Ray, Moose Factory, 1924)

In the mercantile and early industrial fur trades the native people produced nearly all the furs. For this reason the Hudson's Bay Company depended on them for its survival. In turn, throughout much of the nineteenth century the company provided most of the native producers with the hunting and trapping equipment they needed in both prosperous and lean times. In the industrial age this mutually beneficial partnership was strained to the breaking point for many reasons. The years between the two great wars was a time when natives faced increasing hardships because of depletion of fur and game animals and the structural changes that had been taking place in the economy of northern Canada since Confederation. Until the great waves of immigration took place in the late nineteenth and early twentieth centuries, native workers were essential for northern development projects. Before the First World War few white trappers competed with Indians except in the most accessible areas. Thereafter these newcomers became more active, drawn in first by the lure of handsome profits during the war and the boom years of the 1920s. Later, others came out of necessity during the depression. While these new competitors remained mostly in the 'frontier districts' astride the railways, the widespread use of bush planes by the early 1930s meant that white trappers invaded virtually all areas. Their increasing presence at this time exacerbated the difficulties native people experienced as a consequence of the great depression. Meanwhile the reorganization and modernization of the Hudson's Bay Company's fur-trading operations reduced the range of employment that the firm offered to natives.

As their range of alternative opportunities diminished in the 1920s and 1930s, many native groups were forced to become more dependent on commercial trapping than they had been for many years. But, at the same time, they were losing control over fur resources as the federal and provincial governments introduced more comprehensive conservation programs to address the problem of fur and game animal population depletion. Even though these programs were well intended, too often they were implemented with little regard to the circumstances of local native groups. Severe economic hardships often were the end result.

The growing dependence of the native people on imported goods in this century added to their problems. As we have seen, in 1870 a native hunter with a family could equip himself for about $20–$25 dollars per year – about the equivalent of his family's annuity income. Although the purchasing power of $25 of annuity money had risen to $36 by 1900, it dropped sharply thereafter until it was worth only about $10 in 1920 (fig. 45). With the strong deflation that marked the early years of the depression it temporarily increased to $23 in 1931 before declining once again to $15 in 1945. So, over the years inflation seriously eroded the value of the Indians' annuity income.

Meanwhile, the overhead cost of hunting and trapping increased as a greater array of equipment and supplies were needed. By the early 1950s the figure for an autumn outfit had risen to about $96. Gasoline and kerosene alone accounted for over 50 per cent ($49.65) of this amount.[1] Besides these expendable supplies, the capital requirements of a hunter had increased substantially in the early years of this century. By 1940 they amounted to roughly $560 (largely amortized over a ten-year period) for a family head and included a number of items that would not have been needed in the nineteenth century, such as a canvas or freight canoe, an outboard motor, a rifle and a shotgun (in place of a muzzle-loader), and a sewing machine.[2] Additionally, monthly food costs for a family of six had risen to approximately $56 by the early 1950s, and their annual clothing expenses totalled about $140. Taking all these costs into account, anthropologist R.W. Dunning calculated that in the early 1950s the members of a native household

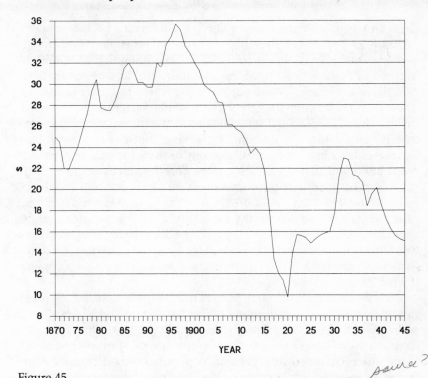

Figure 45
A typical family's annuity, 1870–1945: purchasing power of $25

source?

in northern Ontario needed approximately $1,055.03 per year to sustain themselves.[3]

of assistance

The combined impact of these various developments meant that the incomes native people earned from trapping and other activities too often fell short of their requirements and they had to rely on increasing levels of economic assistance. This dependence aggravated the old tension between the company and the government dating back to the 1870s. Who was responsible for providing this aid outside treaty areas? How was the aid to be delivered inside and outside treaty? Was the assistance adequate? Conflicts also intensified within the company as programs intended to economize and modernize operations worked at cross-purposes with efforts to deliver economic assistance to native producers in traditional ways.

While the general economic trends that were under way between

1920 and 1945 are clear enough, it is very difficult to obtain a precise measure of the impact they had on the native people. The data currently available are only suggestive. Most are found in the voluminous records of the Department of Indian Affairs and in those of the Hudson's Bay Company. The department expected its agents to estimate the amount of income (subsistence and commercial) that Indians collectively earned in the different agencies from various sources. Unfortunately, apparently no documents survive that indicate how these estimates were made. Clearly the quality of some of the agents' calculations are doubtful. For example, in the Fort Resolution statements the same figures were used a number of years in succession suggesting greater stability than undoubtedly was the case.[4] Also, some fluctuations in data resulted from the fact that agency boundaries changed from time to time as the department shifted bands from one jurisdiction to another. If we recognize these limitations, the data do suggest trends which make sense in the light of the structural changes that were taking place.

Probably the most striking picture to emerge is that the aggregate incomes of the agencies examined (Fort Resolution and Isle à la Crosse were excluded because of problems with the data) declined over the fourteen-year period beginning in 1922 (figs 46–8) even though it is generally recognized that the native population had reached a low point by about 1925.[5] The greatest decline in earnings took place in the old Northern Department. Here the total income (expressed in constant dollars) fell by about two-thirds. In Northern Ontario, the decrease was only slightly less severe. Hunting and trapping incomes suffered even more, registering setbacks of 70 to 80 per cent (figs 49 and 50).

What is particularly significant is that the downturn in native hunting incomes in the 1920s took place at a time when the overall economy and the fur industry was strong. Figure 51 shows that while the hunting and trapping incomes of all the agencies combined in 1926 and 1927 were less than 50 per cent of that in 1922, the aggregate value of Canadian wild-fur production (a function of price and volume)[6] exceeded the 1922 figure. In other words, it seems that the Indians of northern portions of the provinces of Alberta, Saskatchewan, Manitoba, and Ontario did not benefit from the price inflation of the 1920s. They also suffered more from the depression.

The likely reason why Indians did so comparatively poorly during the 1920s was that growing numbers of whites were displacing them from their lands, while fur prices were high. For example, in 1926 Dr

buying power?

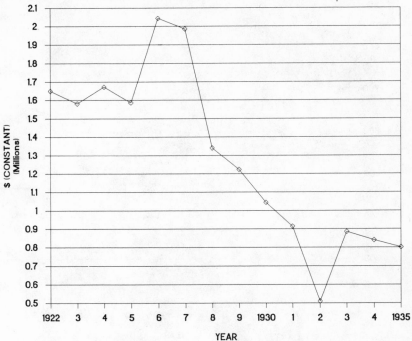

Figure 46
Native income from all sources, 1922–35: woodlands of old Northern and
Southern departments

white trappers

J.J. Wall, who was conducting a medical survey of Indians for the
Department of Indian Affairs along the railway between Cochrane,
Ontario, and La Tuque, Quebec, indicated that white trappers were
using physical force to drive Indians off their traditional trapping
territories. In his account Dr Wall remarked: 'the Indian hunters are
harassed by white trappers who encroach on their traditional hunting
grounds, and in some cases order them to leave. Some of these white
trappers have even gone to the length of poisoning the Indians' dogs,
and each year it becomes harder for the Indians to obtain a living. If
steps are not taken to protect these people, who are now self-support-
ing, they will soon be largely dependent on government bounty.'[7] Wall
added that this was a widespread problem. He stated Indians proposed
to solve the problem by having the Department of Indian Affairs assign

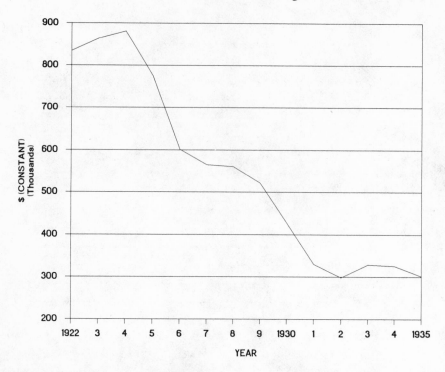

Figure 47
Native income from all sources, 1922–35: northern Alberta, Saskatchewan, and Manitoba

each hunter sole rights to trap eight-square-mile tracts of land. Wall thought this was a reasonable proposal, considering that 'the white trapper ... in contrast to the Indian, has other means of sustenance, such as lumbering, mining and agriculture.'[8] No doubt the trapline registration programs introduced in British Columbia and in the United States were inspirations for this suggestion.

Because whites also turned to hunting and trapping in large numbers during the low points in the business cycle, the Indians failed to regain their position to any significant degree once the depression struck. As we have seen, high unemployment in the cities in 1921 drove many workers into the bush. Of course many of them knew nothing about bush life. To survive they teamed up with experienced trappers.[9] An Edmonton reporter writing about this development for the *Fur Trade*

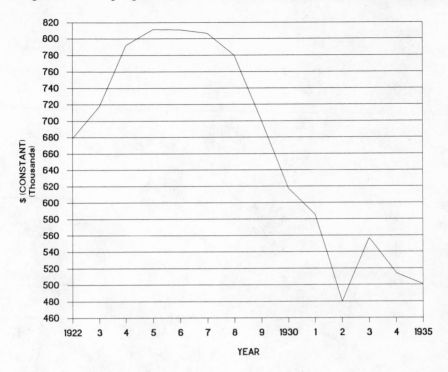

Figure 48
Native income from all sources, 1922–35: northern Ontario

Review in the summer of 1922 stated: 'a feature of the season's operations out of Edmonton has been the fact that more white trappers have
gone into the North than in the previous year. They have not yet
reached the Eskimo country, but they are pushing the Indians back
and have produced a considerable part of the pack in the nearer
Mackenzie region.'[10] The same pattern was repeated in the early
1930s.[11]   *Indian relief*

As the native economic situation deteriorated, government expenditures for relief, medical assistance, and education increased until the
onset of the depression, when they were reduced for the sake of
fiscal restraint. The amounts that were spent on relief in the Yukon,
Manitoba, and the northwest are shown in figure 52. It should be
mentioned that 'remote districts' were those areas lying outside treaties
or beyond the reach of Indian agents. After 1932 the government no

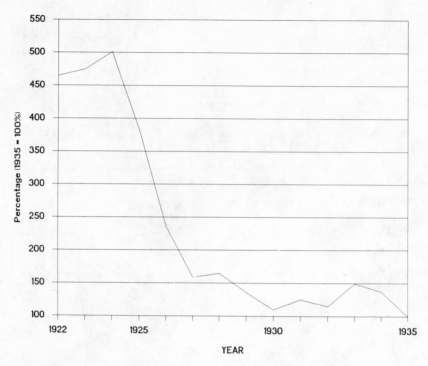

Figure 49
Changing native hunting/trapping income, 1922–35: northern Alberta, Saskatchewan, and Manitoba

longer made this distinction in the accounts. Of interest, aid payments in remote districts show a cyclical pattern rather than any long-term trend. Undoubtedly this was because a substantial portion of such help was given to Inuit and Indians who were almost entirely dependent on arctic fox cycles.

In remote districts the government depended on trading companies and missionaries to distribute its relief following a practice that began on a very limited basis with the Hudson's Bay Company shortly after Confederation. When Chipman served as commissioner, he expected post managers to keep a careful record of 'sick and destitute accounts.'[12] The company then asked the government to reimburse it for the expenditures. As early as 1880 Chief Factor James Fortescue put forward a rationale for shifting this traditional responsibility to the government.

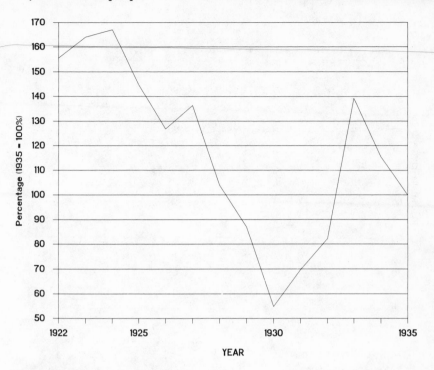

Figure 50
Changing native hunting/trapping income, 1922–35: northern Ontario

He argued that it was reasonable to expect the company to look after the needs of the Indian people in earlier times, when it held the advantages of a monopoly. However, under competitive circumstances this responsibility became an unfair burden.[13] Being a profit-sharing officer when he made his remarks, Fortescue's attitude on this matter is understandable. Later, Chipman adopted Fortescue's outlook, and he pressed the government for compensation.

At the beginning of Chipman's term of office, two regions were causing particular concern – Ungava and James Bay. In both areas the company was forced to make what the commissioner regarded as large expenditures in order to keep the natives from starving. For example, on 18 December 1894 Chipman wrote to Hayter Reed, deputy superintendent-general of Indian affairs, regarding the destitution of the Indians of eastern James Bay. He informed Reed that twelve Indians from

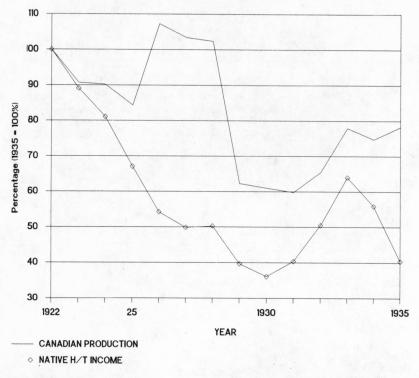

Figure 51
Fur returns and native hunting/trapping, 1922–35: changes in value

Rupert House had starved to death and others were forced to eat their furs even though the company had given them a liberal supply of ammunition in aid.[14] Because of their urgent need to hunt for food, the Indians had little time to trap. Some, particularly those who lived along the coast, were too poor even to hunt. These people had to be fed. Chipman asked Reed to authorize the company to spend $400 on behalf of the Indian Department for that purpose.[15] Chipman ended his request with the observation that: 'the Company had done all that it could afford to do to assist these people, but I leave the matter with confidence in your hands, and feel sure that if the department can see its way to afford assistance, it will readily do so.' Eight days later Reed authorized the expenditure Chipman requested.[16] But, when doing so, Reed wrote to Chipman, saying: 'I need scarcely remind you that the

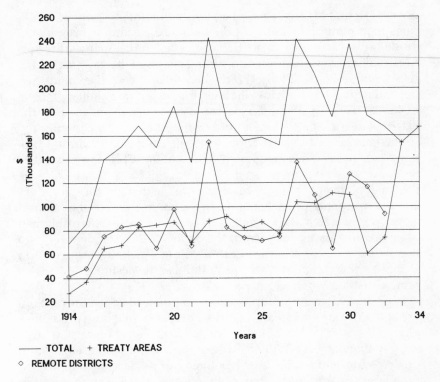

Figure 52
Government relief to northern Indians, 1914–34: inside and outside treaties

greatest care should be used in the expenditure of this money, so that the Indians will not be inclined to call for aid again too readily.'[17] Thus, the old fear of turning the native people into permanent wards of the state continued to lead government officials to move cautiously.

In James Bay, one of the most depleted districts, the problem of destitution was not limited to the isolated outposts. As life became difficult in the outlying areas, native families moved towards the larger settlements, particularly Moose Factory, where they hoped to obtain help from relatives who had steady work with the company. By 1900 Moose Factory had a population of 571 residents. Of these only 193 were permanent employees and members of their immediate families. The other relatives of these men the company regarded as 'hangers on.'[18] Often the post manager had to assist the relatives of these men directly, so that Moose Factory had larger sick and destitute expenditures than most other posts. At the turn of the century this growing burden was one of the worries that compelled the company's directors to seek alternative transportation arrangements in the bay area so that they could close the Moose Works and force the workers and their dependent relatives back into the bush.[19] To deal with a similar problem earlier at York Factory, in 1884 the company had resorted to the extreme measure of physically forcing the Indians to the interior.[20]

The government usually reimbursed the company for the aid provided whenever it was requested to do so, but Chipman wanted to work out an arrangement whereby he did not have to approach the Indian department on a case-by-case basis. He thought this procedure was too costly and time consuming. In the autumn of 1897 the commissioner was able to make the arrangements he wanted. After Chipman discussed the matter with Reed, the deputy superintendent took up the matter with his minister, Clifford Sifton. The minister agreed to authorize the company to furnish supplies to destitute Indians in remote districts when necessary.[21]

In giving Chipman the approval he sought, Reed added the cautionary note: 'You are well aware, of course, that we do not wish to establish a general system of relief, nor do we desire to have it understood that the government intends in any way to provide for distressed Indians, otherwise, as you yourself have pointed out to me, they might go in for a larger quantity than they really need.'[22] In this way the practice developed whereby the government established pre-set limits for local relief. As long as post managers did not exceed them, the company could expect to be fully compensated for the aid given. Eventually competing companies, most notably Revillon Frères, Northern Traders, and Lamson and Hubbard, also provided government-sponsored assistance in this fashion.[23] Missionaries did likewise.

Besides acting as a conduit for the government, the Hudson's Bay Company continued to offer its own economic assistance in the traditional ways – as debt, 'gifts,' and sick and destitute relief. There were several reasons for doing so. Indians who remained loyal believed that the company still had an obligation to look after them even though the legal responsibility may have rested with the Canadian government. For example, in 1920 T.P. O'Kelly filed an inspection report for the Mackenzie River District in which he recorded that a couple of Indians made the pointed observation that 'They were given a medal for long and faithful service, etc., but that did not help them in the least. If they were good and faithful hunters of the Company, they surely deserved some other form of recognition. The men at the posts received pensions, etc., but the hunters got only a medal, which did not prevent furs from getting scarce, or provide for them when they were ill or old.'[24] Reflecting on this observation, O'Kelly added: 'Naturally, this required delicate handling, but in the end, it evidenced that the Indian considered himself Hudson's Bay Company, and desired to remain so.'[25] He thought it would be a good idea for the Hudson's Bay Company to grant old age pensions to Indians, because this action would 'bind younger hunters to the service.' O'Kelly pointed out that it would cost the company little, since the pensions would be paid in goods only to those natives who had always traded with the company, or as the Indians expressed it, had always been 'working for the company.'[26] The commissioners rejected his suggestion.

credit

This episode underscored another problem. There was a widening division of opinion within the company, particularly between the commissioner's office and the men in the field, about whether it was a good idea to continue to look after the economic needs of its trading partners or pass on a larger share of the financial burden to the government. As it had in earlier years, the debate centred on the issue of providing credit to native trappers. Attempts to restrict credit worked at cross-purposes with the traders' goal of providing help to 'deserving' natives. The commissioner's office and some of the district and post managers believed that increasing losses from bad debts primarily were the result of the influence of the growing ranks of opponents who were 'unsteadying' the minds of native customers. Few, if any, company men were willing to help 'disloyal' natives as profit margins continued to shrink in the increasingly competitive trade which created mounting pressure to trim operating expenses as much as possible. Understandably this goal became a preoccupation during the depression.

The snag was that the increasing bad-debt load was not simply the result of Indians' defaulting on their obligations in response to the enticements of rival traders. As demonstrated previously (fig. 23), the native people continued to be very trustworthy, more so than the company's white customers as a group. The major reason for debt losses was the overhunting of fur-bearers and game animals. Making matters worse in the short term, closed trapping seasons in different areas and the establishment of game preserves often severely restricted local natives' earning potential. Until the native people could count on the government to make up for the shortfalls and develop conservation programs that compensated them for immediate losses, they had no choice but to turn to the traders for liberal credit. And, unless the company was prepared to risk the loss of its cheap native labour force, it had to respond positively.

Apart from the issue of native survival, traders still needed to use credit in their fight simply to hold native customers. As in the past, the native people regarded the willingness of the company to extend credit to them as a sign of trust and respect. It had been made clear enough during the First World War that any sudden changes in credit policy were hazardous. When the board instructed its men not to buy any furs during the 1914–15 season, it also ordered them not to extend any credit to the Indians. Philip Godsell said that the Indians felt particularly betrayed by this action and resented the company for many years afterward. In later years Hudson's Bay Company traders referred to 1914 as the 'black year' of the fur trade largely for this reason.[27]

Not surprisingly, there was a tendency for the commissioner's office to stress the need for constraint, whereas the men managing the posts, particularly native outpost managers, were more concerned about native needs and retaining native custom. Conflicts were the inevitable result. The clashes that developed between the commissioner's office and the men in James Bay highlight the underlying problems. More so than any other, this district was plagued by the recurring periods of severe deprivation as a result of poor fox harvests. The early 1920s was a low point in the cycle. Thus, debt losses and gratuity expenses of the James Bay District were very high compared with other regions, which led the commissioner's office to complain to District Manager George Ray about the debt burden. In 1924 Ray justified these costs to Commissioner Angus Brabant by reminding him that the company depended on the natives for its wealth. He then raised a basic issue, undoubtedly a key one on the mind of the fur trade commissioner: 'But the question arises, is it consistent with good business to go on assisting these people to the sum of $25,000 a year till such times as good fox years return to us?' Ray answered his question by citing a number of reasons for continuing the current system: 'Beyond the slight [price] reductions mentioned [for ammunition] I am not in favour of reducing our selling prices for it would be difficult to raise them again when better times shall come to the natives. So it seems the only solution, if it can be called a solution, to the problem, is for us to go on advancing these peoples as if for debt, though they'll have little hope of ever paying it.'[28] Ray added: 'If we continue as I proposed [slight debt reductions], the debt system as a means of keeping the natives alive during the lean years, the Company may – in small measure – be reimbursed by the amounts the natives may be persuaded to pay when the fat years shall come again and in the main, I imagine it will be more easily handled than any system of gratuity we may devise.'[29]

Ray's observations pointed to the heart of the matter. The company had two alternatives. It could return a greater share of the profits to the native people in the form of either better fur prices or lower goods prices. Neither Ray nor the company favoured this solution. On the other hand, these profits could be returned in the form of state or company aid. The advantage of returning it in the form of uncollectable credits was that it gave the company a moral claim on the native peoples' future production, a claim they readily acknowledged. On the other hand, if the state delivered the assistance, the natives had no obligations to the company.

Despite Ray's cogent arguments, Commissioner Brabant and his successor, Charles French, remained preoccupied with cutting debt losses in James Bay and elsewhere. Accordingly, in June of 1927 French issued 'Rules and Regulations Governing Advances to Natives and White Customers.'[30] This directive specified that no Indian or white customer was to receive an advance that exceeded 50 per cent of the value of his average autumn or spring hunt. Until hunters repaid their advances, no additional credit was to be given out under any circumstances. French's directive ended with the remark:

We realize that the Native can get on better when advances are given him and we are willing to continue giving him advances just as long as his conduct warrants it. Should we later on be compelled to entirely discontinue the practice the Native himself will be the cause. His standing with the company is in his own hands. Should he wish to be regarded as a man of his word, honourable and upright, he must live the part and pay his debt when due. If not he is a social outcast and not fit to associate with those of his people who are on the square.[31]

This directive angered J.S.C. Watt, manager of Rupert's House post in James Bay. He took the extraordinary step of sidestepping the chain of command by writing a letter directly to the governor of the company to criticize French's action. Watt noted that making advances to inland Indians was a very profitable investment in the trade, but 'advancing

Coast Indians is, to a large extent, an expense incurred in order to maintain the population, as you [Governor Charles Sale] very aptly described it in your speech [to the shareholders].'[32] After making this point, Watt proceeded to assail French's policy. He caustically remarked: 'one assumes Mr. French is under the impression the natives of the Bay are still in the aboriginal state the Company found them two hundred and fifty eight years ago.' Watt added that the commissioner's statement that those Indians who failed to pay their debts were 'social half-cast[e]s' showed he was under the delusion that it was merely a question of conduct or honesty.[33]

Continuing his attack on the commissioner's office, Watt claimed that the staff in Winnipeg knew little about the conditions in James Bay. He stated that they relied too much on inspectors' reports for external assessments of districts. In Watt's view, even the most painstaking inspection reports were at best superficial and too often the inspectors regarded the Indian merely as ' "a fur producing machine" which left the human element unheeded altogether.'[34] He then detailed the problems that James Bay Indians were facing, criticizing the company for introducing credit restrictions at the very time it was curtailing summer employment opportunities.[35] This action meant Indians needed credit more than ever to survive. In this way the company's own economizing and modernization efforts undermined the struggle to eliminate or sharply reduce credit.

Watt detailed these conflicts of policies in a memo he handed to Mr Innes Wilson (from the Winnipeg office) at Moose Factory on 17 August 1927. He noted: 'Advances to Coast Indians were regarded more as retainers than as advances given out with the prospect of making money on them ... Chief Factor Donald McTavish ... writing Mr. Chipman, then Commissioner ... explained that the coast Indians were necessary in summer in order to freight supplies inland, and like "other beasts of burden" had to be kept alive during Winter.'[36] In other words, the debt system was supporting the Coast Indians (Swampy Cree) primarily as a company summer labour force. They could not survive on the coast strictly by hunting and trapping. Therefore, the elimination of debt and summer work would be catastrophic. Watt's solution to the problem was identical to the one Ray had proposed earlier. He concluded: 'I have proved at least to my own satisfaction, it pays the Company better to carry on, when possible, on the old system, than to eliminate losses on Indian debts, cut the sale prices of merchandise, and pay competitive prices for furs, which of course is the alternative.'[37]

Even though the board had expressed a willingness to absorb increased relief costs in the form of bad debts in 1924, it did not countermand French's 1926 general order regarding credit in spite of Watt's direct appeal. So, the company curtailed credit. Afterward, post managers had to obtain approval from their district manager for the advances they made. At a conference of the district managers held in Winnipeg in November 1932 Fur Trade Commissioner Ralph Parsons reflected on the consequences of this restrictive policy for the James Bay District and decided that there was a close relationship between the volume of furs and the volume of debts. The drastic curtailment of debt to James Bay Indians had reduced their fur hunts to a fraction of what they had been and left them bordering on starvation.[38] Explaining why he thought this was the case, Parsons stated: 'when we cut out debts, the Indians cannot obtain the supplies which would enable them to proceed inland to hunt and trap. The consequence is they hang around the posts, trap out the territories *there* and then exist on relief which they obtain from the government.'[39] The commissioner noted that some post managers had suggested the problem could be resolved by building more inland posts. However, he believed this would merely add to the problem by extending the area of depletion. Similarly, he faulted the attempt by the company to 'control the issue of debt mechanically,' which he said was 'slowly but surely strangling our trade.'[40]

Parsons believed that the solution to the debt / relief problem was to be found not by controlling the amount issued, but rather by improving the ability of post managers to manage the Indians to whom they gave credit. He thought most post managers had lost their grip on the native people because they no longer had the ability and interest in their business or the concern for their customers that their predecessors had. On this topic Parsons remarked: 'these men, back in the 19th century, recognized how dependent our business was on the well-being of their customers and how necessary it was for them to be interested in them.'[41] To make his point, he then quoted to the officers a series of company rules and regulations regarding the treatment of natives which had been in force between 1843 and 1851.

Parsons was only partly correct in his assessment. He failed to note that managers were able to control their native clients a hundred years earlier because the company held a monopoly in most areas and its representatives held great economic power. Furthermore, in that era many of the traders were either relatives of the local natives or at least they spent most, if not all, of their careers in a single district, which enabled them to develop strong social and economic bonds with their customers. By the late 1920s post managers had lost most of these advantages. The changes in company policies discussed in the previous chapter played a considerable part in this development. Parsons's own effort to tighten the control of the department by centralizing authority served to undercut the managers' latitude for action, thereby further-ing the process. In impoverished districts such as Moose Factory Indi-ans often were unable to settle their accounts. For these various reasons the sense of mutual obligation that previously had existed between traders and Indians began to break down.

While the debt / relief problem remained unresolved, the board began to have second thoughts about having company men distribute government relief to native people. On 26 January 1925 they wrote to Brabant, saying: 'we are, however, much concerned by the fact that some of our post managers have distributed relief on government account without that careful and close supervision which it was their duty to exercise.'[42] Acknowledging the staff problems that Brabant faced, they continued: 'We realise the difficulties you have experienced in connection with staff, especially during and since the Great War, but if the subject became a matter of public enquiry, it is not likely that such difficulties would be regarded as a satisfactory excuses, nor should we like to put them forward.'[43] Given that it would be some time before the staff-rebuilding program made much headway, the board wanted Brabant to consider 'whether it would not be better for the Company to make the *major portion* of these disbursements on their own account and to limit any claims for refund from the government to a few very special cases.'[44] The board believed that it was not a question of profit or loss, but 'solely a question of good faith and reputation; that reputation which is beyond price and which we value above all things.'[45]

When they wrote this letter to Brabant, officials of the Fur Trade Department planned to meet with government representatives in Ottawa to discuss concerns about native health conditions. The impending meeting was causing anxiety to the board. The directors were unsure about the range of issues the government wanted to explore. They cautioned Brabant that for the moment his men should avoid any discussions about native economic relief until the company set its house in order. In the meantime, they stressed that every effort should be made to 'live fully up to our responsibilities and even go beyond them in all cases requiring relief.' They added that 'we are quite willing to take into account the expenditure in considering the results of the Posts and Districts concerned, as well as those of the department as a whole.'[46] This last proviso touched on one of the fundamental problems associated with having the company distribute relief for the government according to the terms Chipman had worked out. Earlier I showed that whenever the department was under pressure to cut costs in order to improve profit margins, the men were inclined to stint their aid. One very effective way of doing so involved passing more of the responsibility to the government. The temptation was particularly strong wherever relief expenditures were high.

In 1924 the board instructed Brabant to provide it with data regarding the Canadian government's 'sick and destitute fund' for remote districts along with information about the relief offered by the company at its own expense. The purpose was to obtain some idea of what the additional burden would be to the company if it stopped billing the government. It was suspected that 'the amount involved would add very little to the large sums (about $100,000 annually) given by the Company with the same object in view under the head of Indian Debt.'[47] Until they had examined the information they were requesting from Brabant, the directors deferred making a final decision.[48]

In compliance with the request Brabant sent a report on 14 May 1925 that included statistics regarding 'Relief and Gratuities to Natives' supplied by the company in 'northern districts' during outfits 245 through 254 (1916–25). The districts covered were James Bay, Nelson River, St Lawrence – Labrador (the northern section only), and the Western Arctic. Brabant's data are presented in figure 53 with the exception of those for the Western Arctic. The commissioner said that no detailed sums were available for the latter district, but he added that they totalled about $2,000 annually. According to Brabant's figures, government relief accounted for just under 30 per cent of the total distributed by the company.

In his covering letter Brabant made the additional observation that 'in all other Districts the issue of relief is under the direct control of the Indian Department, and orders for same are signed by the Department's Agents, Police and Missionaries, and these orders are, as a rule, apportioned among our principal competitors and ourselves; the bulk, of course, comes to us.'[49] The commissioner went on to point out that the system 'has been maintained for some years past,' and he claimed that the government regarded it as generally satisfactory. 'The only complaints received have been in connection with prices charged,

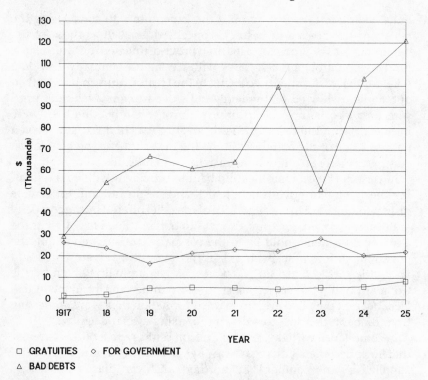

Figure 53
Hudson's Bay Company relief for natives, 1917–25: James Bay and Arctic

but with the consent of the Department these are now fixed at 25% on cost-landed.'[50]

A complaint that the commissioner did not mention was the one the Northwest Territorial government first raised in 1924. Government officials expressed concerns about the highly cyclical nature of the arctic fox economy and the negative impact that it had on the Inuit and Indians. They expressed the view that the company was skimming off the profits in the good years and leaving the government to deal with the shortfalls in lean times. The famous Dr Frederick Banting took up the cause, as did the media.[51] The company was under pressure to do something about the 'feast or famine' aspect of the economy. The territorial government wanted the company to establish a reserve fund when profits were high which could be drawn upon when the fox cycle ebbed. The company was unwilling to establish such a fund and in the end nothing was done. However, the issue lingered and was a matter of concern for the government, the board, and the Canadian Committee again in the early years of the Second World War.[52]

Between the wars some new aspects of company paternalism were explored. In 1925 the board established a Development Department because 'we realised that progress demanded a closer investigation of our opportunities.'[53] This department remained very small (never numbering more than fourteen employees) and its existence was short lived (operations ceased in 1931). None the less, under the direction of Charles Townsend, formerly of the Development Department of the English firm, Lever Brothers, native health and welfare were among the issues examined, and some significant initiatives were undertaken.[54]

On 23 and 24 November 1927 Townsend met with government officials in Ottawa to discuss the policy of the Hudson's Bay Company Development Department vis-à-vis native welfare. As outlined, the policy had two cornerstones – the development of 'home industries' and the improvement of native nutrition. Home industries, mostly the manufacture of native crafts for sale to tourists, were intended to provide native people with a new means of obtaining a livelihood in the summer season as traditional opportunities declined. By discouraging 'idleness,' it was thought that the proposed cottage industries would boost natives' morale and contribute to their physical well-being. The company initiated the program in the summer of 1926, when all post managers were given the directive to do everything in their power to encourage such activity.[55] Townsend showed the government officials a sample of 'toy seals' that the Inuit were making.[56]

Townsend's synopsis of the meeting indicated that the government officials were very impressed with this effort. Dr E.L. Stone, medical superintendent of the Department of Indian Affairs, 'gave his entire approval to this and stated that his Department was really in need of the Company's help, and in fact had only the Company to turn to.'[57] Townsend added that one of Dr Stone's assistants had stated that the Indian Department had no difficulty obtaining work similar to that displayed, but 'there was difficulty in finding and-outlet [sic] for the products.' Townsend assured him that the Hudson's Bay Company 'could take any work of this kind at a tariff rate fixed in conjunction with the Indian Department.'[58]

The other major concern raised at the meeting was native health and nutrition. No doubt this partly reflected the fact that the 1930s was a time when there was a great deal of interest in nutrition and a growing recognition of the importance of vitamins for good health.[59] Townsend detailed a scheme whereby the Hudson's Bay Company proposed to have post managers distribute cod liver oil and a meal made from cod livers to those Indians who were regular customers. Dr Stone endorsed the plan and 'stated his desire of joining us in this and obtaining the product from the company for distribution amongst those Indians with whom the Company was not in contact.'[60] Townsend consented to this proposal. In fact, as early as 1926 the company and the government were co-operating to that end in northeastern Ontario.[61]

Following this conference, Townsend had a meeting with Dr Banting and an associate, a Professor Graham, to review the problem of native health. They, like the public at large, were concerned that the native people were dying at an alarming rate. Tuberculosis was a particularly urgent problem. During the interview Townsend stated that his study of the information he had collected from the company's fur trade officers led him to conclude that: 'the fundamental reason of the greater susceptibility of the native to diseases such as tuberculosis, influenza, etc. was malnutrition.'[62] Townsend reported that Banting 'immediately agreed.' Operating on this assumption Townsend went on to point out that the company was undertaking research in food supplements with the object of restoring the vitality of the natives. In particular, work had been commissioned to try to find a way of processing 'proteins of fresh fish livers' for use 'as part of food which would be distributed amongst the natives.'[63] Townsend agreed to furnish Banting and Graham with samples for testing. Once again he outlined the company's cod liver oil and iodine tablet distribution scheme. Dr Banting indicated that he was very pleased to learn that the company had investigated this matter from a practical point of view. He then gave Townsend a brief résumé of his visit to the United Fruit Growers Association in central America, where some 200 doctors and their staff operated hospitals for native labourers. Banting stated that, by improving the health of its labour force, the United Fruit Growers Association had lowered its production costs.[64] Besides distributing vitamin supplements, by 1928 the Hudson's Bay Company's Development Department also was issuing powdered milk, 'Baysol' antiseptic, and earphones for the deaf. At some posts it even provided 'sunlight treatment' for vitamin D.[65]

By the end of the 1930s company paternalism was no longer adequate. In spite of the fact that the board still expressed concern for the well-being of native people, many of the economizing and modernization schemes that they and the Canadian Committee promoted worked against the attempts of their traders to continue to provide aid to native people. Furthermore, the growing numbers of white trappers meant that natives produced a declining share of the total output of wild furs. It was not possible to do business with white trappers in traditional ways. The efforts to standardize operations in ways acceptable to these newcomers therefore undermined older practices. Stripped of the monopoly for buying furs, selling merchandise, and distributing relief, the company's traders lost the leverage they formerly had enjoyed with their native customers. Discouraged once again from intermarriage, their social bonds with their native clients were also broken. Meanwhile, trading rivals, missionaries, and government officials had become part of the social fabric of many settlements, and they too struggled to gain the confidence of native people. As a result of all these changes, the Hudson's Bay Company obtained fewer benefits by continuing to offer economic and other forms of assistance. For these reasons, the older paternalistic fur trade, a hybrid of European mercantilist and native reciprocal exchange traditions, was crumbling by 1945, and the groundwork for the modern state welfare system so prevalent in the north today was laid.

9

The decline of the old order

Gone are the days of the picturesque and pompous Chief Factors. No longer do cannons roar and flags unfurl in honor of visiting potentates of the fur Trade ... The Fur Lords no longer rule the red Men.
(Philip Godsell, ca 1930)[1]

Canada was transformed from a predominantly agricultural and rural nation to an urban industrial one during the seventy-five years between Confederation and the end of the Second World War. The economic revolution affected all areas of the country, and in the north the fur trade remained in flux. The construction of railway lines and the use of steam-powered riverboats before 1929 and the extension of air service thereafter substantially reduced transportation costs, making it economically feasible for new traders and merchants to enter the north cheaply for the first time. Construction of the telegraph between 1870 and the First World War and the development of radio communication afterward ended the area's relative isolation from world-marketing centres, thereby reducing the risks of engaging in long-distance trading.

While transportation and communication improvements made it possible for newcomers to challenge the venerable company, altered economic circumstances gave them the incentive to do so. Owing to the provisions of their treaties, the Hudson's Bay Company's native clients were among the first residents in the northwest to have disposable cash incomes. The lure of this treaty money drew merchants into the region beginning in the 1870s. Once the depression of the 1870s and 1880s had ended, the rapid expansion of the industrial economies of Europe and North America fuelled a long-term escalation of fur prices which was broken only by the depression of 1920–1 and that of the 1930s. Also, a greater array of peltry was sought as fur dyers and manufacturers developed new processing techniques. This price inflation attracted to the region increasing numbers of white trappers, trapper-traders, traders, and cash fur buyers from the south. The expansion of logging, prospecting, and mining further encouraged this movement, since fur-trapping and trading served to grubstake many of those who participated in these and other new economic ventures.

Meanwhile it became easier for small traders and fur buyers to enter the business. The growth of cities along the southern periphery of old Rupert's Land meant that traders and small companies found it easy to get outfits on credit from local retailers and wholesalers, chiefly those located in Sudbury, Fort William, Kenora, Winnipeg, Prince Albert, and Edmonton. Often the trader and his supplier divided the profits, if any, at the end of the outfit in much the same manner as the Nor' Westers had done in the late eighteenth and early nineteenth centuries. Meanwhile, the emergence of North American cities as major fur-marketing and manufacturing centres (New York was the world leader by the 1920s) helped cash trading on a large scale by sparking intense competition among Canadian, American, and European (particularly English and German) auction houses and brokerage firms. In an effort to draw furs to their respective sales floors, the competitors provided their clients with cheap credit and an array of marketing services. The most important of these services included consignment selling and privileged access to current price information. This meant that independent fur buyers needed less capital to operate and they now could substantially reduce their financial risks by carefully monitoring market trends. As a result, on the eve of the First World War cash fur buying took place on a large scale in the north for the first time. The major problem with this innovation, however, was that easy credit encouraged speculative fur buying during periods of rapidly escalating prices, thereby adding considerably to market volatility. Once cash fur buying became an important component of the northern fur trade, those Indian and white trappers who took advantage of this new opportunity were able to shop around for the best prices for the goods they wanted. This development heightened retail competition in the north.

The complex interplay of economic and technological forces served to undermine the position of the Hudson's Bay Company in the subarctic fur trade. However, the extent of the company's decline in the modern period is not to be explained simply in terms of economic and technological changes. There were internal problems as well. In 1870, for example, senior Hudson's Bay Company officials fully expected the industry to become strongly competitive, and they were confident that their organization would meet the challenge. Yet, apart from authorizing heavy capital investments in riverboat service in the prairies and in the Athabasca-Mackenzie region, they did little to improve the company's aggressive stance. Of critical importance, all too often company officials chose to react to developments rather than seize the initiative. In most districts they let opponents initiate cash fur buying and take the lead in introducing new lines of merchandise. Before the 1930s they took no steps to centralize purchasing so that the company could benefit from the savings gained by bulk buying, even though this had become a standard practice of large wholesalers and retailers in the late nineteenth century. Also, the company continued to add substantial advances to the prime costs of its merchandise in order to cover its high overhead costs. Consequently the Hudson's Bay Company did not price its merchandise competitively.

HBC fur buying

As a fur buyer the company too often lagged behind its opposition. One of the primary reasons was that the London board continued to insist on earmarking most of the Hudson's Bay Company's returns for the London market, even though prices often were higher in North America. Therefore the company was not able to offer trappers as much for their furs as the opposition did. Even worse, the governor and committee halted trading in the autumn of 1914 when the London market was temporarily closed because of the war. Their action gave the company's opponents a tremendous advantage at a crucial time when fur prices soared in wartime North America.

There were other problems with the company's fur-buying operation. The company's traditionally stringent fur-grading policy restricted the ability of its traders to meet their competition because gradings used by North American firms favoured the trapper. Finally, until the First World War the Hudson's Bay Company's fur-purchasing tariffs tended to be not as current as those of other fur buyers because they were set in relation to its auctions which were held semi-annually. The other major auction houses held sales more often – many on a monthly or even a weekly basis during the trapping season. This meant that on rising markets, the type that predominated for much of the period between the 1890s and 1945, the company's price advances lagged behind those of most of its opponents.

It is clear from this study that the increasingly complex nature of the fur trade itself caused particularly serious management problems for a large organization like the Hudson's Bay Company. It seems that the fundamental problem was that two distinctly different fur trades developed after 1885. The older of these was the traditional or remote district trade, which continued to operate predominantly along credit-barter lines; it largely involved the more economically conservative and loyal natives, and competition was weak. The newer was the frontier, or line post business, in which cash trading was commonplace, whites provided a substantial share of the business, and opponents were very active. To direct successfully both types of operations the company needed to have skilled managers, appropriate policies, and an administrative structure that provided both enough central control and enough flexibility at the district level to deal with local circumstances in a coherent fashion. The company largely failed to achieve this objective.

There were several reasons for this failure, not the least of which was its increasing diversification. Before the 1930s the company's directors (the governor and committee) concentrated their attention on other ventures, most notably retailing (where they had made heavy investments) and real estate interests. They neglected the fur trade. It was not until the 1930s that the Canadian Committee undertook a series of detailed studies of the problems of the Fur Trade Department, with the intention of rejuvenating this ailing division. But, by that time the administration of the department had broken down entirely, and the various district managers were conducting their affairs generally as they pleased.

Once the Canadian Committee was ready to take action, it clashed with Fur Trade Commissioner Ralph Parsons and the London board because of differences in basic management philosophies. The Canadian Committee members believed the fur trade should be conducted along 'modern management' lines which involved having the commissioner establish broad policy guidelines, while he delegated operational authority to his assistants, who were experts in the fields of accounting, merchandising, transportation and communications, and fur buying. The trouble was that Parsons was an old-style manager, who had worked his way up through the service in the days when the company expected good post managers to be generalists who had a grasp of all aspects of the business. Reflecting his background, Parsons steadfastly refused to delegate authority. Board members, particularly Governor Cooper, were more sympathetic to Parsons and to the older traditions he represented. As far as the board was concerned, the fur trade was unlike any other business and therefore it had to be managed differently.

The main reason for thinking this way was that the native people supplied all the furs. During the mercantile era the company and its native customers had developed a set of mutually beneficial trading relationships. However, after Confederation these older traditions began to break down rapidly in the frontier areas and new arrangements were needed. The development of new company policies for dealing with native people proved to be one of the most difficult challenges that the company's directors and managers faced.

The pre-Confederation fur trade began as an equal partnership with natives.[2] The company depended on the native people for furs, a portion of the food its men consumed at trading posts, and seasonal labour. Therefore, native loyalty was crucial. Its native clients, on the other hand, became dependent on the company for their basic hunting, trapping, and fishing equipment, a substantial portion of their clothing, and in the late nineteenth century, increasingly, even food. It served the company's interest to make sure that the natives always had these basic necessities. Therefore, in lean years, or when individual hunters suffered misfortunes because of illness or injury, the company provided essential goods as relief, gifts, or uncollectable debts. The old and infirm were also provided for. Besides guaranteeing the physical survival of the native labour force, such company largess also bought loyalty to the company. As the economic position of natives weakened over time, the trade became more paternalistic. However, these arrangements were predicated on economic conditions in which there was a scarcity (at least seasonally) of labourers and employers / trading partners.[3]

After Confederation, when economic circumstances changed rapidly, creating competitive markets for labour, furs, and merchandise, these older arrangements proved ineffective from the company's perspective. Many natives began to sell all (or at least their highest-quality) furs to company challengers. Thus, Hudson's Bay Company officers no longer could count on retaining their Indian trading partners by looking after their well-being in times of need. On the contrary, since the company needed to be more competitive, commissioners tried to cut back on relief and curtail the use of credit to reduce bad-debt losses. In these ways they hoped to trim operating expenses. At the same time the company tried to pass on to the government an increasing share of relief costs for northern natives.

Ultimately these actions were counter-productive, because they served to accelerate the very processes that were undermining native loyalty to the company. For example, the government channelled some of its aid through rival companies and missionary organizations, which meant natives no longer had to depend solely on the company's officers when they needed help. This largely explains why the company's post managers, particularly those in remote districts, were unwilling to risk the loss of trade that might have resulted by eliminating relief or withholding credit. They undermined the efforts of successive commissioners to deal with the 'bad debt problem.'

relief for natives

Before 1945 the Canadian government, for its part, was extremely reluctant to shoulder the burden of native relief. Government officials feared that any general relief program would undermine the willingness of native people to look after themselves. Unfortunately, native people needed more help after the First World War for a number of reasons. Before the war fur price increases had more than offset the depletion of fur resources. Also, native people had found permanent and seasonal employment in a variety of new industries along the railway lines from Ontario to British Columbia. After 1920 the overtrapping of fur-bearers in many areas (especially James Bay and muskrat country), fur conservation measures, job displacement by the waves of immigrants who arrived in Canada at the turn of the century, and the decline of summer employment opportunities with the Hudson's Bay Company brought hardship to increasing numbers of native people. Given the reluctance of the government to respond to their needs, the company had little choice but to continue to render aid, since in many areas it still depended on them. With the encouragement of the government the Hudson's Bay Company's Development Department devised innovative new aid measures aimed at improving native nutrition and promoting craft activities. However, the time had passed when the company could expect that these actions would buy loyalty to the extent they had in earlier days.

In retrospect, the northern natives were better off with the company than with government bureaucrats. Even though the old order had many flaws, the strong personal ties that developed between Indians and traders served to protect each other's basic needs. Government agents did not establish these bonds, and they operated in a very different institutional context. Major policy decisions usually were made by senior bureaucrats who had little familiarity with local problems, and often the various government ministries (federal and provin-

He overlooks the diff. agendas of govt. officials.

cial) worked at cross-purposes with one another in respect to the welfare of the native people. For instance, local conservation efforts (generally provincial initiatives, except in the prairie provinces before 1929) usually deprived natives of much-needed income at the same time as the federal Department of Indian Affairs tried to make natives economically self-sufficient. From its earliest days, the directors on the London board of the Hudson's Bay Company actively sought advice from their men in the field and they gave their officers the authority to modify plans for the sake of local natives whenever doing so seemed to be in the best, long-term interests of the company. It was not until the London group handed over operational control to the Canadian Committee in 1931 that a serious effort was made to eliminate this element of flexibility and humanity. As we have seen, however, district and post managers fought a sustained rearguard action against the imposition of modern business practices. In the end it was a losing struggle, and the company ultimately passed most of the social costs of the northern trade to the state. This action would create new problems for native people which were only fully manifest after the Second World War.

Notes

Abbreviations used in the notes:

BT PRO Board of Trade, Public Record Office, London

Hudson's Bay Company Archives, Provincial Archives of Manitoba. Unless otherwise indicated, all archival references in the notes are to these archives. The following abbreviations have been used for record groups and documentary series in this collection:

ARFTD Annual Reports, Fur Trade Department

CF Confidential Files [London]

CICG Commissioner's Inward Correspondence – General, 1874–1910

COL Commissioner's Outward Letterbooks – London, 1874–1909

COLHBC Commissioner's Outward Letterbooks to Hudson's Bay Company Officials, 1874–92

COMP Commissioner's Office Miscellaneous Papers

DDD Development Department Dossiers, 1925–31

GD Governor's Dossiers

LICHBC London Correspondence Inward – Official Hudson's Bay Company

LFTS London Fur Trade Subject Files

LOCG London Office Correspondence [General]

LOCI London Office Correspondence Inward, 1919–54

MBGC London Minute Books – General Courts and Proprietors

PIR Post Inspection Reports

RG 2 CFTD Canadian Committee, Correspondence – Fur Trade Department, 1919–26

RG 2 CRS Canadian Committee Correspondence (Roneo system), 1904–70

RG 2 NC Canadian Committee, Nanton Correspondence

RG 2 FTC Canadian Committee Fur Trade Conference Minutes [General Manager's Copies], 1931–37

RG 3 AR Fur Trade Department Annual Report

SD Secretary's [London] Dossiers

SDFTC Secretary's [London] Dossiers, Fur Trade Conferences, 1933–34

PAA Provincial Archives of Alberta

PABC Provincial Archives of British Columbia

PREFACE

1 Innis, *Fur Trade in Canada*, 378
2 Ray, 'The Fur Trade in North America,' 29
3 Harold Innis discussed these developments in *The Fur Trade of Canada* and in *The Fur Trade in Canada*.
4 The classic work is Rich, *Hudson's Bay Company*.
5 A lengthy unpublished work on Revillon Frères is Harris, 'Revillon Frères Trading Company Limited.'
6 It should be noted, however, that the company did respond to specific requests for information. Some of the data Innis used in his 1927 work he obtained by correspondence with the company's secretary.
7 MacKay, *Honourable Company*, 310
8 The best short overview of the history of the area is Neatby, 'Exploration and History of the Canadian Arctic.' For a good discussion of the modern fur trade of the western Arctic see Usher, '*Banks Island*' and 'Growth and Decay.' For an account of the Hudson's Bay Company's expansion into Baffin Island see Goldring, 'Inuit Economic Responses.'
9 For expressions of this point of view see Zaslow, *Opening of the Canadian North*, 53–63 and June Helm, Edward S. Rogers, and James G.E. Smith, 'Intercultural Relations and Culture Change in the Shield and Mackenzie Borderlands,' in Helm, *Handbook*, 149

CHAPTER 1 Does the fur trade have a future?

1 MBGC, 1871, A 2 / 18, 33–4. The dissident report has not survived.
2 He was later knighted for the role he played in laying the first transatlantic cable.
3 C. Graham to Sir Stafford Northcote, Fort Garry, 15 March 1871, LICHBC, 1871, A 11 / 100

4 MBGC, 1871, A 2/18, 16. See also Ray, 'Adventurers at the Crossroads,'8

5 Graham to Northcote

6 Ray and Freeman, 'Give Us Good Measure,' 52–62

7 For this aspect of the early fur trade see Ray, Indians in the Fur Trade.

8 Donald Smith to the Governor and Committee, LICHBC, A 11/51, 87–8

9 Ibid., 90

10 Most notable was the appearance of 'wholesale jobbers,' who largely replaced 'consignment merchants' by the 1870s. The jobbers, by taking advantage of the greater speed and regularity offered by railways, were able to supply merchants at much lower rates than middlemen had previously done. See Alfred Chandler, The Visible Hand: The Managerial Revolution in American Business (Cambridge, Mass.: Belknap Press 1977) 216–24

11 Rich, Hudson's Bay Company, vol. 3, 816–90

12 MBGC, 1871, A 2/18, 20, 40–1

13 Banking legislation prevented the company from doing so because of its involvement in land development.

14 The International Financial Society included a number of merchant banking houses in London and Crédit Moblier of Paris which held a one-third interest. The society was formed in the summer of 1863 and financed a number of railway development schemes in England, the British Empire, and Europe. It was also involved in land development schemes in Italy and Mauritius, a trading venture in Egypt, and the conversion of the public debt of Mexico. See Rich, Hudson's Bay Company, vol. 3, 836. According to the prospectus issued in 1863, the company's assets, 'recently and specially valued by competent Valuers,' were placed at £1,023,569 exclusive of its landed territory and cash balance. The latter amounted to £370,000. Prospectus, International Financial Society, 1863, F 27/1, 94

15 Ibid. For a discussion of the Oregon settlement money see Rich, Hudson's Bay Company, vol. 2, 748.

16 The stock was reissued in £20 units, and provision was made for instalment payments. Thus, the new investors represented a wider cross-section of society than had been so in the past.

17 MBGC, 1871, A 2/18

18 Ibid.

19 Prospectus, International Financial Society, 1863

20 General Court, 28 June 1871, MBGC, 1871, A 2/18

21 Ibid.

22 See Ray, 'Adventurers at the Crossroads.'

23 Bowsfield, Letters of Charles John Brydges, xv

24 MacKay, Honourable Company, 302–3

25 Grahame joined the company in 1843.

26 Smith, 'A Desire To Worry Me Out,' 4–11

27 Bowsfield, *Letters of Charles John Brydges*, xxxi–iii

28 Ibid., xxxv. For an excellent discussion of the conflicting assessments about Grahame's effectiveness as chief commissioner see Stardom, 'Adapting to Altered Circumstances,' 53–7

29 Smith greatly resented Brydges and set out successfully to destroy his career with the company. See Smith, 'A Desire To Worry Me Out.'

30 For this reason Smith characterized Grahame as being deficient in imagination and boldness. See Wilson, *Letters of Charles John Brydges*, xxxv.

31 He served in that capacity until his death in 1889, when he was replaced by James H. Lawson. Lawson was given the title of land agent rather than land commissioner. See ibid.

32 Ibid., xl

33 Smith, 'A Desire to Worry Me Out,' 11

34 'Memorandum, 2 May 1932,' GD, A 104/282

35 Smith's most serious charge was that Brydges had speculated in company lands. Smith, 'A Desire to Worry Me Out,' 7–10; Stardom, 'Adapting to Altered Circumstances,' 48

36 Stardom, 'Adapting to Altered Circumstances,' 51–6

37 For an excellent account of this work see ibid., 58–100.

38 For an extended discussion of this effort see den Otter, 'Hudson's Bay Company's Prairie Transportation Problem.' It should be noted that the company had been using steamboats on the west coast since it introduced the steamer *The Beaver* in 1835.

39 Ibid.

40 For a more detailed discussion of this phase of company activity see MacGregor, *Paddle Wheels*, 86–95.

41 This decision had been reached in 1870.

42 Bachrach, *Fur*, 330–1

43 This term was popularized by the explorer, geographer, and trader David Thompson. Glover, *David Thompson's Narrative*

44 Ray, *Indians in the Fur Trade*, 210–12

45 Buffalo hides and robes and various fox pelts were the other primary products of the hunt.

46 For example, beaver prices rose steadily during the middle 1700s, making the trade increasingly profitable. Ray, 'Buying and Selling,' 95–116

47 Fur Trade Commissioner Grahame to Secretary Armit, Fort Garry, 3 April 1875, COL, D 13/1, 172

48 Governor Mactavish Letters Inward from W.J. Christie, Hudson House,

16 April 1867, Governor Mactavish Correspondence Inward, 1866–70, D 10 / 1, 38–40

49 Ibid.

50 Ibid., 179 and Grahame to Armit, 3 April 1875, COL, 1869–80, D 13 / 1, 435

51 Ibid., 435

52 Ibid., 168. The leading opponent was a Métis named La Ronde.

53 Grahame to Belanger, December, 1874, COLHBC, D 14 / 1, 284

54 James Fortescue to Grahame, 10 February 1875, CICG, D 20 / 1 / 5, 165

55 Grahame indicated that Fortescue raised this issue with the commissioner in a postscript of a letter from York Factory dated 16 September 1874. Grahame to Fortescue, 4 December 1874, COLHBC, D 14 / 1, 257. The postscript is missing. CICG, D 20 / 1 / 5, 378–9

56 Ibid., 258

57 Grahame to Armit, 3 April 1875, COL, 1869–80, D 13 / 1, 169

58 Ray, *Indians in the Fur Trade*, 217–28

59 Ibid., 176–7

CHAPTER 2 Laying the groundwork for government involvement

1 *Commons Debates*, 23 April 1880, 1693

2 Morris, *Treaties of Canada*, 43

3 Newell, *Technology on the Frontier*, 59–90

4 Morris, *Treaties of Canada*, 48

5 Ibid., 62

6 Ibid., 65

7 Ibid., 62–3

8 Ibid., 63

9 Ibid., 67

10 Only three headmen per band were eligible. Ibid., 320–4

11 Ray, *Indians in the Fur Trade*; Ray and Freeman, '*Give Us Good Measure*,' 53–78

12 Morris, *Treaties of Canada*, 72

13 Ibid., 73

14 Other provisions were not identical. Chiefs were given only $20 and no allowance was made for headmen. Ibid., 338

15 Ibid., 170–1

16 Ibid., 184

17 Ibid., 185

18 Ibid., 354

19 Auditor General's Reports, *Canada Sessional Papers*, 1868–85

20 *Commons Debates*, 26 April 1882, 1184
21 Ibid.
22 Ibid., 1185
23 *Commons Debates*, 23 April 1880, 1694
24 Sir Richard Cartwright, among others, called for an end to the 'wasteful practice of sustaining large bodies of Indians at public expense.' Ibid., 1694
25 The company kept a careful record of the amount of treaty money paid locally and the share of that money it was able to obtain.
26 *Commons Debates*, Dr Schultz, 23 April 1880, 1694. Schultz was an outspoken opponent of the Hudson's Bay Company and a Canadian annexationist. He played a major role in the troubles at Red River in 1869–70.
27 *Commons Debates*, Mr Donald A. Smith, 23 April 1880, 1697
28 Ibid., 1697
29 Ibid., Sir John A. Macdonald, 11 March 1881, 1351
30 Ibid., 1882, 1186. Mills had served in this capacity as minister of the interior under Prime Minister Alexander Mackenzie between 1876 and 1878.
31 Stanley, *Birth of Western Canada*, 269–94
32 See Auditor General's Reports, *Canada Sessional Papers*, 1880–5. For a discussion of I.G. Baker see Francis, 'Business, Enterprise, and the National Policy.'
33 *Commons Debates*, 9 May 1883, 1109, and Auditor General's Reports, *Canada Sessional Papers*, 1880–5
34 Ibid., 9 May 1883, 1109
35 *Commons Debates*, 9 May 1883, 1103–4
36 Ibid., 1103–4. See also 13 July 1885, 3341.
37 Ibid., 13 July 1885, 3341
38 Ibid., 3341–2
39 Ibid., 19 May 1888, 1698
40 COMP, D 26 / 13, 14–19
41 For example, in 1888 $8,000 was authorized for this purpose. Stardom, 'Adapting to Altered Circumstances,' 132
42 Hudson's Bay Company Reports and Proceedings, 1878–79, Library
43 James Fortescue to Company Secretary W. Armit, 1 December 1880, LICHBC, A 11 / 119a
44 Morris, *Treaties of Canada*, 29
45 Ibid., 218
46 Ibid., 221
47 Ibid., 231
48 *Commons Debates*, 18 April 1877, 1581

49 Morris, *Treaties of Canada*, 73–4
50 Ibid., 174
51 Ibid., 241
52 Ibid.
53 Ibid., 320–4. In Treaties 1 and 2 hunting and fishing rights were not explicitly mentioned. This wording is from Treaty 3. It was used in Treaties 4–7 and subsequently applied to 1 and 2 also. This wording is different from that of the Robinson treaties in that the hunting and fishing clauses of the latter stated that Indians had 'full and free privilege to hunt over the territory now ceded by them, and to fish in the waters thereof as they have heretofore been in the habit of doing, saving and excepting only such portions of the said territory as may from time to time be sold, or leased to individuals, companies of individuals and occupied by them with the consent of the Provincial Government.' Ibid., 302–4
54 This was a significant change in the wording. In 'Her Majesty the Queen against Bert Horseman' (Provincial Court of Alberta) defence lawyers argued that Indians were exempt from provisions of the Wildlife Act of Alberta prohibiting the trafficking in wild game because commercial hunting was a vocation at the time they signed Treaty 8.
55 Cumming and Mickenberg, *Native Rights in Canada*, 213–14
56 In the prairie area the courts have taken the position that the treaties intended only to protect native food sources until they adopted the lifestyle of white settlers. Ibid., 221–33
57 McCandless, *Yukon Wildlife*, 20
58 Cumming and Mickenberg, *Native Rights in Canada*, 209–11
59 Leighton, 'Victorian Civil Servant,' 109–12
60 Ibid., 104–8
61 Stanley, *Birth of Western Canada*, 270–2
62 Ray and Freeman, *'Give Us Good Measure,'* 71
63 Ray, *Indians in the Fur Trade*, 218

CHAPTER 3 The fur trade in transition

1 By 1914 the populations of Ontario and Quebec had become predominantly urban. 1921 was the dividing line for the nation as a whole. For an in-depth study of this period see Brown and Cook, *Canada 1896–1921* and Marr and Paterson, *Canada*, 339–412.
2 The only detailed study of the industry in this period is that of Innis, *Fur Trade of Canada*.
3 Ibid., 21.

4 They were the primary statistical source that Innis used in 1927. 'Fur Trade 1931–44,' GD, A 104/Box 13. He also drew heavily on Jones, *Fur Farming*. Jones employed Hudson's Bay Company data as well.

5 Innis, *Fur Trade of Canada*, 31–2.

6 Jones, *Fur Farming*, 4–5.

7 Ibid., 6

8 Ibid., 8. The term 'electric seal' was applied to seal imitations made from rabbit. Bachrach, *Fur*, 1936, 189

9 Jones, *Fur Farming*, 8.

10 Traditionally the big Leipzig sale took place around Easter. It did not conflict with the timing of the London sales.

11 Clayton, 'Growth and Economic Significance,' 71

12 During this period the fur price index advanced steadily. Innis, *Fur Trade of Canada*, 23

13 Based on DBS, *Annual Reports of the Trade of Canada*

14 See, for example, *Edmonton Bulletin*, 19 June 1886, 1; 10 July 1886, 1. It is clear from this newspaper that several buyers were active in the area throughout the year.

15 Apparently these communiqués were sometimes 'leaked' to the press, since price quotations that were attributed to 'private telegrams' were often printed in the *Edmonton Bulletin*. See, for example, *Edmonton Bulletin*, 29 January 1886, 1.

16 In 1872 Montgomery Ward established the first mail-order firm that distributed a wide variety of dry goods on a national scale. Chandler, *Visible Hand*, 230

17 Memorandum from the Fur Trade Commissioner, 11 April 1914. RG 2 NC, RG 2/6

18 *Edmonton Bulletin*, 13 February 1886, 1

19 Ossenbrugge, of Ossenbrugge, Hibbard and Company was a dealer in hides, pelts, and tallow, who maintained a warehouse and office at Notre Dame St East, Toronto. Other Toronto firms had offices in Winnipeg. *The Commercial* (January 1886), 287–90. *The Commercial* published mostly business news. It was an important source for commodity price information.

20 This firm was created in 1919 and had branches at Fort William, Regina, Edmonton, and Vancouver. The founder, A.B. Shubert, died in 1927. *The Northern Fur Trade* (February 1927), 14. In 1931 A.B. Shubert Canada Ltd was liquidated and replaced by A.B. Shubert Company. *Fur Trade Review* (April 1932), 69

21 By the time of the First World War this averaged about 5 per cent. Funsten Brothers to Norman Bacon, LOCI, A 92/19/104

22 *The Commercial* (January 1888), 282

23 Stardom, 'Adapting to Altered Circumstances,' 105

24 Report of the Commissioner to the Governor, Deputy Governor and Committee of the Hudson's Bay Company on the Trade of the Company, 1885–86. Library, FC 3207.1, R4, 1888, 178

25 Ibid.; Stardom, 'Adapting to Altered Circumstances,' 107

26 Chandler, *Visible Hand*, 223

27 General Court, 29 November 1876, MBGC A 2/31, 10–11. Also, for the first time the company had shouldered the burden of import levies on the inventories that it brought into Canada.

28 He also convinced the governor and committee to leave open annual contracts with suppliers, following government and English railway practices, so that officers had more time to fix the quantities they needed and the company did not have to pay for the goods until they were required. Stardom, 'Adapting to Altered Circumstances,' 117

29 Chandler, *Visible Hand*, 223

30 The company did not calculate depreciation or other kinds of capital accounting. Chandler notes that most merchandisers did not do so at the time because capital investments were small in relation to the total business. Certainly this was the case with the trading posts. Ibid., 223

31 Chipman offered the following example. In the 1897 outfit black bearskins were rated at $8.55, although a skin of the highest quality could cost as much as $25. In London such skins sold for up to $33 in 1897–8. On the other hand, post managers could buy low-grade black bearskins for as little as $1, but the company often sold them for less than that amount. None the less, using the current valuation tariffs, a post would receive credit for the average price, that is, $8.55, even for the poorest-quality skins. C.C. Chipman to Secretary William Ware, 26 May 1899, LFTS, A 12/FT 229/3, 10–11

32 It is clear from advertisements in leading fur trade publications, such as the *British Fur Trade Review* and the *Fur Trade Review*, that many of the large fur-dealing houses had offices in Sudbury.

33 Inspection Reports, R. Hardisty and E. Beeston, 1888, PIR, D 25/4, 42, 56

34 Ibid.

35 Bell and Beeston, Inspection Report, 1886, PIR, D 25/1, 75–7

36 Stardom, 'Adapting to Altered Circumstances,' 118

37 Hardisty and Beeston, Inspection Report, 1888, PIR D 25/4, 217

38 Stardom, 'Adapting to Altered Circumstances,' 118–19

39 They also recommended discontinuing the practice of paying for beaver by the pound, since it encouraged bad dressing. Hardisty and Beeston, Inspection Report, PIR, D 25/4, 217

40 Stardom, 'Adapting to Altered Circumstances,' 119
41 Hardisty and Beeston, Inspection Report, PIR, D 25/4, 215
42 Ibid.
43 Ibid.
44 The cost-landed prices did take into account one-half of the operating expenses of the depot. Stardom, 'Adapting to Altered Circumstances,' 103
45 'Circular from the Commissioner's Office, 15 January 1889' PABC, A D 90 H 86 3–5
46 Ibid., 5–6
47 Stardom, 'Adapting to Altered Circumstances,' 135. The problem with buying on the low end of the market was that there was a risk of accumulating a stock of 'stale' fur which was hard to sell on a rising market when fresh stocks were available.
48 He was born in Amherst, Nova Scotia, on 24 May 1886 and died on 11 February 1924. Between 1867 and 1882 he had served the departments of Agriculture, Public Works, Finance, and Rails and Canals. Between 1884 and 1888 he served as private secretary to Sir Charles Tupper, London high commissioner. From 1888 to 1891 he was chief clerk in the Department of Marine and Fisheries. Search Files
49 Chipman to Ware, 8 June 1898, LFTS, A 12/FT 229/3, 1
50 Ibid., 7
51 Ibid.
52 Ibid. The orders to bring about these changes had been issued by Chipman by the spring of 1899. Chipman to Ware, 26 May 1899, ibid., 38
53 Ibid., 8
54 Ibid., 9
55 They are included as enclosure 'C' in Chipman's letter to Ware, 7 October 1898, ibid., 39.
56 Previously a 20 per cent deduction was made to cover the officers' remuneration, interest on capital employed in the fur trade, and other charges that had to be borne in the London accounts. However, by 1898 the officers' compensation and many of the charges connected with the transportation of furs were entered into the district accounts before the apparent results were calculated, and the question of interest on capital employed in the fur trade was done away with. Chipman to Ware, ibid., 11–12
57 Ibid., 12
58 Ibid. For a discussion of gift giving in the early fur trade see Ray and Freeman, 'Give Us Good Measure.'

59 Chipman to Ware, 7 October 1898, 11
60 Ibid., 12
61 ARFTD, 1913–14, A 74 / 22, 8
62 Fur Trade Conference, 1931, RG 2 FTC, RG 2 / 62, 1
63 Chipman to Ware, 8 June 1898, LFTS, A 12 / FT 22 / 3, 13
64 Hudson's Bay Company 'Rules and Regulations, London, 1887,' Commissioner's Office, Rules and Regulations and Minutes of Meetings of Commissioned Officers, 1843–96, D 24 / 9 Rules 72–6
65 See, for example, District Statements, A 76. The regulations specified that those bad debts that were eventually collected should be credited to the outfit in which they had been written off. The district statements indicate that this was not done. .
66 Chipman to Ware, 30 Oct 1899, LFTS, A 12 / FT 22 / 3, 43
67 Chipman to Ware, 17 November 1899 [enclosure by J. Calder], ibid., 102–12
68 ARFTD, 1903–4, A 74 / 13, 46
69 ARFTD, 1908–9, A 74 / 18, 56–8
70 Chipman to Ware, 17 November 1899, LFTS, A 12 / FT 22 / 3, 111
71 Ibid.
72 Godsell, *Arctic Trader*, 150
73 Bell and Beeston, Inspection Report, Grand Rapids Post, 1886, PIR, D 25 / 1, 87
74 Hardisty and Beeston, Inspection Report, 1888, PIR, D 25 / 4
75 Stardom, 'Adapting to Altered Circumstances,' 103
76 Bell and Beeston, Inspection Report, PIR, D 25 / 1, 217
77 Ibid.
78 Chipman to Ware, 8 June 1898, LFTS, A 12 / FT 22 / 3, 8
79 ARFTD, 1913–14, A 74 / 22, 5–7
80 ARFTD, 1909–10, A 74 / 20, 9
81 ARFTD, 1925, A 74 / 53, 286
82 LICHBC, Moose Factory, 15 September 1891, A 11 / 48, 72
83 Moose Factory District Report, 1886, B 135/e/23
84 R.A. Talbot, 'Paper on Indian Trade' 1933 Fur Trade Conference, A 102 / Box 86, 4–5
85 Harris, 'Revillon Frères,' 41–2
86 MacGregor, *Paddle Wheels*, 116
87 Harris, 'Revillon Frères,' 42
88 Ibid., 13–17
89 Ibid., 14–15
90 Ibid., 39

91 Ibid., 37–8
92 RG 2 NC, 29 May 1913, RG 2 / 2, enclosing an article from the *Winnipeg Free Press* of 24 October 1913

CHAPTER 4 The turning point

1 Godsell, *Arctic Trader*, 150–1
2 Curtis M. Lampson became a very important figure in the British fur industry and he exerted a major influence on the Hudson's Bay Company between 1863–70 while serving as deputy governor.
3 'The Late Emil Teichmann: Death of a Famous Fur Trade Leader,' *British Fur Trade Journal* (April 1924). Lots were often sold in 'strings.' Strings were a series of lots of the same grade.
4 His son, Alfred V. Fraser, joined the firm in 1890 and became a partner of C.M. Lampson & Company in 1912. The latter died in 1931. His brother, George, also a member of Alfred Fraser Incorporated, joined C.M. Lampson & Company as a partner in 1920. *Fur Trade Review* (December 1932), 56. See also *Fur Trade Review* (January 1938), 96.
5 See, for example, *The Commercial*. By the outbreak of the First World War C.M. Lampson & Company also handled large quantities of furs from Africa and Asia. *Fur World* (April, 1910), 4
6 *Fur World* (December 1920). The company was capitalized by selling £50,000 worth of £10 shares. The firm also handled furs from Russia, claiming to have the largest such stocks in London at the end of the war. *Fur World* (July 1920)
7 When it became involved in the fur trade in 1911, operations were managed by A.G. Crosthwaite, who formerly managed Nesbitt's fur business. In 1918 G.P. Pitts was appointed manager and broker. He too came from Nesbitt, bringing with him fifteen years of experience in the fur auction business.
8 *Fur World* (April 1910), 4
9 Norman Bacon to Sir Augustus Nanton, 5 April 1916, RG 2 NC, RG 2 / 2, 2
10 ARFTD, 1915, A 74 / 24, 25–6
11 MacKay, *Honourable Company*, 347
12 Ibid., 306–7
13 Mrs Shirlee Anne Smith, keeper of the records, personal communication, 28 July 1987
14 MacKay, *Honourable Company*, 307–8
15 Nanton to Bacon, 24 July 1916, RG 2 NC, RG 2 / 2 and ARFTD, 1915, A 74 / 24, 5–6

16 ARFTD, 1916, A 74 / 25, 3
17 His failure to negotiate a satisfactory new contract was a contributing reason. Bacon to Nanton, 17 May 1918, RG 2 NC, RG 2 / 4
18 The sales were held in Montreal and were handled by Nicolas F. Monjo for the company. Minutes of Board Meeting, London, 3 January 1924, RG 2 NC, RG 2 / 5
19 *New York Times*, 18 April 1919. Copy in RG 2 NC, RG 2 / 4
20 Fur Trade Commissioner to Governor and Committee, 29 April 1919, LOCI, A 92 / 19 / 2
21 *Fur World* (January 1916)
22 Ibid. Subsequently it was reported that A. Palmer, alien property custodian of the United States government, was liquidating the German assets of fur companies operating in New York and elsewhere and that the money would go to the treasury. *Fur World* (August 1918), 15
23 18 April 1919, RG 2 NC, RG 2 / 4. In the autumn of 1921 Bacon resigned from the New York Fur Auction Sales Company just before the firm was dissolved to create a new organization, and he joined the firm of Joseph Ullman, Inc. of New York. He was sent to London to manage the London branch of the company. *Fur Trade Review* (August 1922), 192
24 Colonel P.B. Fouke of Funsten Brothers played a key role in obtaining the government contract. *Fur Trade Review* (December 1919), 190
25 P.B. Fouke of Funsten Brothers & Company to Bacon, 30 August 1919, LOCI, A 92 / 19 / 104
26 Ibid.
27 The prospectus was sent to the Hudson's Bay Company, since it was a customer of the firm.
28 Memorandum from the Fur Trade Commissioner, 11 April 1914. RG 2 NC, RG 2 / 6
29 Wholesalers often provided small traders with stocks of goods to be bartered for furs. The wholesaler and the trader then divided the profits (if any) from the fur sales.
30 *Fur Trade Review* (December 1919), 244–6
31 The leading fur dealer investors included A. Pierce, president of A. and E. Pierce, Ltd; A.A. Allan, president of A.A. Allan and Company, Ltd; R.S. Coltart, vice-president of Holt Renfrew and Company, Ltd and the Redmond Company, Ltd; J.W. Coristine, president of James Coristine and Company, Ltd; F.W. Gnaedinger, president of L. Gnaedinger, Son and Company; E.E. Cummings of Cummings and Cummings; and F. Cooper, vice-president of Boulter, Waugh, Ltd. *Fur Trade Review* (January 1920), 260; *Fur World* (March 1920), 15–16.

32 *Fur Trade Review* (April 1920), 186

33 At an average commission of 5 per cent, that represented about $1.35 million in commissions.

34 75 per cent of the $32 million sales were by auction.

35 *Women's Wear Daily*, 10 October 1919. The article is included in LOCI, A 92/19/4.

36 It bought the property and warehouses of A. & W. Nesbitt Company for that purpose. *Fur Trade Review* (July 1922), 99. Initially the company was represented in the United States by Nicolas Monjo, who formerly had been in partnership with Albert Monjo when they acted as agents for A. & W. Nesbitt of London. *Fur Trade Review* (April 1921), 213

37 Ibid., 99

38 *Fur Trade Review* (June 1921), 223. Reports in 1922 said the amount was closer to $22 million. In the end all but $2 million in debts was paid off. *Fur Trade Review* (January 1922), 109

39 Ibid. (December 1921), 178

40 8 February 1921, Governor and Committee to the Canadian Advisory Committee, RG 2 NC, RG 2/6. See also 15 July 1921, Fitzgerald to Nanton, RG 2 NC, RG 2/4. The collapse of the St Louis fur auction lead to the bankruptcy of many dealers in that city. For a time afterwards, only limited auctions were held there. See H.P. Warne, 'Paper on Fur Purchasing Agencies,' SDFTC, 1934.

41 *Fur World* (December 1920).

42 J.K. Cornwall, 'Memo Re Fur Trade [of Mackenzie District],' 1946 PABC A D 90 C 81 2–3

43 Fur Trade Commissioner to Governor and Committee 4 February 1919, LOCI, A 92/19/1

44 Cornwall, 'Memo,' 3

45 'Lamson Ltd,' Research Files

46 Fur Trade Commissioner to Governor and Committee, 15 May 1919, LOCI, A 92/19/2

47 Ibid., 27 August 1919

48 Ibid.

49 Innis, *Fur Trade in Canada*, 366

50 MacGregor, *Paddle Wheels*, 116

51 Ibid., 117, 124, 156

52 ARFTD, 1911, RG 3/1, 8–9

53 A. Brabant, Annual Report to the Fur Trade Commissioner, Mackenzie River District, 1918, LOCI, A 92/19/5, 511

54 Cornwall, 'Memo,' 3
55 Godsell, *Arctic Trader*, 149
56 Ibid.
57 Ibid.
58 Ibid., 150
59 Ibid.
60 ARFTD, 1914, A 74/23a, 3–4
61 Ibid.
62 Godsell, *Arctic Trader*, 150–1
63 Cornwall, 'Memo,' 3
64 Ibid., 2
65 Ibid.
66 T.P. O'Kelly, Inspection Report, Mackenzie River District, 11 October 1920, LOCI, A 92/19/18
67 RG 3 AR, 1912, RG 3/1/1, 10
68 The record indicated that they were 'mostly Jews.' A. Brabant, Manager, Mackenzie District to Fur Trade Commissioner, 9 January 1920, LOCI, A 92/5/18
69 O'Kelly, Inspection Report, 1920, 4
70 Ibid., 3
71 Brabant, Annual Report, 1918, 508
72 O'Kelly, Inspection Report, 1920, 20
73 ARFTD, 1918, A 74/26, 6
74 ARFTD, 1925, A 74/53, 259
75 ARFTD, 1923, A 74/52, 17
76 LOCI, 1918/19, A 92/19, 1–5
77 Anderson, *Fur Trader's Story*
78 ARFTD, 1917, A 74/26, 690
79 'Fur Trade Commissions and Indentures,' Memorandum to the governor from the secretary, 2 May 1932, A 104/Box 13, 8
80 Brabant, Annual Report, 1918, 515; Memo of a meeting between Harding of the Western Arctic and Fitzgerald, 23 September 1919. RG 2 NC, RG 2/4
81 ARFTD, 1919, A 74/28, 280
82 ARFTD, 1922, A 74/52, 26
83 LOCI, A 92/19/9
84 Brabant Annual Report, 1918, LOCI, A 92/19/5, 511
85 O'Kelly, Inspection Report, 1920, 22
86 RG 3 AR, 1912, RG 3 1/1, 10 and ARFTD A 74/52, 91
87 O'Kelly, Inspection Report, 1920, 20
88 *Fur Trade Review* (March 1920), 320

89 ARFTD, 1923, A 74/52
90 Fitzgerald, New York Agency [HBC] to Nanton, 21 June 1919, RG 2 NC, RG 2/4
91 Marr and Paterson, *Canada*, 268
92 Bothwell, Drummond, and English, *Canada: 1900–1945*, 1–24; 55–84 and Brown and Cook, *Canada 1896–1921*

CHAPTER 5 The international marketing of Canadian furs

1 Government of Canada, *Statutes*, 57–58 Victoria, 1894, Chapter 31
2 *Fur World* (May, 1911). None of these measures was particularly innovative. The Hudson's Bay Company's beaver conservation schemes of the early nineteenth century included most of these provisions. Ray, 'Some Conservation Schemes'
3 Brody, *Maps and Dreams*, 86–90
4 Novak, 'Future of Trapping,' 92
5 *Fur Trade Review*, (June 1933), 29
6 Ibid. (April 1933), 12
7 Jarvenpa, *Trappers of Patuanak*, 55–6
8 Brody, *Maps and Dreams*, 86–102; 'Report of Medical Service to Indians Located Along the Line of the Canadian National Railways from Cochrane, Ontario to La Tuque,' October 1926, LOCG A 92/Corr/257/1, 21
9 Denmark, 'James Bay Beaver Conservation'
10 Denmark, 'Conservation at Cumberland'
11 *Fur World* (August 1910), 25
12 Ibid., 139
13 Harris, 'Revillon Frères,' 57
14 Innis, *Fur Trade in Canada*, 378n
15 Godsell, *Arctic Trader*, 140–1
16 Fur Trade Conference, 1931 RG 2 FTC, RG 2/62/1, 24
17 Ibid.
18 Watkins, 'World Fur Production, 1945–46,' Report for Hudson's Bay Company, GD, A 104/A8, 11
19 For instance, between 1934 and 1945 Canadian beaver production increased from about 50,000 pelts per year to roughly 131,000 Hudson's Bay Company officials attributed most of the gain to the success of the conservation effort in Ontario between 1934 and 1939. Ibid.
20 Government of Canada, *Fur Farms of Canada*, 4 and *Fur Production of Canada, Annual Report, 1936–7*, 5
21 Government of Canada, *Fur Production of Canada, Annual Report, 1938*, 3 and Beynes and Wilson, 'Canadian Fur Marketing Research'

245 Notes to pages 119–32

22 Government of Canada, *Fur Production of Canada, Annual Report, 1936*, 3
23 Ibid.
24 Beynes and Wilson, 'Canadian Fur Marketing Research'
25 An example was the Canadian National Association, which operated a marketing board. RG2 CRS 7/1-7-1C, 1
26 Bachrach, *Fur*, 109–10 176–7
27 Ibid., 188
28 Ibid., 189, 598
29 Ibid., 184
30 Ibid.
31 McCandless, *Yukon Wildlife*, 133
32 Black, silver, and cross fox are colour phases of this species, but are marketed separately.
33 McCandless, *Yukon Wildlife*, 114–15, 120–1
34 *Fur Trade Review* (January 1938), 66
35 Ibid. (December 1921), 178
36 Ibid. (November 1925), 127–8
37 Ibid. (March 1922), 170; (June 1922), 78
38 Report of John E. Jones, American consul-general, Winnipeg. *Fur World* (July 1910), 30
39 C.G. Wilson, formerly of C.G. Wilson Brokerage Company, Winnipeg, organized the Dominion Fur Auction Company. The new organization took over the net assets of C.G. Wilson Brokerage Company and Winnipeg Fur Auction Sales Ltd. *Fur Trade Review* (September 1931), 96
40 12 February 1921, RG 2 CFTD NC, RG 2/4
41 In 1894 J.W. Peck introduced a new line of fur goods some of which the company manufactured in its Montreal Factory. 'A Handsome Warehouse,' *The Commercial* (16 April 1894), 734
42 *Fur Trade Review* (April 1921), 104 and *Winnipeg Free Press*, 12 February 1921, included in RG 2 NC, RG 2 2/4
43 Ibid.
44 *Fur Trade Review* (May 1921), 150
45 Ibid. (June 1922), 100
46 Ibid. (January 1921), 133–4
47 Ibid.
48 Ibid. (May 1922), 138
49 Ibid. (January 1930), 36; (February 1930), 20
50 'Report on Winnipeg Fur Auction, 14–15 January 1930,' LOCI, A 92/19/209
51 *Northern Fur Trade* (February 1927), 13
52 *Fur Trade Review* (October 1930), 43. Mr Yewdall, founder of Winnipeg

Fur Auction Sales Ltd, retired when Wilson took control. *Fur Trade Review* (September 1930), 28

53 Ibid. (December 1931), 49. At the annual meeting held that year H.W. Bell was elected president and C.G. Wilson vice-president and general manager.

54 Ibid. (January 1930), 34

55 Ibid. (November 1930), 52

56 Beynes and Wilson, 'Canadian Fur Marketing Research,' 27

57 Ibid.

58 Two-thirds of all the mergers that took place between 1900 and 1948 occurred at this time. Marr and Paterson, *Canada*, 415–17

59 'C.M. Lampson & Company Ltd,' Library, Search Files

60 The New York branch had been established in 1923. Two of the senior partners of Huth's retired, and the remaining partners transferred the business to the British Overseas Bank. *Fur Trade Review* (April 1936), 22. The Hudson's Bay Company purchased the firm from the British Overseas Bank. 'C.M. Lampson & Company Ltd,' Library, Search Files

61 Fur Trade Commissioner to the General Manager, 4 March 1936, 'Administration – North America' RG 2 CRS, RG 2/2/7, 1–7-1C

62 *Fur Trade Review* (June 1936), 39; (July 1936), 41; and GD, A 104/Box 13, 'FT 1931–8,' 2

63 *Fur Trade Review* (April 1921), 69. Between 1915 and 1920 these sales disposed of an average of $40,000 worth of furs every year.

64 Ibid. (January 1922), 122

65 Beynes and Wilson, 'Canadian Fur Marketing Research,' 29

66 *Fur Trade Review* (March 1932), 20; (November 1931), 19

67 Ibid. (November 1931), 18–19

68 Beynes and Wilson, 'Canadian Fur Marketing Research,' 10

69 *British Fur Trade* (September 1931)

70 Between 1919 and 1933 Russia was the world's largest fur producer. The bulk of these pelts were disposed of in London until 1931 when the Leningrad auctions began. Chadwick, 'Memo,' 30 July 1943, BT PRO 64/1648

71 *British Fur Trade* (August 1924), 50

72 Ibid. (April 1933), 31

73 Ibid. (June 1933)

74 Ibid. (August 1933). This committee was organized at the request of the American League for the Defense of Jewish Rights.

75 Ibid. (September 1933), 8

76 Ibid.

77 *Stylewear Review,* 15 February 1936 and *The Economist,* 24 March 1945
78 Watkins, 'World Fur Production,' 1–2
79 Chadwick, 'Memo'
80 Barber, 'Policy File, 6 December 1943,' BT PRO 64 / 1648
81 It has been demonstrated that it was very important to have representatives on that board. Newell, 'Politics of Food in Wartime'
82 2 November 1943, BT PRO 64 / 1648
83 Chadwick, 'Memo'
84 It was cut from 100 per cent to 16.33 per cent. *The Economist,* 24 March 1945, 383
85 Ibid.

CHAPTER 6 The struggle for dominance in the Canadian north

1 Governor's Visit to Canada 1934 – Observations,' Administration – North America,' RG 2 CRS, RG 2 / 7, 1-7-1C, 1
2 ARFTD, 1922, A 74 / 52, 68
3 Ibid., 28
4 Ibid., 1923–4, A 74 / 43, 32
5 Ibid., 15
6 Ibid., 16
7 Ibid., 123
8 Ibid.
9 Ibid., 145
10 Ibid., 150
11 Ibid.
12 Ibid., 135
13 Ibid., 119
14 Ibid., 151
15 Ibid., 153
16 Ibid., 1922–3, A 74 / 52, 29
17 Completed in 1913, the government entrusted this rail line to the Canadian Northern Railway in 1918. It became part of the Canadian National Railways in 1923.
18 ARFTD, A 74 / 53, 273
19 Bliss, *Northern Enterprise,* 288–92
20 Sears-Roebuck of Chicago purchased nearly $3 million worth of furs in 1931. RG 2 FTC, 1931, RG 2 / 62
21 Prior to the First World War the Winnipeg store issued a catalogue.
22 RG 2 FTC, 1931, RG 2 / 62, 30–1

23 ARFTD, 1922, A 74 / 52
24 For example, Finkleman of Selkirk backed traders at Norway House, Oxford House, and God's Lake. Ibid., 145
25 Ibid., 144–154
26 McCandless, *Yukon Wildlife*, 124
27 'Report on the Yukon Territory,' RG 2 NC 2 / 2 / 4
28 Marr and Paterson, *Canada*, 415–16
29 Nanton to Commissioner J. Thomson, 7 October 1919, RG 2 NC, RG 2 / 4
30 Louis Romanet, General Inspector, to A. Brabant, Fur Trade Commissioner, 20 October 1920, LOCI, A 92 / 19 / 16
31 Ibid.
32 Lamson and Hubbard Canadian Company, Ltd, Search Files
33 Cornwall 'Memo,' PABC A D 90 C 81, 5–6
34 Millar was a partner in the firm of Millar, Ferguson and Hunter, 59 Yonge Street, Toronto.
35 Royal Trust Company List of Shareholders of the Alberta and Arctic Transportation Company, 14 March 1922, RG 2 CFTD, RG 2 / 4 / 82
36 The 'B-X' was registered at Victoria on 7 June 1910.
37 Cornwall, 'Memo'; Alberta and Arctic Transportation Company Traffic Manager to H.B. McGivirin, MP, Ottawa, 22 December 1923, RG 2 CFTD, RG 2 / 4 / 82
38 W.S. Lecky to Edward Fitzgerald, Deputy Governor, 24 April 1924, RG 2 CFTD, RG 2 / 4 / 82
39 Harris, 'Revillon Frères,' 71
40 Ibid., 66
41 Ibid., 68
42 Ibid.
43 Ibid., 69
44 Ibid., 77–89. The legal arrangements were completed by 31 December 1937.
45 Memo, 23 December 1924, 'Northern Traders Ltd., 1924–38,' SD, A 102 / Box 141, 2
46 Ibid., 1
47 Ibid., 2
48 The steamers and boats operated directly by the Northern Traders were capitalized at $74,000. In addition, the company had craft on the Slave and Athabasca rivers that belonged to a subsidiary called the Northern Transport Company. Memorandum, Winnipeg, 23 December 1924, ibid., 1
49 Fur Trade Commissioner to Governor and Committee, 3 March 1925;

Finklestein to the Hudson's Bay Company, 3 June 1929; 'Draft for discussion, 5 April 1929,' ibid. Moses Finklestein was Max's brother and was a fur dealer in London.

50 Innis, *Fur Trade in Canada*, 366
51 'Notes on discussion with Chester on September 30th, 1931,' 'Northern Traders, 1924–38,' SD, A 102/Box 141
52 Memo, Undated [May], 1930, ibid.
53 Allan Laird Davis Haffner & Hobkirk [solicitors for the Hudson's Bay Company] to Governor and Committee, 10 June 1930, ibid.
54 'Notes on Northern Traders,' 30 September 1931, ibid.
55 The most important of these was the contract to handle the cargo of the Catholic missions. 'Agreement 6 November 1926' ibid.
56 Baker, *Memoirs of an Arctic Arab*, 29–34
57 Ibid., 35
58 Ibid.
59 Ibid., 38
60 Ibid.
61 Ibid.
62 Ibid., 65–6
63 Watkins, 'World Fur Production, 1945–46,' Accounts Department [London], A 103/A8, 2
64 Ibid., 4
65 Beynes and Wilson, 'Canadian Fur Marketing Research,' GD, A 104/Box 13, 17
66 Ibid., 11–12
67 Ibid., 19–33
68 Ibid., 30
69 Ibid., 3

CHAPTER 7 Attempts to revitalize the Hudson's Bay Company's Fur Trade Department

1 Monod, 'Bay Days,' 173–83
2 Nanton served on the boards of directors of Canadian Pacific Railway, Great West Life Assurance Company, Northern Trust Company, Manitoba Bridge and Iron Works, Beaver Lumber Company, Home Investment and Savings Association, and Western Manufacturing. Ibid., 175
3 Report to shareholders, 27 June 1930, *Annual Report*, 11–12, Library
4 The first bonuses were received in 1920 according to the employment

records of senior fur trade officers. 'Notes on Senior Personnel, 23 November 1938,' RG 2 CRS, RG 2/7, 1-7-4a

5 ARFTD, 1925, A 74/54, 2–3; ARFTD, 1924, A 74/53

6 In a letter dated 22 January 1929 [C.C. 5538] the committee made its first series of recommendations for the reorganization of the Fur Trade Department. Governor Charles Sale's copy of a Memo regarding Fur Trade Department, 27 August 1930, CF FTD, A 93/56

7 Report of the Canadian Committee to Governor Charles Sales 27 August 1930, ibid., 2–3

8 RG 2 CRS, RG 2/7, 1-7-4a

9 Memo on 'Fur Trade Department' attached to letter of Canadian Committee to London Board, 27 June 1930, RG 2 CRS, RG 2/7/33, 1-7-1, 3

10 'P.A. Chester,' Library, Search Files

11 Canadian Committee memo on Fur Trade Department, 27 June 1930, ibid., 1–2

12 Inspection, James Bay District, 12 Oct 1920, LOCI, A 92/19/16, 1

13 Ibid., 2

14 'Memo regarding Fur Trade Department' 27 August 1930, CF FTD, A 93/56, 2

15 'Brief Summary of the Hudson's Bay Company's Fur Trade Organization and Activities,' Winnipeg, 30 September 1931, RG 2 CRS, RG 2/7/34, 1-7-1, 2

16 'Governor's Visit to Canada 1934 – Observations,' RG 2 CRS, RG 2/7/73, 1-7-1C, 4

17 Ibid., 3

18 Ibid.

19 Chester's notes were drafted by 8 February 1935. RG 2 CRS, RG 2/7/73, 1-7-1C. Allan became chairman of this committee in 1925. He was one of its founding members.

20 Ibid. He also joined the London board in 1925.

21 'Notes in connection with the Governor's Observations 1934, prepared by Mr. Gasston for Mr. Chester to take to London spring 1935,' 8 February 1935, RG 2 CRS, RG 2/7/73, 1-7-1C, 1

22 'Western Districts,' 29 August 1939, 'Fur Trade Organization, 1936–48,' SD, A 102/Box 86

23 Ibid.

24 'Fur Trade Department, Brief Survey, January, 1942 [Mailed to London, 14 February 1942],' RG 2 CRS, RG 2/7/74, 1-7-1C, 4

25 Ibid., 4

26 'Western Districts'
27 Monod, 'Bay Days,' 182. See also Chandler, *Visible Hand*, 233–6.
28 The creation of these positions was discussed with the London Board in 1933. 'Memorandum of Special Meeting of the Board Held on the 5th May, 1933: Matters Discussed with Chester,' RG 2 CRS, RG 2/7/34, 1-7-1
29 In its 1942 critique to the board the committee noted: 'Thus, not only the district managers, but the senior officials were usually long service post managers and subject to all the limitations imposed by long isolation in the North. Their lack of administrative training was their downfall when confronted with the aggressive influences of the new economic trends.' 'Brief Survey,' 3
30 'Notes on Senior Personnel'
31 Fur Trade Organization, 1936–48, A 102/Box 86, 2
32 Chesshire was born in Parkstone, Dorset, in 1902. He served in that capacity until he was made the general manager of the Bay Stores in 1957. He retired in 1962. Chesshire, Library, Search Files
33 'Fur Trade Apprentices,' George Binney, October 1929, SD, A 102/Box 14, 2
34 Ibid.
35 Ibid., 11
36 Ibid.
37 'Memorandum of Special Meeting'
38 Ibid.
39 Ibid.
40 Ibid.
41 Included were Fort Simpson, Fort Smith, Fort Vermilion, Cumberland House, Portage la Loche, Pine River, Norway House, Split Lake, Oxford House, York Factory, Lac Seul, Fort Hope, Temagami, Fort Albany, Rupert's House, Moose Factory, Seven Islands, Cartwright, Chesterfield, Fort Chimo, and Hershel Island. 'Training Apprentice Clerks,' 25 March 1926, SD, A 102/Box 4
42 Ibid.
43 Ibid.
44 Ralph Parsons to Fur Trade Commissioner, 12 May 1928 (Apprentice Training Schedules), SD, A 102/Box 14
45 George Binney to the Governor and Committee, 28 June 1927, ibid.
46 Charles Sale to George Binney, 19 July 1927, ibid.
47 McKay, *Honourable Company*
48 'Memorandum of Special Meeting'
49 Ibid., enclosure

50 Ibid.
51 Extract, Canadian Committee Minutes [# 9837] 11 April 1940. 'Fur Trade Organization 1936–48,' SD, A 102 / Box 86
52 Memorandum to the Governor, 2 May 1932. 'Fur Trade, 1931–52' GD, A 104 / 282–7
53 Address of Fur Trade Commissioner French to officers at Fur Trade Conference, 21–26 October 1929. GD, A 102 / Box 14, 16
54 Memorandum to the Governor, 1
55 Personnel Records, 'Fur Trade Organization, 1936–48,' SD, A 102 / Box 86, 4
56 G.H. Miles, Director, National Institute of Industrial Psychology, Aldwych House, London, 18 February 1937 to P. Ashley Cooper [governor], Hudson's Bay Company, 'Fur Trade Organization, 1936–48,' SD A 102 / Box 86
57 'Fur Trade Department: District Administration,' Enclosure to letter 332 to Governor and Committee, 6 October 1938, ibid.
58 C.C. Chipman to Ware, 4 November 1901, James Bay District 1901–18, LFTS, A 12 / FT 325 / 1
59 E. Fitzgerald, Deputy Chairman, Canadian Advisory Committee to Governor and Committee, 31 January 1921, 'Governors' Papers,' SD, A 102 / 11–13
60 Ibid., 5 February 1923
61 C.H. French to Governor and Committee, 26 July 1926, ibid.
62 The Secretary to the Governor, 3 March 1930, ibid.
63 Ibid.
64 W.E. Brown, Paper, 'Hudson's Bay Company's Transportation Including Consideration of Aeroplane Transport,' Fur Trade Conference Papers, 1934, CF, A 93 / 43
65 The Imperial Oil Company asked the company to join forces in creating an air service for the Mackenzie River valley. Company officials declined the offer. Meeting, Canadian Advisory Committee, July 1921, 'Governors' Papers' SD, A 102 / 11–13
66 Governor and Committee to Ford Motor Company, 29 May 1930, ibid.
67 'Airplanes,' Enclosure to letter of 22 April 1927, ibid.
68 The price was $47,875 FOB Winnipeg. On 2 October 1941 a second Beechcraft was purchased. Extract of Canadian Committee Minutes, 5 January 1939, and Canadian Committee to the Board, 2 October 1941, ibid.
69 According to reports, the initial trial was successful in that the sleigh did what its maker (Bombardier) guaranteed it would do. Moose Factory Annual Report, 11 October 1923, ARFTD, A 74 / 52
70 Governor and Committee to Canadian Committee, 18 February 1942, 'Administration – North America,' RG 2 CRS, RG 2 / 7 / 40, 1-7-1c

71 'Brief Survey,' 1
72 Edward Fitzgerald, Deputy Chairman, Canadian Committee to the Governor and Committee 21 February 1923, SD, A 102 / Box 214
73 Governor and Committee to Secretary, Canadian Committee 22 December 1987, ibid.
74 Fitzgerald to the Governor and Committee, 21 February 1923, ibid.
75 It should be pointed out that prior to 1920 the company's stores division suffered from the same problem of conservative retailing. Monod, 'Bay Days,' 176–7
76 Anderson, Fur Trader's Story, 20, 90
77 Bishop, Northern Ojibwa, 96; Skinner, 'Notes on Eastern Cree,' 123; Anderson, Fur Trader's Story, 92
78 Bishop, Northern Ojibwa, 96
79 Ibid., 95; Anderson, Fur Trader's Story, 21
80 Anderson, Fur Trader's Story, 5
81 'Brief Survey,' 9. Earlier, in 1934 J. Bartleman of the Mackenzie-Athabasca District presented a paper at the annual manager's conference entitled 'District Merchandising,' in which he made the same points. Fur Trade Conference, 1934, SD, A 102 / Box 86
82 Bartleman, 'District Merchandising,' 1
83 Monod, 'Bay Days,' 176–8
84 Ibid., 6–7
85 J.W. Anderson, 'Management of Line Posts,' Fur Trade Conference, 1933, SD, A 102 / Box 86, 4–5. He also cited Bell in the conclusion of his memoirs. See Anderson, Fur Trader's Story, 232.
86 R.A. Talbot, 'Paper on Indian Trade,' Fur Trade Conference, 1933, SD A 102 / Box 86, 3
87 Ibid., 3–4
88 Following this summary there is a sixteen-page, itemized inventory of goods. Fur Trade Conference, 1936, ibid.
89 'Comprehensive Review,' RG 2 CRS, RG 2 / 7 / 75, 1-7-1C, 11
90 Ibid., 12
91 'Report on Visit to London,' 7 December 1937, ibid.
92 'Comprehensive Review'
93 'Brief Survey'
94 Ibid., 1
95 Monod noted that the committee members blindly followed the latest theories of managment in their attempts to make the retail stores profitable. In the process they failed to consider the needs of the customers and communities they served, to the detriment of the business. Monod, 'Bay Days,' 194–6

96 'Comprehensive Review,' 3

CHAPTER 8 The native people, the Hudson's Bay Company, and the
state in the industrial fur trade

1 Dunning, *Social and Economic Change*, 45
2 Ibid., 44. This figure was arrived at assuming that only one outboard
motor (at $150) was required. Dunning calculated the annual deprecia-
tion rate at nearly $142 per year.
3 Ibid., 46. For a good discussion of the trapping economies of other Ojibwa
bands in northern Ontario in the 1950s and 1960s see Bishop, *Northern
Ojibwa*, 19–76; Rogers, *Round Lake Ojibwa*, c2–78.
4 This area had just been brought under treaty in 1921 with the signing of
Treaty 11.
5 Rogers and Leacock, 'Montagnais-Naskapi,' 173; Young, 'Are Subarctic
Indians Undergoing the Epidemiologic Transition?'
6 The DBS production data were adjusted to eliminate the portion of production supplied by fur ranches.
7 'Report of Medical Service to Indians Located Along the Line of the
Canadian National Railways from Cochrane, Ontario to La Tuque,'
October 1926. LOCG, A 92 / Corr / 257 / 1, 21
8 Ibid., 22
9 *Fur Trade Review* (December 1921), 134
10 Ibid. (July 1922), 142
11 Ibid. (January/February 1930), 34 and (June 1933), 29
12 A partial record of these accounts survives in the company archives. See
Sick and Destitute Accounts, Commissioner's Office Accounts Received
from District Headquarters, D 30 / 18b.
13 Fortescue also wanted the company to pressure the government to bring
his area under treaty so that new wealth would be available in the form
of annuity money. James J. Fortescue to Hudson's Bay Company Secretary Armit, 1 December 1880. LICHBC, A 11 / 119a
14 C.C. Chipman to Hayter Reed, LFTS, A 12 / FT, 243 / 1, 5
15 LFTS, A 12 / FT, 243 / 1
16 Reed to Chipman, 26 December 1894, ibid., 6
17 Ibid.
18 The presence of these dependants was another reason why the company
decided to open the Charlton Depot. By laying off the labour force,
officials hoped that the factory would stop drawing Indians from the
interior. Moose Factory District Report, 1899, B 135 / e / 33

19 Chipman to Ware, 4 November 1901, LFTS, A 12 / FT, 325 / 1
20 Tough, 'Native People,' 184–5
21 Reed to Chipman, 23 September 1897. Copy included in letter of Chipman to Hudson's Bay Company Secretary Ware, 1 October 1897, LFTS, A 12 / FT, 49
22 Ibid.
23 These expenditures can be found in the Auditor General's Annual Reports in *Canada Sessional Papers* and in the Department of Indian Affairs Annual Reports.
24 O'Kelly, Inspection Report, 1920, LOCI A 92 / 19 / 18
25 Ibid.
26 Ibid.
27 Godsell, *Arctic Trader*, 149
28 'Annual Report, James Bay, 1924' ARFTD, A 74 / 53, 341
29 Ibid.
30 CF, A 93 / 45
31 Ibid., 2
32 J. Watt to Governor Charles Sale, 1 September 1927, ibid., 1. The speech Watt referred to was one that Governor Sale had delivered to the general court of the company on 28 June 1927. Copies of this speech were sent to post managers.
33 Ibid., 3
34 Ibid., 4
35 Hay making for the company had been worth $3,000 to the Rupert House Indians. Ibid., 4
36 'Notes on Coast Indians, Rupert House, James Bay District, 17 August 1927,' ibid.
37 Ibid.
38 Fur Trade Conference, 1932, SD, A 102 / Box 86, 9–10
39 Ibid.
40 Ibid.
41 Ibid.
42 Deputy Governor Charles Sale to Angus Brabant, 26 January 1925, 'Indian Department, Ottawa, Relief of Natives,' SD, A 102 / Box 107, 2
43 Ibid.
44 Ibid.
45 Ibid.
46 Ibid., 3
47 Sterling to Brabant, 18 December 1924, ibid.
48 Ibid.

49 Angus Brabant to the Governor and Committee, 14 May 1925, ibid. The amounts distributed at each post by the various companies can be found in the Auditor General's Annual Reports in *Canada Sessional Papers*.
50 Brabant to Governor and Committee, 14 May 1925, ibid.
51 J. Chadwick Brooks, Secretary to the Canadian Committee 18 February 1942, RG 2 CRS, RG 2/7/75, 1-7-1C, 5
52 Ibid.; 'Brief Survey,' 15–16
53 Hudson's Bay Company *Annual Report*, 1926, Library
54 Morton, 'We Are Still Adventurers'
55 'Home Industries,' enclosure to letter of 10 July 1928, Ralph Parsons to Manager, Hudson's Bay Company, LOCG, A 92/Corr/257/1
56 'Résumé of conference Held in Ottawa 23rd & 24th November 1927,' 'Native Welfare, 1926–28,' DDD, A 95/52, 1–2
57 Ibid.
58 Ibid.
59 Newell, 'The Politics of Food,' 183
60 Ibid.
61 'Report of Medical Service'
62 'Interview with Dr. Banting, 30 December 1927,' DDD A 95/52, 1–2
63 Ibid.
64 Ibid.
65 Memo, Fur Trade Department No. 586, 'Welfare,' 14 June 1928 DDD, A 95/53

CHAPTER 9 The decline of the old order

1 Godsell, *Arctic Trader*, 309
2 The economist Claire Pentland described it as system of personal labour relations in which the employer or trading company assumed the social overhead costs of its workers or clients in return for their loyalty. See Pentland, *Labour and Capital in Canada, 1650–1860*, 28–33.
3 Ibid.

Appendix:
Figure references and data notes

FIGURE 1 Source: MBGC, 1878 HBCA PAM A 2/5, 28. These data, included in the 1878 report to the shareholders, updated those presented in 1871.

FIGURE 2 Source: Urquhart and Buckley, *Historical Statistics of Canada*, 291. I selected 1870 as the base year because of the important decisions about the company's future that were made in the economic context of 1870–1. Also, in the 1870s and early 1880s the shareholders continued to use these years as the reference point in their deliberations about the company's progress.

FIGURE 3 Source: *Annual Reports* (published) to the shareholders, 1870–1945. Library, HBCA PAM.

FIGURES 4 and 5 Source: 'Northern Department fur returns, York Factory, 1870,' HBCA PAM B 239/h/3 and 'Comparative of the Southern Department Returns, 1871,' Accounts from the Headquarters of the Northern, Southern, Montreal and Western Departments, 1871–90, HBCA PAM D 29/13. There are no good maps of the department and district boundaries for this period so I approximated them, taking into account the posts assigned to the various districts.

FIGURES 6 and 7 *Annual Reports*, 1870–85

FIGURE 8 George Brown and Ron Maguire, *Indian Treaties in Historical Perspective* (Ottawa: Research Branch, Department of Indian and Northern Affairs 1979) xxvi

FIGURE 9 Public Accounts, Part 1, Canada, *Sessional Papers*, 1883, xxiv

FIGURE 10 Annual Report of the Auditor General, Consolidated Indian Fund,

Expenditures under supply, Canada, *Sessional Papers*, 1870–1905. These data were submitted to the auditor-general's office by the Department of Indian Affairs. Also they can be obtained from the statistical summaries in the annual reports of the latter department which are published in the *Sessional Papers*.

FIGURES 11–18 Jones, *Fur Farming*, 148–59 and GD HBCA PAM A 104 / Box 13. The Hudson's Bay Company supplied the data to Jones and later to Harold Innis for his *Fur Trade of Canada*. It is the material the secretary sent to Innis that is contained in this file in the company's archives.

FIGURES 19 and 20 Canada, *Sessional Papers*, 1900–40.

FIGURES 21 and 22 ARFTD, 1890–91, HBCA PAM A 74 / 1. These annual reports were compiled in the commissioner's office from the routine summaries provided by the various district managers.

FIGURES 23 and 24 ARFTD, 1890–1920, HBCA PAM A 74 / 1–30

FIGURE 25 ARFTD, 1911–12, HBCA PAM A 74 / 21

FIGURE 26 The changing price of a hypothetical bale of furs was calculated from fur production and price data provided by Novak et al., *Furbearer Harvests*. Novak used constant (1970) dollars to compensate for inflationary / deflationary trends. I calculated a weighted price for the bale by considering the share each species made to the returns.

FIGURE 27 Dominion Bureau of Statistics, *Fur Production of Canada, Annual Reports*, 1926–45

FIGURES 28–37 Novak et al., *Furbearer Harvests*

FIGURE 38 I drafted this figure taking into account commentaries contained in the annual reports of the Hudson's Bay Company Fur Trade Department during the preceding five years. It shows how company officials perceived the north at that time.

FIGURE 39 ARFTD, 1921–22 HBCA PAM A 74 / 29–30

FIGURE 40 ARFTD, A 74 / 52.

FIGURE 41 Novak, *Furbearer Harvests*

FIGURE 42 GD HBCA PAM A 104 / Box 13

FIGURE 43 SD HBCA PAM A 102 / Box 86. This illustration is a simplification of the company's diagram.

FIGURE 44 HBCA PAM G 3/121. This map summarizes information contained on a 1933 map that the company prepared to portray its operations.

FIGURE 45 The changing value of the annuities were calculated by using the wholesale price index in Urquhart and Buckley, *Historical Statistics*, 293–4.

FIGURES 46–50 Department of Indian Affairs Annual Reports, Canada, *Sessional Papers*, 1922–35. The current dollar amounts were converted to constant dollars using wholesale price index number 35 (1935–9 = 100) in Urquhart and Buckley, *Historical Statistics*, 293. The agencies included in figure 46 are Chapleau, Fort Francis, Kenora, Lesser Slave Lake, Norway House, Onion Lake, Sault Ste Marie, Savanne, The Pas, Timiskaming, and Fort William. Incorporated in figure 47 are Lesser Slave Lake, Norway House, The Pas, and Onion Lake; those in figure 48 are Chapleau, Fort Francis, Kenora, Sault Ste Marie, Savanne, and Timiskaming. Figure 49 encompasses Battleford, Lesser Slave Lake, Onion Lake, and Norway House. Those in figure 50 are Chapleau, Fort Francis, Kenora, Sault Ste Marie, Savanne, Timiskaming, and Fort William. I did not use the data for Fort Resolution because it appears that the agents submitted the same estimates for several years in a row before changing them. The Fort Chipewyan data are incomplete, so I excluded them also.

FIGURE 51 The data for the annual fur production of Canada are from Dominion Bureau of Statistics, *Fur Production Annual Report, 1948*. The data for native hunting and trapping returns are from the Department of Indian Affairs annual reports, 1922–35. These data were converted to constant dollars using the wholesale price index of Urquhart and Buckley, *Historical Statistics*, 293.

FIGURE 52 Annual Report of the Auditor General, Canada, *Sessional Papers, 1889–1934*. The reporting units were Remote Districts, Berens River, Edmonton, Fisher River, Fort Simpson, Fort Smith, Isle à la Crosse, Lesser Slave Lake, Manitopah, Norway House, The Pas, Fort Churchill, and York Factory, Fort Resolution, Treaty Number 8, Chapleau, and James Bay.

FIGURE 53 SD HBCA PAM A 102/Box 107

Picture credits

Hudson's Bay Company Archives, Provincial Archives of Manitoba: Joseph Wrigley and senior officers in Winnipeg 1987/363-E-710 (N7783); site plan or Norway House B.154/e/25, fo.8; unidentified native paddlers 1987/363-G-130/161 (N7738); advertisements from Bernstein Fur Company, A.B. Shubert, and Canadian Fur Auction Sales Company A.92/19/8; CAA test vehicle at Moose Factory 1987/363-M-145/2B; twin-engined Beechcraft 1987/363-C-521 (5606); hauling supplies from Moose Factory 1987/363-M-145/7; Isaiah Clark 1987/363-T-220.1/3 (N7266); Allan Fraser and Clark 1987/363-T-220.1/49 (N7282); Lac La Ronge 1987/363-L-5 (N7798)

Glenbow Archives: HBC's *Grahame* NA 4035-98; Peace River Jim NA 2760-8; trading post at Fort St John NA 2617-48; Fort Smith, NWT NB-6-11; launching the *Northland Pioneer* and *Northland Trader* NA 2786-9; Lamson and Hubbard fur shipment, Edmonton NA 3006-1; R.D. Ferrier NA 3006-3; Northern Traders' post at Fort Providence NA 3844-15; Treaty 9 payment at Lansdowne House NA 3235-70; Charles N. Stephen NA 3235-65

RCMP Museum: Grand Rapids, Athabasca River NA 949-78

Fur Trade Review **(New York):** International Fur Exchange, St Louis, Missouri (Feb. 1920); map of Lamson and Hubbard operations (Feb. 1920); 'cute little animals' cartoon (Nov. 1919); sketch of ermine cape (Aug. 1919); Sonja Henie (Jan. 1938); twin silver fox scarf (Feb. 1938)

The British Fur Trade: silk coat (Feb. 1925)

National Archives of Canada: 'Moose Works' at Moose Factory C1717

Bibliography

PUBLISHED SOURCES

A. Government of Canada Publications
Auditor General's Reports. *Canada Sessional Papers*, 1870–1922, 52 vols
Bowsfield, H., ed. *The Letters of Charles John Brydges, 1879–1882.* Winnipeg: Hudson's Bay Record Society 1977
Brown, George and Ron Maguire. *Indian Treaties in Historical Perspective.* Ottawa: Department of Indian and Northern Affairs 1979
Commons Debates, 1877–94
Daniel, Richard. *A History of Native Claims Processes in Canada, 1867–1979.* Ottawa: Department of Indian and Northern Affairs 1980
Department of Indian Affairs Annual Reports. *Sessional Papers*
Department of Trade and Commerce, 'Exports from Canada,' *Sessional Papers*, 1900–40
Dominion Bureau of Statistics (DBS), Agricultural Division. *Fur Farms of Canada, 1925.* Ottawa 1927
– Agricultural Division, *Fur Production of Canada, Annual Reports.* Ottawa 1926–48
– Agricultural Division, *Statistics of Hides, Skins and Leather.* Ottawa 1954
– General Statistics Branch, *Recent Economic Tendencies in Canada, 1919–34.* Ottawa 1935
– National Accounts and Balances Division, Industry Output Section, *Indexes of Real Domestic Production by Industry of Origin, 1935–61.* Ottawa 1963
Indian Department. *Facts Respecting Indian Affairs in the North-West.* Ottawa 1886

Usher, Peter J. *Banks Island: An Area Economic Survey.* Ottawa: Department of Indian Affairs and Northern Development 1966

B. *Provincial Governments*
Northwestern Ontario. Toronto 1879
Revised Statutes of Ontario. Toronto 1951
Statutes, 57–58 Victoria, 1894, chapter 31, Ontario

C. *Books*
Anderson, J.W. *Fur Trader's Story.* Toronto: Ryerson 1961
Bachrach, Max. *Fur: A Practical Treatise.* London: Prentice-Hall 1936
Baker, Peter. *Memoirs of An Arctic Arab: The Story of a Free-trader in Northern Canada.* Yellowknife: Yellowknife Publishing 1976
Berger, Carl. *The Writing of Canadian History: Aspects of English-Canadian Historical Writing: 1900 to 1970.* Toronto: Oxford University Press 1976
Bishop, Charles A. *The Northern Ojibwa and the Fur Trade.* Toronto: Holt, Rinehart and Winston of Canada 1974
Bliss, Michael. *Northern Enterprise: Five Centuries of Canadian Business.* Toronto: McClelland and Stewart 1987
Bothwell, Robert, I. Drummond, and John English. *Canada: 1900–1945.* Toronto: University of Toronto Press 1987
Boulanger, Tom. *An Indian Remembers: My Life As A Trapper in Northern Manitoba.* Winnipeg: Peguis 1971
Brody, Hugh. *Maps and Dreams.* Pelican: Suffolk 1981
Brown, Craig and Ramsay Cook. *Canada 1896–1921: A Nation Transformed.* Toronto: McClelland and Stewart 1974
Cameron, Duncan, ed. *Explorations in Canadian Economic History: Essays in Honour of Irene M. Spry.* Ottawa: University of Ottawa Press 1985
Cumming, P.A. and N.H. Mickenberg. *Native Rights in Canada.* Toronto: Indian-Eskimo Association 1972
Dunning, R.W. *Social and Economic Change Among the Northern Ojibwa.* Toronto: University of Toronto Press 1959
Foster, John E., ed. *The Developing West.* Edmonton: University of Alberta Press 1983
Friesen, Gerald. *The Canadian Prairies: A History.* Toronto: University of Toronto Press 1984
Getty, A. and A. Lussier, eds. *As Long as the Sun Shines and Water Flows: A Reader in Canadian Native Studies.* Vancouver: University of British Columbia Press 1983
Glover, R., ed. *David Thompson's Narrative 1784–1812.* Toronto: Champlain Society 1962

Godsell, Philip. *Arctic Trader.* London: Travel Book Club, n.d.

Helm, June, ed. *Handbook of North American Indians.* Volume 6, *Subarctic.* Washington DC: Smithsonian 1981

Hodgetts, J.E. *The Canadian Public Service: A Physiology of Government, 1867–1970.* Toronto: University of Toronto Press 1973

Innis, H.A. *The Fur Trade of Canada.* Toronto: University of Toronto Library 1927

– *The Fur Trade in Canada.* Toronto: University of Toronto Press (revised edition) 1970 [1930]

Jarvenpa, Robert. *The Trappers of Patuanak: Toward a Spatial Ecology of Modern Hunters,* Mercury Series, Canadian Ethnology Service Paper 67. Ottawa: National Museums of Canada 1980

Jones, J. Walter. *Fur Farming in Canada.* Montreal: The Mortimor Company 1913

Keighley, Sydney Augustus. *Trader-Tripper-Trapper: The Life of a Bay Man.* Winnipeg: Rupert's Land Research Centre and Watson and Dwyer 1989

Links, J.G. *The Book of Fur.* London: J. Barrie 1956

McCandless, Robert G. *Yukon Wildlife: A Social History.* Edmonton: University of Alberta Press 1985

MacGregor, J.G. *Paddle Wheels to Bucket-Wheels on the Athabasca.* Toronto: McClelland and Stewart 1974

MacKay, Douglas. *The Honourable Company: A History of the Hudson's Bay Company.* Toronto: The Musson Book Company 1938

Marr, William and Donald Paterson. *Canada: An Economic History.* Toronto: Gage 1980

Morris, Alexander. *The Treaties of Canada with the Indians of Manitoba and the North-West Territories Including the Negotiations on which they were based, and other information relating thereto.* Toronto: Coles 1979 [1862]

Morse, Bradford, ed. *Native Peoples and the Law: Indian, Metis and Inuit Rights in Canada.* Ottawa: Carleton University Press 1985

Newell, Dianne. *Technology on the Frontier: Mining in Old Ontario.* Vancouver: University of British Columbia Press 1986

Novak, Milan et al., eds. *Wild Furbearer Management and Conservation in North America.* Toronto: Ontario Ministry of Natural Resources 1988

– *Furbearer Harvests in North America.* Toronto: Ontario Ministry of Natural Resources, 1987

Pentland, Claire. *Labour and Capital in Canada, 1650–1860.* Toronto: University of Toronto Press 1981

Ray, Arthur J. *Indians in the Fur Trade.* Toronto: University of Toronto Press 1974

Ray, Arthur J. and Donald B. Freeman. *'Give Us Good Measure.': An Economic Analysis of Relations between the Indians and The Hudson's Bay Company before 1763*. Toronto: University of Toronto Press 1978

Rich, E.E. *Hudson's Bay Company, 1670–1870*, 3 vols. Toronto: McClelland and Stewart 1960

Rogers, Edward S. *The Round Lake Ojibwa*, Occasional Paper 5. Toronto: Royal Ontario Museum 1962

Ross, Hugh Mackay. *The Apprentice's Tale*. Winnipeg: Watson and Dwyer 1986

Seton, E.T. *The Arctic Prairies*. London: Constable & Co. 1912

Skinner, Alanson. 'Notes on the Eastern Cree and Northern Saulteaux,' *Anthropological Papers of the American Museum of Natural History* 9 (1911)

Stanley, George F.G. *The Birth of Western Canada*. Toronto: University of Toronto Press 1961 [1936]

Tanner, Adrian. *Bringing Home Animals: Religious Ideology and Mode of Production of the Mistassini Cree*. St John's: Memorial University of Newfoundland 1979

Tetso, John, *Trapping Is My Life*. Toronto: Peter Martin Associates 1970

Urquhart, M.C. and K.A.H. Buckley, eds. *Historical Statistics of Canada*. Toronto: Macmillan 1965

Zaslow, Morris. *The Opening of the Canadian North, 1870–1914*. Toronto: McClelland and Stewart 1971

– *The Northward Expansion of Canada, 1914–1967*. Toronto: McClelland and Stewart 1988

D. Contemporary Newspapers and Periodicals
British Fur Trade Journal (London), 1923–57
British Fur Trade Review (London), 1924–33
Chamber of Commerce Journal, London Chamber of Commerce, 1911–22
The Commercial (Winnipeg), January 1886, 4 (No. 15)
Dry Goods Review, 1931
The Economist, 1945
Edmonton Bulletin, 19 June 1886 (No. 33); 29 January 1886 (No. 13); 13 February 1886 (No. 15); 10 July 1886 (No. 36)
Fur Trade Review (New York), 1919–39
Fur Weekly News, 1933
Fur World, April, 1910–20
The Northern Fur Trade, 1927
Stylewear Review, 1936
Women's Wear Daily, 1919

E. *Articles*

Bishop, Charles A. and Arthur J. Ray. 'Ethnohistoric Research in the Central Subarctic: Some Conceptual and Methodological Problems.' *Western Canadian Journal of Anthropology* 6 (1976): 116–44

Clayton, James L. 'The Growth and Economic Significance of the American Fur Trade, 1790–1890.' In *Aspects of the Fur Trade: Selected Papers of the 1965 North American Fur Trade Conference.* St Paul: Minnesota Historical Society 1967

Denmark, D.E. 'James Bay Beaver Conservation.' *The Beaver* (September 1948): 36–43

– 'Conservation at Cumberland.' *The Beaver* (March 1940): 47–49

Goldring, Philip. 'Inuit Economic Responses to Euro-American contacts: Southeast Baffin Island, 1824–1940.' *Historical Papers* (1986): 146–72

Helm, June and David Damas. 'The Contact-traditional All-Native Community of the Canadian North: The Upper Mackenzie "Bush" Athapaskans and the Igluligmiut.' *Anthropologica* (new series), 5 (1963): 9–21

Leighton, Douglas. 'A Victorian Civil Servant at Work: Lawrence Vankoughnet and the Canadian Indian Department, 1874–1893.' In Getty and Lussier, eds, *As Long as the Sun Shines*

Monod, David. 'Bay Days: The Managerial Revolution and the Hudson's Bay Company Department Stores, 1912–39.' *Historical Papers* (1986): 173–96

Morton, Anne. 'We are still Adventurers: The Records of the Hudson's Bay Company's Development Department and Fish and Fish Products Department, 1925–1940.' *Archivaria* 21 (Winter 1985–6): 158–9

Neatby, H., 'Exploration and History of the Canadian Arctic.' In *Handbook of North American Indians*. Volume 5, *Arctic*. Washington, DC: Smithsonian Institution, 1978: 377–90

Newell, Dianne. 'Published Government Documents as a Source for Interdisciplinary History: A Canadian Case Study.' *Government Publications Review* (1981): 381–93

– 'The Politics of Food in World War II: Great Britain's Grip on Canada's Pacific Fishery.' *Historical Papers* (1988): 178–97

Novak, Milan. 'The Future of Trapping.' In Novak et al., eds, *Wild Furbearer Management*

den Otter, A.A. 'The Hudson's Bay Company's Prairie Transportation Problem, 1870–85.' In Foster, ed., *The Developing West*

Ray, Arthur J. 'Some Conservation Schemes of the Hudson's Bay Company, 1820–50: An Examination of the Problems of Resource Management in the Fur Trade.' *Journal of Historical Geography* 1 (1975): 49–68

- 'The Northern Great Plains: Pantry of the Northwestern Fur Trade, 1774–1885.' *Prairie Forum* 9 (1984): 263–80
- 'Buying and Selling Hudson's Bay Company Furs in the Eighteenth Century.' In Cameron, ed., *Explorations in Canadian Economic History*
- 'Adventurers at the Crossroads.' *The Beaver* 8 (April / May 1986): 4–12
- 'The Fur Trade in North America: An Overview from A Historical Geographical Perspective.' In Novak et al., eds, *Wild Furbearer Management*
- 'The Hudson's Bay Company and Native People.' *Handbook of North American Indians*. Volume 4, *History of Indian White Relations*. Washington, DC: Smithsonian Institution, 1988: 335–50

Ray, Arthur J. and Arthur Roberts. 'Approaches to the Ethnohistory of the Subarctic: A Review of the Handbook of North American Indians: Subarctic.' *Ethnohistory* 32 (1986): 270–80

Rogers, Edward S. and Eleanor Leacock. 'Montagnais-Naskapi.' In Helm, ed., *Handbook*

Smith, Shirlee Anne. 'A Desire to Worry Me Out.' *The Beaver* (December 1987): 4–11

Usher, Peter J. 'The Growth and Decay of the Trading and Trapping Frontiers in the Western Canadian Arctic.' *Canadian Geographer* 19 (4): 308–20

Young, T. Kue. 'Are Subarctic Indians Undergoing the Epidemiologic Transition?' *Social Science Medicine* (1988): 659–71

UNPUBLISHED SOURCES

A. Hudson's Bay Company Archives, Provincial Archives of Manitoba
To aid the reader the documents from this collection are grouped in the order in which they appear in the archives catalogues rather than alphabetically.

Record Class A. London Headquarters Records:
A 1, London Minute Books
A 2, London Minute Books – General Courts and Proprietors (Verbatim Transcripts), 1871–83, A 2 / 18–44
A 11, London Correspondence Inward – Official Hudson's Bay Company, 1871–81, A 11 / 47–119
A 12, London Correspondence Inward from Commissioners, 1874, A 12 / 16
A 12 / FT, Fur Trade Subject Files: Correspondence Inward from the Commissioner:
  1891–96, A 12 / FT, 341[2]
  1894–18, A 12 / FT, 229 / 3–325 / 1

A 20, Fur Department Accounts, 1905, A 20 / 105
A 74, Fur Trade Department Annual Reports, 1891–1922 (42 vols), A 74 / 1–42
A 76, Fur Trade Districts and Post Balance Sheets, 1890–1915, A 76 / 5–32
A 92, London Office Correspondence, 1919–54:
  Correspondence Inward to London, 1919–27, A 92 / 19 / 1–102
  Correspondence Outward From London, 1919–27, A 92 / 102–143
  Fur Cycles, 1930, A 92 / 102–143
  Correspondence [General], 1926–28, A 92 / Corr:
    'Report of Medical Service to Indians Located Along the Line of the
      Canadian National Railways from Cochrane, Ontario to La Tuque,'
      October 1926, A 92 / Corr / 257 / 1
A 93 Confidential Files:
  Brown, W.E. 'Hudson's Bay Company Transportation Including Consider-
    ation of Aeroplane Transport,' Presented at 1934 Fur Trade Confer-
    ence, A 93 / 43
  Fur Trade Conference, 1928, A 93 / 43
  Fur Trade Conference, 1929, A 93 / 44
  Fur Trade Department, A 93 / 56
A 94, Development Department Correspondence, 1925–31
A 95, Development Department Dossiers, 1925–31:
  Native Welfare, 1926–28, A 95 / 52–55
  Organization, 1926–30, A 95 / 65
A 96, Development Department Management Dossiers
A 97, Development Department Reports and Miscellaneous
A 102, London Secretary's Dossiers:
  Accounts Department, 1931–57, A 102 / 1–7
  Aeroplane Transport, 1921–50, A 102 / 11–13
  George Binney, 1926–31, A 102 / 294–96
  Fur Cycles, 1930–50, A 102 / Box 81
  Fur Production, C.S. Elton, 1927–31, A 102 / Box 85
  Fur Preserves, 1939, A 102 / Box 85
  Fur Trade Bonus, Canada, 1922–37, A 102 / Box 86
  Fur Trade Conferences, 1931–7 (see also RG 2 FTC), A 102 / Box 86
  Fur Trade Conference Papers, A 102 / Box 86:
    Anderson, J.W. 'Management of Line Posts,' 1933
    Bartleman, J. 'District Merchandising,' 1934
    Cooper, H.E. 'Merchandising,' 1934
    Cooper, the Rev. J.M. 'Aboriginal Land Holding systems' [read by J.W.
      Anderson], 1933

Cowan, M. 'Line Post Trade,' 1934,

Talbot, R.A. 'Paper on Indian Trade,' 1933

Warne, H.P. 'Paper on Fur Purchasing Agencies'

'Fur Trade in America, 1924' by N.H. Bacon, A 102 / Box 86 (see also A 92)

Furs, Farming, Dressing, Dyeing, 1914–46, A / 102 / Box 79a

Indian Department, Ottawa, Relief of Natives, 1924–29, A 102 / Box 107

Lamson, Ltd, Purchase of Interest, 1924, A 102 / Box 118

Montreal Fur Sales, 1945–58, A 102 / Box 230

Northern Traders Ltd, 1924–38, A 102 / Box 141

Personnel Records, Fur Trade Organization, 1936–48, A 102 / Box 86

Radio at Hudson's Bay Company Posts, 1939–41, A 102 / Box 168

Revillon Trading Company, 1926–35, A 102 / Box 176

Tractor Transportation, 1921–35, A 102 / Box 200

A 103 Accounts Department Dead Dossiers:

Watkins, F.W. 'World Fur Production, 1944–46,' Report for Hudson's Bay
Company, A 103–A8. Copy also in CC CRS, RG 2 / 7 / 189, 5-3-36

A 104 Governors' Dossiers:

Fur Trade 1931–48, A 104 / 282–87 [Box 13]

Beynes. N. and C.G. Wilson, 'Canadian Fur Marketing Research, 1948' A
104 / 288

Fur Trade Organization, 1936–48, A 104 / Boxes 4–86

Miscellaneous Subjects: Natives and Native Welfare, 1933–46, A 104 / 216–
29

'Fur Trade Commissions and Indentures,' Memorandum to the governor
from the secretary, 2 May 1932, A 104 / Box 13

Chesshire Correspondence, 1944–54, FTD Unclassified, 54 / 2, 54 / 10, and
54 / 11

P.A. Chester Correspondence:

9 / 31–12 / 32, A 104 / 77

1 / 33–12 / 33, A 104 / 78

1 / 34–12 / 34, A 104 / 79

1 / 35–12 / 37, A 104 / 80

1 / 38–2 / 39, A 104 / 81

3 / 39–12 / 40, A 104 / 82

1 / 41–10 / 41, A 104 / 83

1 / 42–10 / 43, A 104 / 84

1 / 44–10 / 46, A 104 / 85

Record Class B. Trading Post Records:

Moose Factory District Report, 1899, B 135 / e / 33

Northern Department Fur Returns, 1870, B 239 / h / 3

Record Class D. Canadian Governor's and Commissioner's Office Papers:
D 9 / 1 Governor Mactavish Outward, 1865–67
D 10 / 1 Governor Mactavish Inward, 1866–70
D 11 Donald Smith's Correspondence Outward, 1869–80
D 12 Donald Smith's Correspondence Inward, 1870–79
D 13 Outward Letterbooks – London, 1874–1909, 1875, D 13 / 1, 172
D 14 Outward Letterbooks to Hudson's Bay Company Officials, 1874–92
D 15 Outward Letterbooks – General, 1874–89
D 16 Private and Confidential Letterbooks, 1872–83 and 1887–93
D 17 Outward Letterbooks to Canadian Sub-committee and Hudson's Bay
  Company Governor, 1884–94
D 19 Inward Correspondence from London, 1874–95 and 1897–1910
D 20 Inward Correspondence – General, 1874–1910
D 24 Rules and Regulations and Minutes of Meetings of Commissioned
  Officers, 1843–96
D 25 Post Inspection Reports, 1886–94, Undated:
  P.W. Bell and E.K. Beeston, 1886, D 25 / 1
  E.K. Beeston, 1887, D 25 / 2
  R. Hardisty and E.K. Beeston, 1888, D 25 / 3
  R. Hardisty and E. Beeston, 1888, D 25 / 4
  J. McDougall and E.K. Beeston, 1890, D 25 / 10
  P.M. McKenzie, 1890, D 25 / 12
D 26 Miscellaneous Papers, 1857–1913, Undated:
  Rules and Regulations, London, 1887, D 26 / 3
  Papers Relating to Transport, 1874–93, D 26 / 9
D 27 Fur Trade Papers and Accounts, 1874–91, Undated:
  Abstract of Average Prices of Northern Department Returns, 1870–74, D
  27 / 1
D 29 Accounts from the Headquarters of the Northern, Southern, Montreal
  and Western Departments, 1871–1900:
  Comparative Statement of Returns of the Southern Department, 1872–3,
  D 29 / 13
D 30 Accounts Received from District Headquarters, 1872–1900:
  Athabasca District Accounts, 1874–90, D 30 / 1
  Athabasca Sick and Destitute Accounts, 1887–90, D 30 / 18
D 31 District and Post balance Sheets and Trading Accounts Current, 1886–
  1915
D 34 District Statements, 1892–1900

Record Series F: International Financial Society:
Hudson's Bay Company Stock Application Form, F 27 / 1 / 95
International Financial Society Prospectus, F 27 / 1 / 94
Memorandum of Agreement Between Edward Watkin and Richard Potter
[Governor of the Hudson's Bay Company], F 27 / 1 / 89

Record Group 2: Canadian Committee
Sir Augustus Nanton's Correspondence, 1911–24:
    Index to Nanton Correspondence, RG 2 / 2 / 1
    Nanton Correspondence, 1913–23, RG 2 / 2–6
    'Report on the Yukon Territory' RG 2 / 2 / 4
Correspondence – Fur Trade Department, 1919–26, RG 2 / 4
Correspondence (Roneo system), 1904–70, RG 2 / 7:
    33, 1-7-1 Administration – North America – Canadian Committee and the
        Board, 26 / 9 / 26–25 / 7 / 31
    34, 1-7-1 Administration – North America – Canadian Committee and the
        Board, 9 / 7 / 31–25 / 4 / 34
    37, 1-7-1 Administration – North America – Canadian Committee and the
        Board, 9 / 7 / 34–1 / 11 / 36
    38, 1-7-1 Administration – North America – Canadian Committee and the
        Board, 20 / 11 / 36–14 / 3 / 38
    39, 1-7-1 Administration – North America – Canadian Committee and the
        Board, 13 / 3 / 38–26 / 9 / 41
    40, 1-7-1 Administration – North America – Canadian Committee and the
        Board, 16 / 10 / 41–31 / 12 / 42
    41, 1-7-1 Administration – North America – Canadian Committee and the
        Board, 7 / 1 / 43–10 / 1 / 46
    73, 1-7-1c Administration – North America – Canadian Committee and the
        London Board – Fur Trade Department, 23 / 10 / 34–29 / 3 / 37
    74, 1-7-1c Administration – North America – Canadian Committee and the
        London Board – Fur Trade Department, 1 / 6 / 37–29 / 3 / 37
    75, 1-7-1c Administration – North America – Canadian Committee and the
        London Board – Fur Trade Department, 12 / 3 / 42–10 / 46
P.A. Chester's Private Files, 1930–70, RG 2 / 11 /
    Lamson & Hubbard Canadian Co. RG 2 / 56G
    Fur Trade Conference Minutes (General Manager's Copies), 1931–37, RG
    2 / 62 /

Record Group 3: Fur Trade Department
Library: Hudson's Bay Company Archives

Search Files:
  Chesshire, Robert H.
  Chester, P.A.
  Graham, Sir Cyril
  Lamson and Hubbard Canadian Company, Ltd
  Published Annual Reports of Hudson's Bay Company
  Report of the Commissioner to the Governor, Deputy Governor and
    Committee of the Hudson's Bay Company on the Trade of the Com-
    pany, 1885–86. Library, FC 3207.1, R4, 1888

B. *Provincial Archives of Alberta*
An Act Respecting Game in the Northwest Territories of Canada, MR 200 /
  55
Bartleman, J., Manager, Superior-Huron District, Hudson's Bay Company.
  'Inspection of Posts, 1929,' 73.551 / 1

C. *Provincial Archives of British Columbia*
Circular from the Commissioner's [Hudson's Bay Company] Office, 15 January 1889,' A D 90 H 86 3–5
Cornwall, J.K. 'Memo Re Fur Trade [of Mackenzie District]' 1946, A D 90 C 81
  2–3

D. *Public Record Office, London, England*
Beynes, N.R. 'Memo to the Board of Trade' 2 November 1943 BT PRO 64 /
  1648
Board of Trade, 'Policy File, Minute sheet' 6 December 1943' BT PRO 64 / 1648
'Confidential Replies by the Fur Trade to the Board of Trade Questionnaire
  on Post-war Reconstruction' 30 July 1943 BT PRO 64 / 1648

E. *Other*
Francis, James M. 'Business, Enterprise, and the National Policy: the Role of
  T.C. Power & Brothers and I.G. Baker & Company in the Political and
  Economic Development of the Southwestern Canadian Prairies and
  Northern Montana, 1870–1893.' MA thesis, History Department, Univer-
  sity of British Columbia 1978
Harris, Lynda. 'Revillon Frères Trading Company Limited: Fur Traders of
  the North, 1901–1936.' Vol. 1, Historical Planning and Research Branch,
  Ministry of Culture and Recreation, Province of Ontario, Toronto 1976
'Her Majesty the Queen against Bert Horseman,' Provincial Court of Alberta,
  26 September 1985

Stardom, E.J. 'Adapting to Altered Circumstances: Commissioner Joseph Wrigley and the Hudson's Bay Company 1884–1891.' MA thesis, University of Manitoba 1987

Tough, Frank. 'Native People and the Regional Economy of Northern Manitoba: 1870–1930s.' PHD dissertation, Geography Department, York University 1987

Index